HIGHLAND SHEPHERD

James MacGregor, Father of the Scottish Enlightenment in Nova Scotia

ALAN WILSON

Highland Shepherd

James MacGregor, Father of the Scottish Enlightenment in Nova Scotia

UNIVERSITY OF TORONTO PRESS
Toronto Buffalo London

ISBN 978-1-4426-4451-9

∞

Library and Archives Canada Cataloguing in Publication

Wilson, Alan, 1927–, author
Highland shepherd : James MacGregor, father of the
Scottish enlightenment in Nova Scotia / Alan Wilson.

Includes bibliographical references and index.
ISBN 978-1-4426-4451-9 (bound)

1. MacGregor, James, 1759-1830. 2. Presbyterian Church of Nova
Scotia—Clergy—Biography. 3. Presbyterians—Nova Scotia—Biography.
4. Scottish Canadians—Nova Scotia—Biography. 5. Presbyterian Church
of Nova Scotia—Nova Scotia—History. 6. Nova Scotia—Biography. I. Title.

BX9225.M255W44 2015   285'.1092   C2015-902454-4

University of Toronto Press acknowledges the financial assistance to its
publishing program of the Canada Council for the Arts and the
Ontario Arts Council, an agency of the Government of Ontario.

 **Canada Council   Conseil des Arts
for the Arts   du Canada**

 ONTARIO ARTS COUNCIL
CONSEIL DES ARTS DE L'ONTARIO
an Ontario government agency
un organisme du gouvernement de l'Ontario

University of Toronto Press acknowledges the financial support of the
Government of Canada through the Canada Book Fund for its
publishing activities.

For Budge, Barry Cahill, and Jack MacCormack:
three faithful supporters

Contents

Contents

Part Four: Partnering

Part Five: Community and Union

Preface and Acknowledgements

James MacGregor was a man of mind, spirit, and "of his hands":[1] teacher, scholar, poet, reviewer, translator, amateur scientist, farmer/improver, inventor, and above all wide-ranging mission-driven evangelist, church organizer, and ecclesiastical diplomat. Context counts with MacGregor.

No scholarly life of MacGregor has yet appeared. Like others, this account reflects in part the pioneering work of his grandson, Rev. George Patterson, although the book was mistitled *Memoir of the Life of the Rev. James MacGregor, D.D.* 2. Much of it is a transcription of MacGregor's unfinished and unpublished autobiography, starting from his departure for Nova Scotia in 1786 until he suffered a stroke in 1823. To complete the account, Patterson relied on his grandfather's drafts and other notes, on newspapers, on family recollections, and on oral accounts from those who had known him or had heard stories of him.

The *Memoir* was published in Philadelphia in 1859, nearly thirty years after the death of MacGregor and on the centenary of his birth. It was published by his old Perthshire friend Joseph Wilson, who in the same year published *A Few Remains of the Rev. James MacGregor, D.D., prints of essays, addresses and public letters, with selected private correspondence.*[2] Patterson provided a brief preface to the *Remains*. By contrast, in the *Memoir* he annotated and supplemented MacGregor's manuscript extensively, presenting it in a hagiographic, Victorian style that tests the modern reader's patience and credulity. I have compared MacGregor's originals in the Archives of the Maritime Conference of the United Church of Canada with Patterson's published record. Patterson made only minor textual changes, scoring out some personal names and in a few places garnishing the original style, but much remains a true transcription, a printed primary source. I have frequently cited the published *Memoir*, believing it to be more accessible to the reader than the originals at Sackville. Copies exist on microfilm in Halifax at Nova Scotia Archives (hereafter NSA).

In the mid-nineteenth century,[3] while studying at Edinburgh, Patterson visited many places associated with his grandfather's first twenty-seven years, the Scottish years. I visited them, too, and aided by recent Scottish historical production, enquired extensively into his early life and education – his formative setting.

One of the best sources of early Maritime Presbyterian history is Rev. James Robertson's *History of the Mission of the Secession Church to Nova Scotia and Prince Edward Island ...*, published in Edinburgh in 1847,[4] twelve years before Patterson's *Memoir*. When Patterson was a student at Edinburgh, he took with him MacGregor's papers, and Robertson used them. Patterson owed a great deal to Robertson for deciphering and arranging his grandfather's notes, and for insights into the growth of the Secessionist Church of Scotland. Their accounts run closely parallel in words and ideas.

Unfortunately, not all of MacGregor's correspondence came down even to Patterson, and after 1823, MacGregor's journal lapsed into fragmented notes. The minutes of the Pictou Presbytery were not recorded for the first five years to 1800, and they falter after 1823. MacGregor wrote the Session books until 1823, but they were not resumed until after his death in 1830. In this account, collections of correspondence and many other papers helped round out the archival record. MacGregor's publications are listed in the bibliography; his frequent reports home appeared in his Scottish Church's journal, *The Christian Magazine*.

Susan Buggey's 1987 entry in the *Dictionary of Canadian Biography*, is the most reliable short account of MacGregor. Many academic articles concerning MacGregor have appeared. Among the best are those by Barry Cahill, archivist and authority on Presbyterian history. A member of the Committee on History of the Presbyterian Church in Canada, he has kindly written an introduction, contrasting MacGregor's and Thomas McCulloch's enduring reputations. He and I have long shared the conviction that James's evangelicalism was linked to his Scottish Enlightenment background – a specific example of a general proposition raised by Brian McKillop of Carleton University, regarding the formation of the "Anglo-Canadian 'mind.'" I have also tried to push beyond the customary enquiry into the theological, intellectual, and political activities of a Canadian minister and to examine, as well, the loneliness and difficulties of early pastoral life. They helped form the Canadian "mind," too.

The general reader may find the chart useful, for it reviews various divisions of Presbyterianism at the time, together with the maps.

MacGregor appears in several works of fiction: Thomas McCulloch's two novellas, *William* and *Melville*, published in 1826 as *Colonial Gleanings*; an unpublished novel by McCulloch, "Morton," in manuscript in NSA;[5] and Frank Baird's novel, *Rob MacNab, A Story of Old Pictou*, illustrated by C.W. Jeffreys and published in 1923.[6] The fullest of these, "Morton" comes from one who knew him closely and was his steady admirer, and who would deplore today's academic rivalry in evaluating their roles at Pictou, given how much McCulloch respected James and his ideas, how close were their views on education, and how deeply their lives interlocked. Their differences were often of means, not ends, their temperaments contrasting sharply.

In setting the Scottish background for MacGregor's work in Nova Scotia, I have suggested his parents' influence, portraying his childhood in Strathearn, Strathallan, and Strathclyde; the young man in the intellectual, social, and economic ferment of Scotland's industrial and intellectual revolution, especially in Glasgow's distinctive place in the Scottish Enlightenment; together with the driven catechist in Scotland, Pictou, and beyond – the bush pilot of his day, which is the only part of his work acknowledged by most writers.

My debt to old and new schools of Scottish history is reflected in the endnotes, and I acknowledge gratefully the work of many recent scholars appearing in the *Dictionary of Canadian Biography* and elsewhere.

I have especially to thank my wife, Budge Wilson C.M., O.N.S., LL.D., D.Hum. L., from whom I have learned much about writing and about life.

My deepest thanks for scholarly direction go to Barry Cahill, and for his introduction and preparing the index. His wise and informed criticism as colleague and friend has often recharged me. Thanks, too, to Dr. Charles H.H. Scobie, Professor Emeritus of Religious Studies at Mount Allison University, who read the early manuscript to my great profit, and whose wife, Jean, served shortbreads in the manse at Comrie, Perthshire. Fittingly, it was there that Rev. Sam Gilfillan, MacGregor's friend and steady correspondent, resided when James needed him.

In Pictou at my beginning, Vangie Way, Nedra Wilson, and Fern MacDonald made MacGregor's footprints across Pictou County visible, while John Ashton kindly gave me a plaque made from the MacGregor Elm.

In Scotland, thanks go to Liz and Russell Cunningham and David Morrison of St. Fillans, MacGregor's birthplace. In Whitburn, thanks to Craig Hunter, webmaster;. to David Alston of Nigg, Ross-shire; to Erskine Duncan, Leighton Library, Dunblane; and to the late Professor Rosalind Mitchison, Edinburgh.

Thanks to the late Professor Jack MacCormack, my oldest and closest friend, for his knowledge of Highland and religious history; and to Tom and Sheila Sheppard who have given careful reading and encouragement to yet another manuscript.

Thanks, too, to Kirsten Franklin and Lucas Jarche for unfailing support – and to Michael Colborne, Allan Marble, both of Halifax; Sandy and Nick Smith, Stouffville, ON; Maria Darragh, Toronto; John Gammell, Midland, ON; Archie Killawee and Edith Patterson, Truro, N.S.; Douglas Graham, Rockville, Maryland; Rev. Sherman Isbell, Fairfax, Virginia; Terris Howard; Professor Edward MacDonald, U.P.E.I.; Richard MacNeil, Pictou GenWeb; and Effie Rankin, Mabou Gaelic and Historical Society.

A writer is sustained by many librarians and archivists – for me, at Glasgow University's Special Collections; Glasgow's Mitchell Library; Whitburn Public Library; New College Library, Edinburgh; the Innerpeffray Library, near Crieff; the Leighton Library, Dunblane; New Glasgow Public Library; Hector Research Centre, Pictou; Old Court House Museum, Guysborough, N.S.; Sherbrooke Branch Library, N.S.; United Church Maritime Conference Archives, Sackville, New Brunswick; and Nova Scotia Archives, Halifax.

Lastly, I cannot forget my cheerful, exacting editors, Krystyna Budd and Elizabeth King, and at an early stage, Tom Roach of Waterloo, ON,.

I have adopted the later spelling "MacGregor," although James used "McGregor." Jacob and James MacGregor started a five-generation dynasty of Presbyterian religious and educational leaders. This is the story of the first two.

Historiographical Introduction

BARRY CAHILL

The whole-cloth Presbyterian contribution to colonial Atlantic Canada in education, culture, and economic and intellectual life was implicit in the forty-year career of the Reverend James MacGregor (1759–1830), a dissenting minister and the father of Scottish Reformation Christianity in the region.[1]

MacGregor was Presbyterianism's lead contributor to the development of the Maritimes during the Loyalist Ascendancy, but never before *Highland Shepherd* has he been recognized as such, nor indeed much recognized at all, except as a pioneer missionary – a "coureur de bois of the Kingdom of Heaven."[2] Over the years, he has been either ignored by historians or celebrated by his co-religionists. In July 1936, for example, the Maritimes (now Atlantic) Synod of the Presbyterian Church in Canada dedicated a cairn to MacGregor's memory on the occasion of the sesquicentenary of his arrival in Pictou. The celebration was a commemoration of MacGregor as a "great spiritual leader" – both a religious and an ethnocultural hero. A book followed, which included substantial papers on MacGregor as a "prophet, pastor and [Gaelic] poet and as an 'apostle.'" The former president of Dalhousie University – Nova Scotia's answer to the Scottish universities – spoke on "Pictou's contribution to the intellectual life of Canada," but only hinted at MacGregor's significance: "It early came home to Dr. MacGregor that the provision of a native ministry was the only real solution of the religious problem. This meant education, and this meant schools. MacGregor himself was no mean scholar; but his time was fully occupied."[3]

Public history has been more considerate of James MacGregor than church history, where he is adversely judged in relation to his younger contemporary, Thomas McCulloch. Indeed, much of the credit given McCulloch (who, unlike MacGregor was not an itinerant missionary) in light of his greater opportunities, fewer responsibilities, wider field of activity, and less onerous demands on his time and energy properly belongs to MacGregor. The chief casualty of the McCulloch myth has been MacGregor history.

This devaluation is most evident in the scholarship that devotes these and other articles to McCulloch but largely overlooks MacGregor. In the end, McCulloch provides historical context for MacGregor, rather than the reverse. It goes unremarked in the literature that McCulloch was a follower and fulfiller, carrying out MacGregor's ideas and initiatives and realizing his educational vision. Without James MacGregor we might never have heard of Thomas McCulloch, whose forty-year career is properly contextualized as homage to MacGregor. McCulloch was in large measure the creation of MacGregor, who was the single most important influence on the younger man's career. Yet important as MacGregor's paternal mentoring of McCulloch may have been, the dynamic of the relationship between them is part of McCulloch's history, not MacGregor's. There is a reluctance toward recognizing either MacGregor's personal significance beyond his missions or his significance for McCulloch.

Students of the Presbyterian intelligentsia tend to see MacGregor as the rough-hewn minister and Highland mystic, and McCulloch as the thinker and critic. The true picture, presented in *Highland Shepherd*, is much richer and more complex. The history of the Scottish Enlightenment in Nova Scotia has needed to reclaim the more conventional ministerial aspects of McCulloch's career as well as the scientific rationalist aspects of MacGregor, as it appears here, both of which have been downplayed. MacGregor stands at the beginning and McCulloch at the end of what Daniel Cobb Harvey called Nova Scotia's "intellectual awakening." Harvey dispatches MacGregor in two words, "pioneer missionary," whereas McCulloch gets four paragraphs and is treated as if he were sui generis. Attempting to explain why Scottish immigrants had so profound an influence on Nova Scotia's economic and intellectual life, Harvey sought clues in the arrival of men like MacGregor, but above all in the accidental sojourn of Rev. Thomas McCulloch: "He it was who stirred his illiterate countrymen into action, provided the means of training against tremendous odds, produced a highly stimulating group of distinguished scholars, and left to Pictou county and the Nova Scotian Scots that intellectual tradition of which they are so justly proud."[4]

More of the same or similar appears in H.H. Walsh's "Church and Sect in the Maritime Provinces": "The arrival of Dr. Thomas McCulloch in Nova Scotia was a momentous event not only in the history of Canadian Presbyterian but in the social and cultural development of the Maritime Provinces." While this is a gross overstatement, Walsh demonstrated a clearer sense of the relationship between and relative importance of MacGregor and McCulloch than have historians of either of them before or since: "MacGregor soon recognized in him [McCulloch] a great educator, and was quick to take the opportunity to being to fruition a plan that had long been brewing in his mind – to found an academy from which it would be possible to recruit young men for the ministry."[5]

A telling and typical example of the persistent disequilibrium between historical evaluations of MacGregor and McCulloch is found in Philip Buckner and John Reid's 1994 edited collection of essays, *The Atlantic Region to Confederation: A History*. There MacGregor is rightly credited with Pictou's becoming "the centre for Presbyterianism in Nova Scotia." But we are further told that "the great creative contribution of Presbyterianism to the culture of the Atlantic colonies would begin just after the turn of the [nineteenth] century with the arrival of Thomas McCulloch and his profound sense of educational mission."[6] This is precisely where the MacGregor of history collides with the McCulloch of faith. MacGregor's sense of educational mission was more profound than McCulloch's, and the process, as described in *Highland Shepherd*, began nearly two decades earlier, under MacGregor. Even more revealing is the secondary source cited in support: Douglas Campbell and Ray MacLean limit MacGregor's significance to his laying "the seedbed of Presbyterianism in the country."[7]

Another example of this disequilibrium is the late George Rawlyk's 1997 edited collection of essays, *Aspects of the Canadian Evangelical Experience*, which reduces MacGregor even further – to a mere "Gael," a sort of ministerial Rob Roy or Scottish Paul Bunyan. While there is no question that MacGregor, unlike McCulloch, is integral to the "portrait of the Scottish Gael in Nova Scotia,"[8] there was much more to MacGregor's mission and ministry than "the evangelical confidence in religious experience that protected [him] from Old World Moderatism and New World latitudinarianism."[9]

MacGregor was the sophisticated intellectual everyman, a true child and product of the Scottish Enlightenment and the Scottish Realist philosophy propounded by Thomas Reid, Adam Smith's successor as professor of moral philosophy at Glasgow during MacGregor's undergraduate years.[10] Indeed, what Sir Robert Falconer called "Scottish influence in the higher education of Canada" began with MacGregor.[11]

By comparison with McCulloch, MacGregor wrote little and published less; he did not live to complete his own memoirs, which survive in manuscript and were printed in extension in James Robertson's 1847 *History of the Mission of the Secession Church to Nova Scotia and Prince Edward Island, from Its Commencement in 1765*. There is no monograph on him except the 1859 centenary filiopietistic offering of his grandson, the Reverend George Patterson, whose 533-page *Memoir of the Rev. James MacGregor, D.D.*, is a memoir in the narrow technical sense of "a historical account or biography written from personal knowledge or special sources."[12] The work is an ambitious life-and-times essay, but for reasons unknown Patterson led many astray by placing MacGregor at the University of Edinburgh (which he himself had attended) rather than at Glasgow, alma mater to MacGregor, McCulloch, and many of their colleagues at Pictou.

Patterson's work had a chilling effect on MacGregor's memory in that it discouraged scholarship for well over a century, deterring mainstream historians and preventing MacGregor's being seen as anything more than a Great Man, a figure of the heroic past rather than of history, and of interest chiefly to his descendants and co-religionists. Only a few specialized studies of aspects of his career have appeared, and Patterson's legacy of "Presbyterian propagandism" (Allan Dunlop) has been largely negative in its effect.

Pride of place belongs to Susan Buggey, whose 1987 article in volume 6 of the Dictionary of Canadian Biography (*DCB*) was, at the time of its publication, the only MacGregor scholarship worthy of the name. As Buggey points out, "A great deal has been written about MacGregor. The vast majority of these writings are based on George Patterson's *Memoir of the Rev. James MacGregor, D.D.* ... and have not been included in this bibliography."[13] She could hardly have damned more judiciously or with fainter praise, though her own concept of MacGregor is oversimplistic ("minister, author and composer"). MacGregor was also a scholar, educator, public intellectual, scientific agriculturalist, and experimental inventor.

It is instructive to compare Buggey's *DCB* 6 article on MacGregor with her *DCB* 7 article on McCulloch, co-written with Gwendolyn Davies and published in 1988. From this otherwise excellent work

MacGregor is conspicuous by his near-total absence. He may have been the first to think of training a native-born ministeriate but, it seems, McCulloch was the first to do something about it. Apart from having a good idea on which McCulloch afterwards capitalized, MacGregor is limited here to the character he inspired in McCulloch's fiction. Yet much of what is said about McCulloch in this article applies equally to MacGregor, who was no less "driven by his intellect, his Calvinist faith, his philosophical liberalism and his enormous energy"[14] than was McCulloch. Many of the scholarly works cited in the bibliography are relevant to MacGregor, as are the concepts behind them; for example, S.G. McMullin's "Evolution of a Liberal Mind." One cannot imagine a liberal mind more highly evolved than MacGregor's. Nor does the article address McCulloch's intellectual debt to MacGregor or their sometimes complicated and difficult relationship over twenty-seven years between McCulloch's unscheduled arrival at Pictou in 1803, when MacGregor was at the height of his powers, and MacGregor's death in 1830. This writing-out of MacGregor from McCulloch's career also reflects a tendency to exaggerate the breadth and importance of the latter: neither during MacGregor's lifetime nor afterwards was McCulloch ever the "undisputed leader" of the Presbyterian Church of Nova Scotia. He was far too Gaullist and uncollegial for that.

There is still no thesis at the MA, much less the PhD, level, on MacGregor in the round or on any aspect of his career. In the autumn of 1994 the Department of Religious Studies at Mount Allison University hosted an academic conference, "The Contribution of Presbyterianism to Atlantic Canada."[15] No assessment of the contribution of Presbyterianism to the history and culture of the Maritime Provinces would have been complete without MacGregor, though only three of twenty-one papers presented addressed him directly. One dealt with his antislavery activism, another with his "fictional valorization" by Thomas McCulloch, and a third with his radical evangelical persona. No attempt was made to assess MacGregor as the *fons et origo* of Presbyterianism in Atlantic Canada or to assess his personal contribution to the wider contribution of Presbyterianism.

A book of scholarly essays, *The Presbyterian Contribution to Canadian Life and Culture*, published on the occasion of the conference, does not address MacGregor directly but rates him and McCulloch as standing out prominently "in early Nova Scotia Presbyterianism." An essay by the editor, Dr. William Klempa (then principal of Presbyterian College, Montreal), on the history of Presbyterian theology before the 1875 establishment of the Presbyterian Church in Canada, allows that MacGregor and McCulloch were "far from being intellectual pygmies."[16] Klempa's essay covers the primitive and pentecostal Henry Alline (whose theology MacGregor described as "a mixture of Calvinism, Antinomianism and Enthusiasm") and McCulloch (the "outstanding figure" during early settlement), while excluding MacGregor altogether. The balance is tipped too heavily in favour of McCulloch – the famous as opposed to the important – whose index references outnumber MacGregor's four to one. Yet, an argument could be made that unlike MacGregor, McCulloch was not a theologian at all. Moreover, on the face of it there seems no reason why Alline, a "New Light" Congregationalist, should appear in a history of Presbyterian theology, with which he had little in common and to which he was much opposed.

Writing circa 1941, Judge George Geddie Patterson, MacGregor's great-grandson, observed of Thomas McCulloch that "adequate justice has never yet been done him."[17] Since that time perhaps McCulloch has been done more than justice.

Now, *Highland Shepherd* is finally doing more than "adequate justice" to James MacGregor. In Alan Wilson, MacGregor has finally found a historian worthy of his deeds and personality. The book goes beyond a conventional or an intellectual biography. It is a fully realized social history of MacGregor's public life and times in Scotland and in Canada, where he was one of the foremost developers of the Scottish tradition. Scottish Presbyterianism, agriculture, artisanship and industry, Gaelic literature, higher education, and politics all owe something to him.

In his magisterial biography of George Munro Grant, D.B. Mack speaks engagingly of Grant as "Pictou man."[18] Grant was one of this new species – *homo intellectualis* – of which James MacGregor was the real progenitor.

Presbyterian Organization Relating to Macgregor's Life

1560 John Knox leads the Scottish Reformation.

1638 Adoption of the National Covenant

1647 Adoption of the Westminister Confession of Faith

1690 Religious settlement guarantees the Presbyterian foundation of the Scottish National Church ("Kirk"), known today as "The Church of Scotland."

1733 Rev. Ebenezer Erskine and his supporters, who oppose lay and state patronage appointments to Kirk churches, and who support a more active evangelicalism, are suspended by the Kirk's General Assembly.

1740 Erskine and colleagues secede from the Kirk to form the Associate Synod in a new "Secession Church."

1747 Controversy arises over enforcement of the "Burgess Oath," requiring town burghers (or burgesses) to defer to the Established Church of Scotland and to resist Catholic resurgence. Many fear that it must mean closer church-state relations, especially in matters of patronage, thereby reinforcing the Kirk's powers. This leads to a division among Secessionists between supporters of the oath – the Associate Synod (the "Burghers") – and those who oppose it, who then form a new "General Associate Synod," based at Glasgow, the "Anti-Burghers."

1817 The Secessionists' separation in Nova Scotia is healed by the formation of the "Presbyterian Church of Nova Scotia" in 1817.

1820 Burgher and Anti-Burgher elements reunite as United Secession Church of Scotland.

PART ONE

Getting There

Chapter One

Awaiting the Verdict

Glasgow, Scotland. 4 May 1786. The young man sat alone, shifting on the hard bench, staring at the closed doors opposite him. His face, normally dark, seemed pale against the black of his clerical coat. Through the tall casement windows, a wind-tossed sky showed patches of blue between billows of white clouds. It was a Scottish spring, sun and rain playing mischievously with people's spirits. For James MacGregor these shifts matched his mercurial mood as he awaited the verdict.

Through the great double doors he could hear muted sounds of the impassioned argument typical of meetings of Synod, for he knew the rhetoric of men of strong Anti-Burgher conviction – sounds he had grown up with at home for over twenty-five years, and which Scotland had heard for more than a half-century. He leaned forward, straining to discover whether they had reached a decision, but the doors were stout and his desire to listen was tempered by fear of what he might hear. This was the moment he and his family had long worked for, and he prayed that his father would not be disappointed. James had told Synod, "I had considered it a case clear, not to myself only, but to the majority of the Synod, that I was called to preach to the Highlanders of Scotland, and of course that I could not be sent abroad."[1]

Torn between duty to family and to God – yet knowing that he must submit to God's will in Synod's instructions – he asked himself, "What is Pictou? And what have I to offer it?"

He shifted restlessly, crossing his long, powerful legs. His face was long and showing colour as his pulse quickened with his mounting anxiety. No one had accompanied him, nor would there be any meeting of the Class of '86, for his had been a lonely path. When not in Glasgow or later, Alloa, near Perth, pursuing his studies, he had walked the Highlands and his own *ling*, heather, even to the north at Nigg in Ross-shire, teaching and preaching to fulfil his probation and earn his keep. Settling into the garret of a grateful dissenter or of a student's respectful parents, he had consoled himself that in making his own way, he was also broadening his knowledge of his native land and of the Gaelic language.

Now, his studies behind him, he must take up a post. He drew his feet under the bench, for his shoes were poor, worn thin from five years on mission, building a reputation as one of Synod's most versatile candidates. But, he must obey Synod, for apart from the Bible it was as close as one could come to God's Word. He longed to work beside his father in the Highland vineyards, jointly bringing in a harvest of souls. The family had talked the evenings away in prospect of that partnership, as they had spoken of the Highlander's need for leadership in increasingly troubled times.

Like his father, James wanted to stem the tide of departing Highlanders, some of them the most enterprising. A generation ago, after Culloden, there had been "Butcher" Cumberland's brutal "mopping up" of the glens. Culloden had been more than a military defeat, the beginning of a final assault on clanship. Now the means was foreclosure, eviction, seizure of land by Scots and English landlords with plans for commercial development.

Yet ironically, Highlanders were on the increase.[2] The end of the clan wars, better medical practices, and the introduction of the potato had reinforced their penchant for large families.[3] Many with money or seeking a trade were flocking south to set up commercially, to work as navvies on the vast lowland canal projects, or to learn new skills like industrial weaving. Highland border districts like south Perthshire were twice as populous now, and Perth would grow by 20 per cent by 1800. Argyle would follow. There was, however, another side to this emigration as the small, tough Highland cattle gave way to sheep, and food crops to fodder. Greedy landholders were pushing the Highlands in new directions: glens would be emptied to provide wintering-over for sheep, and rentals would rise from £700 to £1,500. Faced with such threats – or simply feeling ambitious – many were moving overseas in hope of owning their own land in new economies and societies.

In time, voluntary emigration would be overridden by the flight of refugees fleeing west to an uncertain fishery and a waning kelp trade; south to the cities; or in hope or desperation to North America and beyond. Even in the late 1770s, in parts of the Highlands voluntary emigration was yielding to exodus under duress.

The ancient feudal culture was wasting away; many chieftains and tacksmen had already gone. The Highlands had not known a conventional economy – or the "tenants" would have been no better than peasants, as dependent as the shepherds with their sheep now moving in around them. But, they prided themselves as crofters and on being next in line after their chiefs and tacksmen. Kinship and loyalty lay at the heart of Highland society, but it was threatened by a growing subordination to industrialization and the commercial culture of the Lowlands and of England.[4] Although kin-based societies had disappeared in much of Europe, in Scotland "about one in each twenty-four people were actually members of a titled or chiefly house, and … about one-half of the Scottish nation consciously regarded themselves as members of the aristocracy."[5] A tectonic shift was underway in Highland culture, but pride, tradition, cultural nationalism, and old rivalries would leap the Atlantic to places as far removed as Nova Scotia.

The Campbells, spread from Argyll to Breadalbane, set a positive example, as J.M. Bumsted highlights in his emigration story, by adopting cattle and timber export and even taking up American land and Caribbean plantations – and now they were pressing their countrymen.[6] In James's gateway country of south Perthshire, Highland ways had always been under threat from the Lowlands. Local clan spirit might be kept alive by the legends of Rob Roy and would survive even into Victorian times in what David Daiches deftly calls the region's "Balmoralization,"[7] encouraged by Walter Scott's fictions and the Queen's visits with Mr. Brown. But some, like James's father, Jacob, had seen where events were leading and resolved to rebuild old ways at home, as well as to save souls. Emigration by the educated and enterprising must be staunched before panic drove out even more.

James stirred again, thinking of how he had sought a ministry to "his brethren, his kinsmen according to the flesh." He longed for Comrie or a little farther north, Craigdam. Either would allow him to work with his father. Besides, while Highlanders needed God's Word, they also needed letters and learning, which a well-schooled young man could provide.

He had, besides, an independent spirit that soon led him to renounce his father's surname, "Drummond," one of the sept names of the earls of Perth, the MacGregors' protectors, after James VI declared them "altogidder banished" for acts of murder, poaching, robbery, and more.[8]

Rob Roy had plunged the name back into infamy, and after Culloden it had been banned again. In 1774, however, the proscription was lifted, and Jemmy Drummond boldly assumed the name "James McGregor."

Still the time moved leadenly. He stood up, tall and spare, stretching and quietly pacing the hall. At twenty-seven, his energies drove him towards his life's work. Like his father he would serve God and restore Highland culture and pride, especially in the Gaelic. And he had chosen a good time. Lowlanders considered Highland poetry little more than bad verse and Highland culture backward and lacking refinement,[9] but this was a period of great output in Gaelic people and poetry, and James rejoiced in both.

As he waited, he prayed again to be called home, not banished to some foreign frontier in the north of God knew where. At home Jacob, too, sat waiting, willing Synod to agree to what he and Jemmy had dreamed of for years.

Chapter Two

Honour Thy Father

On a morning in the early 1730s James's father, Jacob Drummond, then a teenager, lay sleeping in his father's house in the Perthshire *clachan*, hamlet, of Portmore, on the shores of Loch Earn. He was awakened by the *acainean*, the sobs, of a woman outside. Peering out in the grey dawn, he watched the misery of many newcomers straggling down from the surrounding hills. The woman turned to him, wailing through her tears,

> We were asleep in our beds when they came with *armachd*, torches, and swords to do us violence. They stole our *ainmhidhean*, animals, killed our *aighean*, cows, put our roofs to the flame, and drove us away before we could gather to us anything that was ours. Help us, for we're *airsneaclach*, weary and in despair.

It was not an unusual event: another village sacked by the agents of greedy Scots landlords and English business interests to "free" the land and turn it to other purposes. Such accounts unsettled Jacob, who was no *niddering*, coward, but intent on improving his lot. He had often considered moving south and now set out for the port town of Alloa, county seat of Clackmannan at the head of the Firth of Forth.

There, he apprenticed to a weaver, for Alloa and nearby Stirling, the old Royal Town, were becoming major textile centres.[1] Alloa would soon account for 20 per cent of Scotland's textile production, and Jacob, intent on improving his skills, applied himself steadily. Some of his clansmen supported the Stewarts in the '45,[2] but Jacob and Alloa wanted nothing to do with the Jacobites or the Bonnie Prince. To them, "Ilka thing hath its time, And so had kings of the Stewart line." The shoemakers of Alloa stuck to their lasts – and Jacob to his weaving.

He pursued two goals: a sound trade and a passionate evangelical-ism. His master weaver had introduced him to a church near Stirling, guided by one of Scotland's great preachers, Rev. Ebenezer Erskine, and his conversion would prove the most empowering moment in his life. Indeed, Jacob's impact upon his son Jemmy helps to account for MacGregor's later religious and social message, his strength of will, and his legendary evangelicalism.

Besides becoming a centre for textiles, Alloa was a growing coal-mining, industrial, and shipping centre, spawning a large working class. Change was everywhere, the Erskines championing waterfront development, coal mining, and agricultural "improvement." Clack-mannanshire, Scotland's smallest county, was becoming powerful in an industrial and trading world.

The Erskines' record was long and distinguished: keepers of the royal castles; James V's guardians after Flodden; baronets of Nova Scotia; hosts to Mary, Queen of Scots for six years. To be an Erskine was of consequence, and Rev. Ebenezer Erskine was a leader in a further family enterprise, the Church of Scotland, the Kirk. By midcentury, however, their reputation began to dim as Sir Thomas lost miners and blamed the workers: "There is," he complained, "much too little of the custom of punishing Coalli-ers." Exploitation and long indentures were common among the men of "the black stone," and Jacob shared their spirit of discontent.[3] Crowded industrial towns and pollution belied the idea of progress. Miners and weavers looked for respect and better conditions through education and invention. Prescient improvers like the Erskines linked agricultural progress with industrial growth and social stability. Urban workers needed ample and cheap food supplies.[4] Later, this yearning for social and eco-nomic harmony guided James MacGregor in his mission in Nova Scotia.

Many employers regarded the workers as "ignorant," "outcast from the church," especially Highlanders, who complained of the great distance between their living quarters and the churches.[5] They also rebelled against patronage in settling ministers.

> In 1740, when it was proposed ... that the minister of Monimail be transferred to the large and flourishing parish of Inveresk, a body of weavers ... protested. The transfer would, they claimed be based on love of money, not on spiritual edification, and they did not want a minister open to such influences.[6]

Militant or simply discouraged, weavers made up a large part of Scottish emigration.[7]

Jacob Drummond was distressed, but he returned to his people with new skills and a new religious enthusiasm. Experienced weavers' earnings were relatively high, but in the towns they endured what Christopher Whatley calls "voluntary slavery."[8] Worsening working and living conditions bred a culture of wage slavery, fatalism, and despair, which Jacob rejected. Freedom, independence, and optimism were hallmarks of his religious and social convictions. Accordingly, he returned to Strathearn, where by working hard as an independent he could earn more than those on urban wages,[9] and he could live in familiar and agreeable surroundings. Jacob's progressive agrarian vision directed him to a renewed Gaelic spirit, culture, and concern for his Highland neighbours. The later letters of his minister at Comrie, Rev. Samuel Gilfillan, sent to Jacob's son in Pictou, confirm his lifelong consistency.[10]

Jacob began again – as shepherd, farmer, weaver, preacher, catechist, and distiller. Through assurance and faith, he pursued social harmony for himself and his people, encouraging them to remain at home. His vision arose from two passions: his religious faith and the belief that social reform, especially literacy and education, could effect general improvement and bring individual success. Those ambitions, nurtured at Alloa and pursued in the Highlands, fostered a passion for general reform in his son and later in his grandson, Rev. Peter Gordon MacGregor in nineteenth-century Halifax.

Meanwhile, while Alloa had given Jacob a trade and a spiritual beginning, Ebenezer Erskine was about to rock the Kirk, and the shock waves of that activity were felt in Nova Scotia and in the early relations between Pictou and Truro, where his son would encounter them.

Erskine aimed his protest at a set of self-appointed reformers within the Kirk. These self-styled "Moderates" were pressing for elitist change, many being men of learning and the professions.[11] Calling for change in traditionally puritanical Scottish Presbyterianism,[12] they would replace scripture and grace with "good works." From the "New Towns" – the upper-middle-class districts of Glasgow and Edinburgh – they decried a rigid Sabbatarianism. Moderates dined out on Saturday night, instead of preparing for the solemnity of the Sabbath. Some even attended the theatre, challenging the hypocrisy of attending "a concert of musick with a play between acts."[13] Academics, ministers, lawyers, literary luminaries, they reflected educated, upper-class values and derided the "provincial" clergy for appeals to emotion and enthusiasm to arouse the guilt they believed must precede salvation. The Moderates offered "reason and moderation," but as David Daiches observes, "Sometimes they spoke like Deists rather than Christians."[14]

Their "Society for Promoting Christian Knowledge" urged Lowland Kirk ministers to "convert the [Highland] peasantry from the Gaelic and their heathenish religion and culture,"[15] meaning Catholic, for in places the Scottish Reformation had not penetrated the Highlands. But, Jacob Drummond saw in their contempt for Highland ways an offence to his religion and culture.

The Moderates condoned private and state appointments to Kirk pulpits, defying the Evangelicals' goal of an elective ministry and stipulating that they should be the only ones appointed. Patronage of this sort alarmed Ebenezer Erskine and threatened the freedom and independence of men like Jacob.

Similar criticisms were raised by John Wesley in England, as the two "national" churches came under attack. T.C. Smout deftly describes those churches:

> Both believed that the social order was already organized in a way highly satisfactory to God and both assumed the Lord to be as moderate in His religious views as they were themselves. Many ministers began to drop their primitive character of eager reprovers, and to adopt the personae of polite and unenthusiastic gentlemen, able to embellish God's word in an elegant address indicating to the poor the prime virtues of obedience and industry.[16]

The Moderates' leader, Rev. William Robertson, principal of Edinburgh and historian second only to Edward Gibbon, was opposed to the century-old Presbyterian Covenanting tradition, which regarded bishops or patrons of any kind as an affront to the Gospel liberty in which Presbyterian pastors and elders were traditionally rooted. "Covenanting," he sniffed, "had its origins in banditry." Then he drew another line in the sand: "There can be no society where there is no subordination."[17]

But Jacob Drummond wanted no part of a system where a laird appointed one of his own to the pulpit in his bailiwick. He balked at settled ministers and challenges to traditional public disciplinary procedures like "stooling."[18] Ebenezer Erskine rallied those who clung to evangelicalism and the great sermon tradition. Caught up by this so-called affectionate ministry that drew tears of remorse during long sermons studded with graphic pictures of the dangers of sin and the prospect of hell, Jacob Drummond followed Erskine. "Good works" must not displace faith, for as Wallace Notestein remarks, "It was not in the Scot to be satisfied with good works. He demanded more poetry in his religion and more passion."[19] Jacob gave himself to their cause.

Erskine vilified the Moderates' cosy connections with the state and their collusion with many town burgesses, calling for a renewal of Scottishness and loyalty to the Gaelic language. His revolt combined religion, culture, class, and politics – elements that appeared years later in the dispute over Pictou Academy. Erskinites rebuked the new intellectual aristocracy, like David Hume, who spoke a broader Scots than Robbie Burns and "sent his manuscripts to English friends to be corrected of any Scotticisms."[20]

As Richard Finlay observes, Erskine's radical conservative revolt stemmed from the Covenanters' egalitarian rejection of "theocratic privilege and patronage."[21] Erskine especially condemned the Moderates' support of class privilege: "I can find no warrant from the word of God to confer the spiritual privileges of His house upon the rich beyond the poor: whereas by the [Patronage] Act, the man with the gold ring and the gay clothing is preferred unto the man with the vile raiment and poor attire."[22] But the Moderates ignored such injunctions.

A century later, these struggles resurfaced in Scotland and in British North America when Rev. Thomas Chalmers reprised Erskine, and three hundred clergy and thousands of laity left the Kirk to form the Free Church. The 1840s jingle of the "Great Disruption" could have applied to Erskine's eighteenth-century renegades:

> The new kirk, the wee kirk
> The kirk wi'out the steeple;
> The auld kirk, the cauld kirk,
> The kirk without the people.

Thus, Erskine's populism reflected Dissenting Presbyterianism's democratic streak, appealing to tradesmen like Jacob and to distressed labour. Defying the Kirk, they formed an "Associate Presbytery." But if these "Seceders" were conservative in customs and in matters like grace and good works, their social policies were liberal. They questioned the inertia inherent in the doctrine of predestination. Change was in the air: an emerging middle class and a beleaguered working class rejected the view that they must accept the station to which God was reputed to have assigned them. The Seceders gave them hope without abandoning grace or the need for a personal piety. Thus, Jacob became a "reader," or "catechist," on mission "to exhort and to explain the scriptures" until he was qualified or superseded by trained ministers. He might have remained at Erskine's call forever.

In 1747, however, a second disruption arose, this time among the Seceders themselves, an event that sent Jacob home to become a self-appointed Secessionist missionary. He returned, however, as an "Anti-Burgher" Secessionist, a distinction that would touch his son in Nova Scotia, and which remains the last piece of religious baggage brought by James to Pictou to be examined.

The new controversy centred on old state-church quarrels.[23] In certain towns, burgesses (burghers) were required to swear a "Burgess Oath," sealing Kirk-state ties. The oath also implied that the Kirk was the bulwark against a mythically resurgent popery, but sceptics saw it as an excuse to restore the Kirk's waning fortunes. Jacob was as much against papists as the next man, but he spurned the oath for implicitly acknowledging the Kirk as being by law established. But Ebenezer Erskine confounded them all by agreeing to the oath. The appeal played to his weak suit, for Ebenezer could find a papist plot around any corner. To many, he seemed to have knuckled under to the Moderates. Or why secede at all? What Edmund Burke called "the natural dissidence of dissent" manifested itself in waves of indignation.

So, the Associated Presbytery disassociated itself, dividing over the oath. Two Seceder churches emerged with separate assemblies: the Associate Assembly of Burghers (Erskinites), and a "General Associate Assembly" of Anti-Burghers, with Jacob an adherent. Jacob took sad leave of the man who had brought him into the fellowship of believers, but he, too, was a man of principle. Thus he joined one of the more puritanical groups in the country.

In the New World, Jemmy Drummond (MacGregor) would face the ghosts of Kirk Moderatism at Halifax and in the power of the Established Church of England in Nova Scotia, and he would have his early differences with Truro's Burgher Presbytery. For although such issues may appear petty and distant in an age that questions formal religion, the Reformation came late to Scotland, and memories were still fresh. Disruption was imbedded in clan rivalries, struggles over succession, tensions with an officially Protestant England, and fear of interference by France, Spain, and the papacy. Defiant positions were common, and issues over church and state led to conflict among a fractious people. James MacGregor would bring to Nova Scotia the inspiration – and some of the burden – of his Secessionist ways and his paternal roots, a legacy that during his early years would sometimes put him to the test at Pictou.

Chapter Three

New Beginnings for Father and Son

Jacob Drummond returned home in the mid-1740s, settling at Portmore on Loch Earn in the Kirk parish of Comrie, which lay a few miles to the east. Portmore had a Kirk shelter – akin to a *tigh an leughaidh*, reading-house[1] – but the closest Anti-Burgher congregation was 29 kilometres (18 miles) southwest at Kinkell, well beyond Comrie and the thriving town of Crieff.

Jacob's was a lonely, unrecognized mission, but he was determined to grow Anti-Burgher congregations in his own district, no matter how long it took. Secession had hardly reached the lower Highlands, but as an independent farmer-weaver he resolved to raise a family, with sons to support him and to succeed him in farm and mission.

Strathearn's natural beauty would draw any unattached man home, and Jacob's heart was light as he rounded the Ochils into Bridge-of-Allan, thence into Strathallan and the ancient cathedral town of Dunblane, perched on the southern foothills of the Highland massif.[2] He was bound for Loch Earn, where at its western end "the eagle, he was lord above, And Rob was lord below." But Jacob's goal was the eastern end, where the Earn waters tumble past Comrie and Crieff, ultimately entering the Tay estuary near Perth. At home, he looked again in awe at the grandeur of Ben Fuith across the loch and westward where the peaks were always snow-covered. There he began a new life in peaceful containment.

The legends surrounding Rob Roy had brought renown to western Strathearn, but to the east, at Comrie, Muthill, and Crieff, there had been excitement of a different kind. Comrie sits at the epicentre of the great Highland Border Fault and is deservedly called "The earthquake capital of Scotland" and "The Shakin' Toun." There were rich historical associations as well, for the district lay across another line, where the Roman legions had been turned back. Portmore was associated with St. Fillan (*Faelan*), Robert the Bruce's patron saint at Bannockburn, and Jemmy grew up with stories of that tireless early evangelist for another, competing cause – the Scottish crown and country. Further, the road through Strathearn connected all north-south commerce. Crieff was the site of Scotland's great interior cattle market with its cattle drives, called "trysts," an entrepot for Stirling and Falkirk, which ensured a lively local economy. A tryst could witness thirty thousand guineas changing hands: thus, Crieff was also a major banking centre.[3]

Strathearn is a magical country: above it on the moorlands lie *lochans*, lakes and ponds, reaching north to Loch Tay, a country of chattering burns, splendid bogs, bold crags, and all alive with birds and game. Jacob would remain there for the rest of his life, finding a wife in a cousin, Jannet Dochart (another MacGregor sobriquet). Courting her, he walked down the lovely river path to the vale of Duniera (now Dunira), described by Sarah Murray as "the most singular spot … in the world."[4] Jannet's parents worked on the 20,000-acre estate of James Drummond VII, and it was at Comrie that Jacob and Jannet were married on 1 December 1748.[5]

A daughter, also Jannet, was born in 1749, and two other sisters arrived, but neither of their older brothers survived. Jemmy, the youngest, was born in December 1759, with the family's hopes pinned on him. His brothers' deaths had projected him into a common Highland succession: dedicating the eldest son to the ministry, Catholic and Protestant alike.

Among the locals Jacob was dubbed "Nathanael,"[6] the true Israelite, who, after doubting, had acknowledged that "good could come out of Nazareth." He was unsparing in encouraging Strathearn and Jemmy to that end. Years later, as patriarch at Pictou, Jemmy followed his father's example.

Jemmy's equally spiritual mother had the practical nature that Jacob sometimes lacked. Through her good management, Jemmy received the religious education he needed,[7] while also pursuing classics and languages. From John Knox and Jacob, Jemmy learned that education was tied to spiritual advance. By his parents' and sisters' labour, he would follow the course his father and custom set for him.

MacGregor left little record of his childhood, but his love of Strathearn is evident in his papers. A map he drew, detailing every stream that entered Loch Earn, is still extant.[8] Exploring the shores and hills about him, he earned a reputation for fun, energy, and initiative; someone described him as "a fine frank lad," whose friends often gathered at his cottage where "he would keep them the whole evening in amusement."[9]

Drummond means "the far side of the hill," and with his companions, Jemmy climbed the steep slopes to burns teeming with trout; he glimpsed hare and red deer, stags and ptarmigan, and watched the soaring majesty of eagles and peregrines. In spring, along with orange-billed oystercatchers came runs of North Sea salmon and char, as men and boys lined the banks, restoring empty larders. In summer, he swam in the loch's frigid waters, sometimes swimming out to Neish Island and the ruins of Loch Earn Castle. The massacre of the MacNeishes, their enemies carrying boats over the mountains at night, was a story to thrill any youngster.

With the warming of the days there appeared banks of heath and heather; rowan blossomed; strawberry and harebell beckoned; and in the woods, the last of the wild hyacinths bloomed. Downriver, Jemmy climbed Dunfillan, visiting the mounded Pictish *cathair*, fort, and the legendary St. Fillan's Chair, *Tom nan Glun*, "Hillock of the Knees," where, it was said, the faithful had left their mark while kneeling in prayer.

Nearer home he followed the peat road, climbed the sharp goat track, and after crossing the scree slope and travelling under giant oaks, came to the rolling moorlands with their bogs and lochans, their wild orchids, and a feeling of removal from all human company. It remains a wild and deeply moving land – one to prepare him for the even wilder beauty of Nova Scotia.

When summer folded into fall, there was the excitement of the trysts as hundreds of cattle drovers worked their way down the Sma' Glen or Glen Boltachan to the bustling market place at Crieff. With his friends Jemmy stared in awe at these men from the Western Isles – Oban, Skye, and Harris – who had driven their charges across Scotland. Thirty thousand head was not uncommon, spilling in and out of Crieff. The noisy scene was made for small boys, who tempted fate by slipping as close to the passing beasts as they dared. Jacob and Jannet brought their vegetables, their weaving, and their whisky in hopes of brisk sales to herders whose pockets were lined with fresh pay. The grand Hebridean parade excited the young people, leading them to wonder about life beyond their lovely loch and the snug world of Strathearn.

Loch Earn and St Fillans. (Souvenir of Scotland: Its Cities, Lakes and Mountains. T. Nelson and Sons, London, Edinburgh, and New York. 1894, [n.p.].)

For Jemmy, this tireless activity would be repeated in Nova Scotia, where he would often depend for food and safety on his strength, his long legs, his sense of direction, his agility, and his gathering skills. It nurtured his endurance and height: he grew to over six feet (described as "rather above the middle size," for Highlanders were tall). Later, men marveled at his energy, but he had been strengthened by a strenuous childhood on the hills of Strathearn.

For eight years this enchanted world filled Jemmy's days, while his parents and sisters prepared him for his schooling. He watched his father's unceasing efforts, learning not to be discouraged by a catechist's slow progress, and from him he caught the importance of literacy, for on many nights after his day labours, Jacob tramped the hills, bringing tracts, reading the Bible, tutoring – reminding his people that to read the Word directly was to approach the realms of God. No one should intervene between the believer and the Truth. He spoke with the fire of an old Covenanter, seeing education and religion as twin pillars of a righteous life – and a free one.

Often on Sundays the family rose before dawn to walk the 29 kilometres (18 miles) east to Kinkell, where the Earn was spanned by a handsome stone bridge.[10] Arriving around nine, they rested until the service, which was held in the open on a green that slopes to the quiet river. Later, retracing their steps, they talked of matters raised by the minister, and Jacob stopped all whom they met, describing the meeting – but he encountered plenty of critics. One doubter remarked, "Here comes that great Seceder, we canna get a word said." A more charitable voice countered, "The woods on the side of Loch Earne, if they could speak would testify how often he wrestled with god for his church, and especially for this benighted part of the country."[11]

Not far from the Kinkell bridge stands the Innerpeffray Library, Scotland's oldest free public lending library, founded in 1680 by David Drummond. It was completed in 1762, when Jacob and his family were attending the meetings close by. One of Jemmy's ministers appears in the borrowers' list, which reflects the varied backgrounds of its users: gentlemen, carpenters, mechanics, and weavers.[12] Strathearn attended to learning for all levels and classes – another lesson to take to Pictou.

Later, when Kinkell's Seceder minister, Rev. James Barlas, began regular visitations to Portmore, Jacob became his leading elder, and later still, Barlas became one of MacGregor's chief correspondents overseas, as did his son-in-law and successor, Rev. Samuel Gilfillan, Jemmy's contemporary.

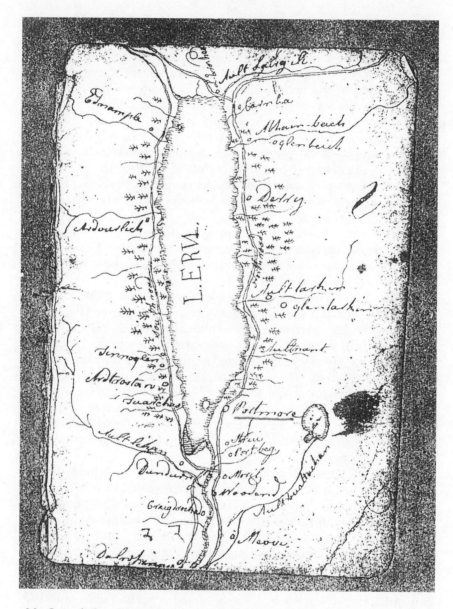

MacGregor's Own Map of Loch Earn. (Original in MacGregor Papers, Archives of Maritime Conference, United Church of Canada, Sackville, NB; with permission.)

While Jannet and the girls worked the farm, selling their produce and sewing in the community, Jacob tended the sheep, wove, and operated a still to raise money to educate the future abstentionist. Together they had three aims: to provide for the family, to ensure Jemmy's schooling, and to further Jacob's mission. In their culture everything was directed to establishing the oldest male. Girls got short shrift.

In 1767 Jemmy was sent to grammar school at Kinkell, where Rev. Barlas was also dominie.[13] He boarded with an elder, earning his keep by daily reeling dozens of knots of linen thread. Here, too, he began his interest in folklore. Recognizing his good spirits and cleverness, his host remarked, "He'll show blood."[14]

For secondary learning, he moved farther east to the cathedral town of Dunblane in Strathallan.[15] Dunblane was well suited for a boy bound for the pulpit and the study, for in the sixth century St Blane had founded a college there, and Dunblane preserved ancient customs and held learning in great regard. It was a picture book community, with narrow, sloping streets, stone buildings, and always the rush of the Allan Water. The school stood in Smithy Loan, on a knoll above the cathedral. Jemmy's transition in this town of tradition, religion, and learning was a significant part of his maturing, as he grew in sophistication with an unusual facility for languages, especially Hebrew and Gaelic.

After Dunblane, he entered the University of Glasgow in 1776, which proved another formative experience.

Chapter Four

Glasgow and Alloa

James MacGregor's grandson, Rev. George Patterson, who published the *Memoir*, claimed falsely that James attended the University of Edinburgh, as he would himself do. James attended Glasgow, and it makes all the difference. A son of Jacob Drummond would not have been sent to a university dominated by Kirk Moderates. Glasgow – college and town – had a lasting effect upon him, and Pictou read the Glasgow papers first.

Glasgow University in the late eighteenth century – "The College" – was one of Scotland's four noted universities.[1] Founded in 1451, it contrasted with Edinburgh, established over a century later. Their differences were rooted in their different societies and economies.

After Scotland's union with England in 1707, Edinburgh was associated with government, the professions, and a literary flowering. Glasgow followed a more industrial and commercial pattern, holding its college to a more classical curriculum. During the eighteenth century, however, the college broadened out, reflecting the town's economic growth and boasting a new intelligentsia: scientific, technological, philosophic, and economic, even mercantile under Adam Smith.

When Jemmy entered Glasgow, the town was small and the college tiny, with fewer than three hundred students. Besides having an interest in divinity, Jemmy was attracted to language and moral philosophy, which was well established in ways that anticipated the social sciences. T.C. Smout reminds us that "if philosophy was about morals, and morals affected the whole of society, then all the social sciences could legitimately become the philosopher's field."[2]

David Daiches agrees: "Moral philosophy and history are both products of an interest in the science of man."[3] The greatest promoter of the "science of man" at the time was David Hume,[4] but while he and many advocates of the Scottish Common Sense philosophy wanted to remove religion from considerations of morality and social conduct, their emphasis on social progress could engage an enquiring young student of divinity. The watchword was "improvement," and Scotland had proportionately more schools than the rest of Britain and Europe.[5] Across Lowland Scotland a new intellectualism elevated and Europeanized upper-middle-class interests and tastes; new cultural and intellectual clubs were appearing. At Edinburgh, training in fields like law and medicine held priority. There, too, town and gown were linked in the patronage and power surrounding the Kirk, the Established Church of Scotland. Many divinity students attended Edinburgh because they felt more certain of a good posting.

By contrast, R.N. Smart observes that until the nineteenth century, "Glasgow reflected the industrial and commercial nature of its province, ... Edinburgh the professional and legal nature of its province."[6] Roger Emerson notes that each of the three leading Scottish universities – Edinburgh, Glasgow, and Aberdeen – had its own interests and supports, and therefore each enjoyed fairly defined roles in the making of the Scottish Enlightenment. Glasgow was "a merchant town, but the merchants had little to do with the polite professors until near the end of the century," although Smith and John Millar mingled regularly with townspeople.[7]

By contrast with Edinburgh, Glasgow was less concerned about *working* with Establishments, civic or religious, than about *understanding* them – their origins and makeup, the roots of their power. Faculty and curriculum focused on questions of human nature, the sources of authority and morality, civic responsibility, social and juridical issues, and human rights. Glasgow town was still a centre for the trade in slaves, but an antislavery movement was developing swiftly in town and college. In a word, Glasgow sought "the moral politician." Emerson argues that there were really two Enlightenments at Glasgow: that in science, politics, history, and education; and an "evangelical enlightenment," less Tory and more sympathetic to the American rebels and the early French revolutionaries. They also believed that learning should be useful and should support true religion.[8] This was the world into which Jemmy MacGregor entered in 1776.

N.E. Phillipson identifies the 1770s and 1780s as the zenith of the Enlightenment at Glasgow, the years that Jemmy attended or was working out of Glasgow.[9] "Auld Reekie" soon became one of Britain's fastest-growing cities, surpassing sixty thousand during his residency.[10] Some grew rich from linen and tobacco, some from slaves, others from manufacturing. West of the old Glasgow Cross district, imposing mansions rose up in New Town, around George Square. But most people were small traders, craftspeople, and shopkeepers, making only modest gains.

Everywhere there was new architectural, cultural, and intellectual excitement, and at the college, the attraction of great lecturers. Irene Maver observes, "Most of the College professors fell into the exclusive ranks of the highly taxed, showing the prestige of the institution and the profitable returns for senior academics."[11] Hume received £5,000 sterling (2009 CAN $700,000) for the first volume of his history of Britain, and Principal Robertson £4,500 for his second book.[12]

Robert Turnbull describes the entry to the old college through its ornate sixteenth-century west front:

> Passing up the High Street, we come to an arched gateway, [and] ... a quadrangle court, with antique looking buildings on each side. Beyond this ... another quadrangle, this surrounded by buildings of perhaps more recent date ... Beyond us is the college-green, ornamented with trees, and divided into two parts by a sluggish stream ... A number of the students, having laid aside their scarlet gowns, are playing at football, a violent but delightful and invigorating exercise.[13]

Jemmy was caught up by Glasgow's wonders and vibrancy, but he found another appeal, too: "There was a keen philosophical edge to the ideas emanating from Glasgow, which related to the quest for social harmony and the concept of civil and religious liberty."[14] Glasgow had its faculty and student clubs, and from the political economy club Adam Smith had encouraged interaction between town and gown.[15] As at Edinburgh, the civic government worked with the Kirk and large landowners, but at Glasgow this was often honoured in the breach. Many newcomers were Secessionists – very many Anti-Burghers. By 1819, 40 per cent of Glasgow's population would be dissenters,[16] and the city had become the administrative and rallying centre for the Anti-Burgher Synod, whose divinity school would soon open at nearby Whitburn.

As at Edinburgh, the governors of Glasgow University were largely Kirk Moderates, but as Maver observes, "There came to be a significant dissenting base in Glasgow because of the patronage issue, predominantly in the Secession churches."[17] The mix of passion and piety in the evangelicals and their vision of "the godly, ordered society" suited this sprawling urban scene, where "the pace of change was seen as threatening the intricate social balance."[18] For the evangelicals, principles and profession without performance were not enough, but Roger Emerson cautions not to separate too sharply thinkers and improvers.[19]

Edinburgh became a haute-bourgeois capital, noted for its distinguished writers, distinct from London in that professionalism outnumbered and presided over the leisured and aristocratic class. Glasgow showed a practical and scientific side as a centre of social, economic, linguistic, and philosophic and related theological inquiry.

Into this probing, even radical scene came a boy of fifteen from peaceful Portmore. Here, Jemmy Drummond would absorb and take to the New World Glasgow's optimism and its concern for human improvement, perhaps in part because the college drew its teachers heavily "from the manse and the counting-house."[20]

Although their philosophies were somewhat opposed, two of Glasgow's outstanding teachers, John Millar and Thomas Reid, may have had the greatest influence upon him. Millar professed, "There is thus, in human society, a natural progress from ignorance to knowledge, and from rude, to civilized manners."[21] David Daiches observes, "The moral philosophy of the men of the Scottish Enlightenment, from Hume to Adam Smith, took on the whole an optimistic view of human nature and placed great emphasis on man's innate quality of sympathy and benevolence."[22]

Millar rejected Hume's scepticism, arguing that improvement could alter a people's manners, laws, and governance, specifically "the emancipation of social inferiors, women, slaves and children from their barbarous condition in rude times through the emergence of liberal societies and governments."[23] MacGregor's later missions reflected this conviction.

But Thomas Reid's examination of the roots of morality would also have appealed to an earnest student like Jemmy. Reid's contribution to moral philosophy, as Richard Sher notes, was to examine "the rational and improvable aspects of the moral faculty."[24] This was the search for individual improvement and social harmony, which was Jacob Drummond's simple goal and a mark of Glasgow's intellectual and religious life.

But how did a boy from a tiny rural setting fit into this crowded city and into the college's scarlet-gowned scene? Of course, he had already made adjustments at Kinkell and Dunblane, and his peers were not all strangers. Many Glasgow students were the sons neither of nobles nor of rich lawyers but came from the homes of rural merchants and even of tenant farmers – "parents of low estate but justifiable pride from skill or function in society."[25] To attempt university in Scotland was a smaller gamble than it would have been earlier or elsewhere. "Throughout the Highlands and Islands ... there was a deep concern to have children instructed."[26] Improvements in burgh, parish, and grammar schools ensured a youthful stream into the universities. Boys came to university from more diverse backgrounds than in England. John Millar entered Glasgow at twelve, and it was common to complete university at nineteen.[27]

Attendance also sprang from the attraction of great lecturers, from the nation's new prosperity, and from the influence of the "Improvers" in agriculture and industry.[28] Whereas in England "young gentlemen of leisure" were sent to Oxford or Cambridge to develop as they might in congenial surroundings, Scottish youth were sent "to be equipped with knowledge and provided with tools and to develop a frame of mind and habits of application."[29] There were also no Test Acts to keep out Dissenters and Catholics. Consequently, a far higher proportion of boys from a smaller population entered university.

Even fairly poor boys could find a niche. There were few student residences, but digs were cheap and distances home not great. Fees were low and seldom required of divinity students. A good student might be helped by his dominie or minister, especially if he proposed teaching or the church. A dominie was part of the church's infrastructure, and Jemmy benefited from this tradition.[30]

Accommodation was especially cheap if one accepted mean rooms, lived off produce and oatmeal from home, and helped in the household. Even in the twentieth century, midway through the first term "Meal Monday" was still ceremonially held, a time when needy students could return home for a fresh bag to carry them to the end of term.[31] Glasgow's runaway expansion in the eighteenth century also opened up short-term employment, which Jemmy pursued for a decade. Discipline and application, learned at Glasgow, were apparent throughout his life, and emphasis on religious and notably nonsectarian education anticipated Pictou. In 1776, then, Jemmy Drummond entered Glasgow, which had barely three hundred students.[32]

He lived in the shadow of Trongate: nearby, off the High Street, was the college. On the hill above stood the thirteenth-century Kirk cathedral of St. Mungo's. His landlady was a family friend, and his mother probably sent him off with local products: lamb, venison, grouse, pheasants, and wild berries and with Jacob's wool and fine weaving. For leisure, there were the College Green and nearby Glasgow Green, running along the Clyde just beyond the Barras. Both offered respite from the Old Town's industrial crowding and population.

For, Lower High Street was a neighbourhood to escape from: tenements swarmed in the shadow of factories, and "over-building" shaded the streets from both sides, transforming narrow lanes into sunless, stinking gutters. The new-old Glasgow was a mixed blessing as it careened into a new age. Jemmy, accustomed to wild spaces, open moors, and mountain views, was challenged, but he had always adjusted, and coming to terms with Glasgow proved good preparation for the radically different scene in Nova Scotia. Resilience was bred into clan and country.

With his early teachers' dedication and Dunblane's rigorous training, he was well prepared for the college, even to following lectures in Latin, though English was by then largely in force. There were no tutorials, as at "Oxbridge," but the Scottish universities were renowned for great lecturers. At Glasgow, there was competition even to listen to some courses.

Jemmy's syllabus followed a familiar pattern: Latin ("Humanity"), moral philosophy, logic, mathematics, and some science ("Natural Philosophy"). In preparation for the ministry, he took Greek and Hebrew, and his shorthand combined Hebrew, Greek, and Gaelic, the languages he knew best. The college's original Enlightenment luminary, Francis Hutcheson, had once graced the chair of moral philosophy. Thomas Miller observes that Hutcheson departed from the classical civic humanist tradition, going back to Cicero, while developing "an eclectic system, incorporating the values of civic humanism and the methods and principles of the natural rights tradition."[33] Hutcheson had been followed by his brilliant pupil, Adam Smith, but now Smith too had retired and was succeeded by his student Thomas Reid. Reid's moral philosophy class was subscribed by more than a third of the student body, and Jemmy would have been among them. There was a great appeal in Reid's eloquent defence of man's moral nature against Thomas Hobbes's proposition that all men are moved to benevolence only from "lively expectation of favours to come."

Although in some respects Reid shared Hume's scepticism, in matters of religion he was a conservative. His "Common Sense" philosophy did not oppose strong religious convictions. He had a flexible mind

and recognized "mental events or mental acts of which we are uncon-
scious."[34] Samuel Fleischker concludes, "Reid was ... well suited for ...
reconciling Enlightenment thought with Christian faith."[35]

When Jemmy came to Glasgow, Adam Smith had recently published
an appendix to his *Theory of Moral Sentiments* (1767), titled *"Considerations concerning the First Formation of Languages,"* a common inquiry
among Scottish writers, although Dugald Stewart dismissed it as "con-
jectural history."[36] But Smith infused historical inquiry into subjects that
had long rested on abstraction and undirected speculation.[37] Although
men like the Moderate William Robertson rejected it, Reid and Millar probed the nature and origin of man's mind and society with new
resourcefulness and imagination. Reid believed that languages, "especially their syntax," were the route to philosophic truth: "There are
certain common opinions of mankind, upon which the structure and
grammar of all languages are founded. While these opinions are common to all men, there will be a great similarity in all languages ... an
uniformity among men in those opinions upon which the structure of
language is founded."[38]

Reid's introductory course in rhetoric and belles-lettres included an
examination of the origins and progress of language. Jemmy, immersed
in the etymology of Gaelic, was bound to respond. After Dunblane,
he spoke a smoother English, some French, was at home in Latin and
Greek, and Hebrew had become his strongest suit. But he had greatly
extended his Gaelic through travel, developing confidence in the spoken and written language. Soon he would undertake Irish, Welsh and
even Basque; Celtic appears in many notes extant at Glasgow.[39] In Nova
Scotia, he would add Mi'kmaq to his list. Thus, at Glasgow, the Scottish
Enlightenment ventured beyond the formerly limited republic of letters, and Jemmy related to its probing into the human mind by means
of comparative philology. It became a lifelong pursuit.

He was also drawn to it by a friend, John Jamieson, who shared his
enthusiasm. Jamieson was a prodigy: Jemmy's age, he had entered Glasgow at nine, the son of an Anti-Burgher minister and destined to become
one himself. His reputation stands as the compiler of the first comprehensive Gaelic dictionary – a feat rivalling Dr. Johnson's. As boys, they
found a common interest in the roots of languages, and fifty years later
they were still corresponding. Probably Jemmy attended Duke Street's
Anti-Burgher church, where Jamieson's father was the incumbent.

He must have lived a fairly quiet social life, having neither the time
nor the money for the student dining and debating clubs where wits

and reputations were made. When he could, he returned home, but mostly he followed a common Scottish pattern: "Young men on vacation ... could teach the rudiments to children of the lesser tenantry who farmed at considerable distance from the nearest parochial school."[40] Jemmy did so extensively.

Glasgow's small size and its mission of questioning the roots of orthodoxy and custom made it a great decade to be at the college – and at forty, John Millar, professor of civil law, was in his prime. Edinburgh's secularism and professionalism contrasted with Glasgow's moral and natural philosophy where, Millar's biographer William Lehmann argues, Millar was a pioneer in sociological analysis. But Millar was more than that in those heady days at Glasgow.[41]

Certain teachers in small liberal colleges can exercise great influence over their colleagues and students – even those who do not study under them but are drawn, as Lehmann observes, by "the mere vivacity of [their thought]." John Rae, Adam Smith's biographer, described Millar as "the most celebrated and most successful teacher of his time, ... the most effective apostle of liberalism in Scotland in that age."[42] Miller, says Lehmann, had "a rare combination of moral seriousness, with yet a spriteliness and good humour" in his lectures and in his easy conversation with students.[43] His presence at the tiny college was enormous: he taught civil law, yet his classes were always oversubscribed, for he offered something to the lawyer, the future statesman, and the general student. John Cairns observes that Millar saw the law "as a liberal and enlightened science."[44] Students from all over Britain came to hear him, and he lectured over two hundred and fifty times a year, three hours a day, five days a week. Forty-six of those lectures were designed for students like Jemmy, who wanted a broad arts course.[45] On Sunday evenings Millar's lectures were free.

In a college where many pursued "broad enquiries into the nature of society, frequently with ethical overtones," Millar stood out, and on his small estate, he was a model farmer – an Improver. He belonged to the liberal Society of Friends of the People. He chaired a committee that recommended an LLD for the antislavery crusader William Wilberforce, and he instigated Glasgow's appeal to Parliament to end the slave trade.[46] His position on slavery was later reflected in one of MacGregor's finest achievements.

Lehmann concludes, "[Millar's] writings ... made up the principal diet of a rising generation ... who led the Scottish agitation for reform, ... a remarkable awakening, not only in the intellectual, but also in the moral and political, the literary and artistic, the cultural, and even, in a measure, the religious life of Scotland."[47] Further, Millar regarded Seceders more favourably than other organized religious groups:

> [They] recommend themselves to the people rather than cultivate the patronage of men in power. They could, therefore, be of little service to the sovereign in supporting his prerogative, and, in consequence, had little to expect from his favour. On the contrary, as their interest and habits connected them with the populace, they entered with alacrity into the popular feelings and views, beheld with jealousy and apprehension the lofty pretensions of the crown, and sounded throughout the kingdom the alarm of regal usurpation.[48]

Welcome words to a burgeoning population of Seceder Glaswegians, as they must have been to those like Jemmy, who crowded his classes.

Just before Jemmy's arrival at Glasgow, Millar published his masterpiece, *Origin of the Distinction of Ranks*, probing how humankind's earliest customs led not only to the development of authority, class structure, and governance but also to woman's subjugation, serfdom, class distinctions, and wage and black slavery. But reaching beyond social theory, he argued, "The ideal social leader was to be the public-spirited, eloquent, active and learned citizen."[49] Parallels with Plato's *Republic* are obvious, for Glasgow's Enlightenment stemmed in part from the classics. The minister as public servant is only a step away.

Although others excluded religion from Hume's "science of man," Millar acknowledged the power of an educated clergy in fostering "civic moralism."[50] Recognizing the independent route of Seceders, he admired their activist clergy for addressing public issues, attributing their influence to their learning.[51] Like Knox in the *First Book of Discipline*, writes Lehmann, Millar paid "a great deal of attention to education, and especially to religious educational establishments, in his writings." Although always the Enlightenment rationalist, he recognized "the element of mystery in life and in the universe, and man's weakness and his dependence on "the author of our being."[52]

Millar was perhaps the most radical member of Glasgow's faculty, but his words were usually temperate. Anand Chitnis says of him, "Millar's eloquence fixed deeply in their minds the principles of free constitutional government."[53] Chitnis also recognizes the deep social conscience in this typical Millarite statement: "It is plainly the interest of the higher ranks to assist in cultivating the minds of the common people and in restoring to them the knowledge which they may be said to have sacrificed to the general prosperity."[54]

At Glasgow, Jemmy came under the influence of such teachers, men who probed the links among education, power, governance, and progress, and several of whom examined religion's place in these dynamic questions so central to Glasgow's Enlightenment. These were issues at the heart of MacGregor's later ambition for an academy at Pictou, founded in this spirit.

Roger Emerson observes that there were at Glasgow "the best educated and most widely travelled members of the eighteenth-century professoriate ... Professors elsewhere were often as independent, but nowhere else did they use their freedom as responsibly."[55] These were Glasgow's *philosophes*.

Through Hutcheson, Reid, and Millar, Glasgow added to intellect and discourse the elements of intuition and common experience. Reid, father of the Scottish Common Sense (or Realist) School, believed that some part of the truth arises in the beliefs of large numbers of men and women who together produce a consensus, a socially constructed truth. Millar, differing from Reid in some respects, recognized the mystery of understanding. "Common Sense" might better be called "Common Sensibility," that is, perceptions common to many. This validation of thought by its efficacy, an early modernist perception, anticipated C.S. Pierce. Thus, the rationalist, poet, and evangelical in James MacGregor as scholar and preacher found a potent combination of ideas and activism at Glasgow, which later fuelled his urge to create a parallel culture in the wilds of Nova Scotia.

At Glasgow the sheep-master's son had entered a world of culture, linguistics, natural and social science, and moral philosophy that would transform him into a sophisticated, highly cultivated individual – all of which would later be channelled into the homely intimacies of a primitive pastorate.

The college year at Glasgow ran from October to June, but during the long break, Jemmy helped earn his way by teaching, incidentally extending his Gaelic and his knowledge of Scottish history. At Glenlednock, north of Comrie, he was recognized for his learning, organization, and good spirits: "an active sprightly lad, full of life and activity, very sociable in the family, and so full of fun, as sometimes to elicit a reproof from the dour but pious old man with whom he lodged."[56]

There, Jemmy pursued the Comrie district's legends, laying the groundwork for his interest in folklore and local dialects. Even in old age James believed in the fairy folk, the fearful *kelpies* and *uruisgs* (water bulls and horses) of Highland lore, and the *Daoine Sith* – Men of Peace, who were anything but, being parallel figures to the Norse trolls. Isabel Grant observes that it was not unusual for an educated Scot to hold such beliefs and that as late as 1845, "it could be seriously written in the New Statistical Account that a late Principal of Aberdeen had contributed by his benevolent exertions ... to the expulsion of fairies from the Highland Hills."[57]

MacGregor's great literary passions, however, were poetry and the Gaelic. In two centuries the Highlands produced one hundred and thirty poets, some "outstanding,"[58] and Perthshire was a historic centre for Gaelic poetry. A seventeenth-century Perthshire James MacGregor had compiled *The Book of the Dean of Lismore* – songs of the "strollers," the county's wandering bards. Jemmy grew up in a rich tradition of creativity and poetry, carrying many songs with him to the New World. At Glenlednock, he also translated Proverbs from Greek to Gaelic, which proved invaluable to father and son.

Later he taught at Morebattle in the Border country, under a Seceder minister whose granddaughter recalled for George Patterson "a tall dark, fine looking man, of very cheerful disposition," who sang Gaelic songs, wrote poetry for them, but did not stay long, for his heart was in the Highlands.[59]

He graduated in 1779: at nineteen, Jemmy Drummond had become the man James McGregor.[60] Shortly after, he began training for the ministry at the Associate Synod Theological Hall at Alloa, where his father had begun his religious life. He faced five years of preparation before ordination, but the school year was short: two intensive months in early autumn under the respected Rev. William Moncrieff, son of Ebenezer Erskine's old colleague Alexander. Like Jacob, however, the Moncrieffs had parted from Ebenezer, becoming leaders in the Anti-Burgher breakaway.

During these five years Jemmy worked in the field with a surveyor in Perthshire, but largely as a roving tutor and probationer, gaining pastoral and teaching experience and preparing for ordination. He served at sixteen locations, ranging from the Border to Argyle, through Aberdeen, and in the north at Nigg in Ross-shire. There, he absorbed other Highland scenes and people, continuing his studies in etymology and philology, and progressing beyond his Perthshire "border Gaelic." He stayed longest in Argyllshire, where he gathered more Gaelic songs and folklore, which later led to his cognomen, "MacGregor of the Verses." He also researched the history of the clans; the resulting knowledge served him well in Nova Scotia, where many from those regions had settled.

As his studies came to an end, he received several calls. One was from Craigdam in Aberdeenshire, where he had served as a probationer; another came from Nigg in the north. A third, more tentative, came from home, at Comrie. He savoured the prospect of working with his father out of Craigdam or Comrie, but then there arose a fourth call, one that raised very different prospects and threw him into alarm.

Chapter Five

In Passage

The management of overseas missions was haphazard when James was called to Pictou. Order awaited the great mission surge of the Victorians, when a man might be dispatched by his denomination or by several societies that would administer and finance the project. Working with other churches was not an Anti-Burgher trait, however: Synod determined its own agents, and while it was unusual in its zeal for foreign missions, sometimes it fell short in their administration.

Nor did many ministers recognize an obligation or honour in serving beyond their presbytery or county: the imperialists' "white-man's burden" lay in the future. Yet Seceder missions to America had begun twenty years earlier – perhaps in hope of greater success overseas than in the Highlands, where some had not yet been touched by the Reformation.

Now, Synod was approached by two Greenock shippers, John Pagan and John Buchanan, authorized to arrange for a minister for a struggling settlement in Nova Scotia. In 1773 Pagan, a co-sponsor of this "Philadelphia Company," Pictou's colonizing agency, had delivered settlers in his ship, *Hector*. It might have been assumed that James would be properly treated, given Pagan's relationship with the company. For James, however, the prospect of Pictou came as a blow.

He had considered it "a case clear" that Synod would send him to nearby Craigdam, or respect his father's wishes and assign him to Comrie to complement Jacob's labours.[1] He left no doubt of his own preference, worrying over undertaking his first charge in such an alien scene.

The Pictou petition of 8 November 1784 had been signed by five men: Robert Patterson, John Patterson, Robert Marshall, William Smith, and

Donald MacKay,[2] but it had been addressed to the *Burgher* Synod. The petitioners observed that for twenty years they had known only sporadic visits from Burgher Truro's Rev. Daniel Cock and his associate, Rev. David Smith. Indeed, Cock had written the eloquent petition:

> Many, very many silent Sabbaths have passed … to our very great grief, and the great prejudice of … religion. [We] earnestly request the Presbytery, in the bowels of our Lord Jesus Christ … for the advancement of his kingdom, and the salvation of precious perishing souls in this wilderness – that you … send us with all convenient speed a minister. That he who has the stars of the Churches in his Right hand may direct you to a proper object, and put it in his heart to come over to our Macedonia.[3]

The committee pledged £80 currency per annum for the first and second year; £90 for the third and fourth years, and thereafter £90 sterling annually, one-half in cash and the other in produce. They would also build a house and barn and provide a glebe lot.[4] It was almost a foolhardy offer, for the incumbent could become a rich man.

Rebuffed by the Burghers, they turned to Anti-Burgher Perth Presbytery,[5] but it lacked jurisdiction and referred them to Synod at Glasgow, where MacGregor's fine probationary record and his facility in Gaelic probably ensured his selection. Nor could Synod have been aware of what a wily manipulator Pagan was, filling the decrepit *Hector* with passengers wholly unprepared for the wilderness. So many settlers had deserted that the company was still regrouping.

Withholding information may have been Pagan's strategy again, for James complained that he could learn nothing about the community.[6] No one told him that most of his prospective flock were Highland Kirkmen, and some illiterate. But Synod was satisfied, and it required James to appear before it on 4 May 1786, and there we first found him sitting on a bench awaiting their decision. They faced a difficult challenge, for ordained men were needed at home, too. James had advised Pagan and Buchanan and Synod:

> I think some person … is clearly called upon to go to their assistance, but I am not so clear if I be the person … From the petition itself, it appears that it was never designed to be presented to the Associate Synod. Perhaps the petitioners do not know whether there be any Associate Synod … I know nothing of the Presbyterian ministers there, but is there any reason to hope that they are all sound, and especially that they are all friends of a

covenanted Reformation? [If Mr. Pagan would inform me], then he would
see the reasonableness of my shunning such a situation.[7]

His anxiety was well founded, for he knew the Scots were a tribal
people whose religious life was an important part of their culture. Not
everyone in Nova Scotia would have forgotten the grounds of conflict in
Scotland, and dealing with strangers could be intimidating for a newly
ordained minister alone and far from home. Most Presbyterian clergy
in Nova Scotia were Burgher, while the Kirk was hardly represented,
and certainly not represented outside Halifax or Shelburne. Still, if it
must happen, James hoped that he would win respect at Pictou. Synod
split hairs: he was not being "sent to make Seceders, but Christians."[8]
Friction, however, was endemic in the situation, and James found it all
very uncertain.

In fact, after questioning him, Synod had quickly agreed upon him.
What was taking so long was a debate over supply in principle. Suddenly, however, the door was hurriedly opened and an apologetic
clerk, Rev. John Buist, summoned him before the conclave. Although
his mind had been focused on his father and their dreams, it took all of
his self-discipline to face Synod's unanimous decision:

> I was thunderstruck ... I by no means expected it, though I was not without
> fears of it ... I did not know what to say or think ... I had never met with
> an event to deprive me wholly of a night's sleep ... Through the [next]
> day several friends helped much to reconcile me to Synod's appointment.
> Upon reflection I observed that there was at present no opening of great
> consequence for my preaching to the Highlanders at home, that souls
> were equally precious wherever they were, and that I might be as success-
> ful abroad as at home. I resolved to go, but still overwhelming difficulties
> were before me. The mission was vastly important, and I was alone and
> weakness itself. I had to go among strangers, probably prejudiced against
> [my] religious denomination ... I felt as an exile from the church. Besides
> Nova Scotia was accounted so barren, cold, and dreary, that there was no
> living in it with comfort.[9]

He professed himself a frail vessel to do God's work in such surroundings, urging that he might have succeeded at home, his name and
reputation ensuring support, but what could he do in a land known
only by an exotic name, and one that knew nothing of him? He wanted
to talk to his father, but there was so little time. He thought of Jacob,

now past seventy, still deepening in faith and anxiously awaiting word that his son would soon be home, where Jacob could serve under him.

But first James must conduct a promised service in Glasgow, and time was running out. He faced a final oral examination before Glasgow Presbytery, and his sailing date was three weeks away. Had he known that he would never again see Scotland or his parents, his anxiety might have been beyond bearing.

At last he could hurry home for a bittersweet leave-taking, gathering together his material and spiritual resources, and bidding farewell to family and lifelong friends. He was troubled, but he and Jacob found consolation in the belief that God's will had been revealed to them. He chided his bereft mother gently, "Do not wish to hinder me, for if I remained I might be a heart-break to you."[10] He could not spurn what he believed to be God's will.

Practical preparations he left to his mother and sisters. It seemed impossible that they could sew and pack all that he would need for what they feared was the sub-Arctic climate of Nova Scotia. A local shirt-maker gave her time freely, but in the event they had to ship the rest a year later, there being no other voyage that season.

First, however, he prepared for his exam, and then, at Samuel Gilfillan's invitation and amidst the great urgency of his last hours at home, he presented a farewell sermon at Crieff. He took for his text Hagar's words: "Thou, God, seest me" (Genesis 16:7). *Hagar* means "emigrant"; she who had borne Ishmael of Abraham and moved into the desert until Ishmael could fulfil the prophecy that he would become the founder of the twelve tribes. Now, James affirmed that God had assigned him as surely as He had Hagar. Later Gilfillan's wife, Rachel, reported, "It was a beautiful and serious discourse. He left Crieff the next day. Our family were in tears, even the servants. He was very much about our house, and was very familiar and amiable in his manners."[11]

Meanwhile, his finances were a problem. Missionaries paid their own passage, provided for their needs and equipment, and could only hope that they would be regularly paid. His family had little to offer in currency, but a local collection was taken; a brother-in-law lent him £20, and a sister borrowed two guineas to lend to him – and later received it back. But he had to buy books, writing materials, clothing, and other supplies. On the eve of his departure, when James was back in Glasgow with only a guinea left, someone asked him to support a good cause: nothing ventured, he gave the guinea, and then met a friend who observed, "Well, you are not going with that hat. Come in here."

They entered a store, and he was invited to pick the hat of his choice. He left Scotland with £5, borrowed and later returned with interest, and a strikingly new hat. To those who asked, he replied, "Trust in Providence."

He might have added – "and John Buist" – for there was no infrastructure to support overseas missions, no annual report required, and if payment of stipends fell off, or differences arose, no arbiter. A missionary was sustained by his faith and his courage. MacGregor was fortunate, however, in John Buist, Clerk of Synod and minister at Greenock, who arranged his examination, ordination, and embarkation and would remain a regular correspondent and lifeline for many years.[12]

On 27 May he left his parents and sisters forever. On 30 May he excelled at his ministerial trials before Glasgow Presbytery, and on the following day he was ordained and appointed to Pictou, leaving a list of what was required at the open exam.

1 Deliver a lecture on *Matthew* XXVIII, verses 19–20 – Christ's exhortation to his disciples to go forth and spread His word.
2 Deliver a popular sermon on the last clause of verse 20, above – Christ's assurance that He will always be with you.
3 Offer an exegesis on the proposition that "Christ is God."
4 Offer an account of the first half of the first year of church history.
5 Read the first psalm in Hebrew.
6 Read in Greek and on sight any text from the Greek testament.
7 Answer ex tempore questions.[13]

He passed readily, and on 1 June Dr. James Robertson preached on the trials of a missionary and of how the church knew "what Israel ought to do."[14] The church might know, but James professed that he did not and returned to "a depression of spirits from unbelieving fears of my weakness, as if God could do nothing by my means."[15] Based on Job 8:7, Robertson had urged on him a proverb, "Great events have often small beginnings."

On Saturday, 3 June 1786, the tide on the wane, he left Greenock on the brig *Lily*, Captain Smith, for Halifax. For seven weeks he shared a makeshift cabin with five service officers and two "gentlemen emigrants." They were respectful, but he found them rowdy and profane, and on Sunday, when the crew showed no disposition to observe the Sabbath, he held service on deck with a few steerage passengers attending him. One Sunday, he prayed alone in a "brisk brattling of wind" with no one on deck but the helmsman.

He dismissed the voyage as not "worth mentioning,"[16] although it was probably nothing of the kind. Those in steerage may have joined his services because prayer was their only remaining resort, or they failed to attend because they were too ill. Their food and medicines were probably spoiled, and on such voyages child mortality was often appalling: eighteen children had died on the *Hector*. But the *Lily* was more fortunate,[17] and James's physical strength, self-discipline, and spiritual powers sustained him.

He debarked at Halifax on 11 July, and after two days began the final leg of his long journey. He sent his luggage ahead by boat, asking Squire Patterson to pay the guinea until he arrived.[18] Leaving Halifax was no hardship: "[Its] immorality shocked me not a little, and I hastened out of it hoping better things of the country."[19] It was an accurate assessment of a town slipping into doldrums and drink between wars.

A farmer from Truro, 95 kilometres (60 miles) away, offered to escort him on horseback. Ironically, his guide belonged to Rev. Daniel Cock's congregation. Thus, James faced his first New World awakening: someone he had expected to be wary of him had gone out of his way to help a fellow Dissenter.[20]

He had some time to prepare for Daniel Cock, however, for the journey took three days. He would have preferred shank's mare, but after leaving Halifax ill at ease on a hired horse, they travelled a passable road to the head of Bedford Basin. Then they plunged into the forest on a poor trail. James was struck by the majesty of the trees, comparing it to a ducal estate in Scotland. But soon the trail worsened, becoming poorer than the wildest Highland track. He looked for a hospitable Highlander, but there was none, and by evening they had covered only 12 kilometres (8 miles). Bivouacking in a rocky clearing, they caught some trout for supper and added bread and bohea tea, the fine black tea from Foochow.[21]

Next morning, the trail maundered even worse among deadfalls and slash, and all favourable comparisons to Scotland ceased. His guide had insisted that they cover as much distance as possible before breakfast, and they rode a further 12 kilometres before eating. It was good advice in the mosquito-filled woods of Nova Scotia during a wet July.

And it *was* wet. Their horses were often over their knees in water and mud, with twisted branches and roots ready to spill horse and rider. MacGregor tried to manoeuvre in the tracks of the lead horse, but then we came to a place so apparently dangerous, that it seemed quite impossible to escape without broken bones. There was no way to get to a side, or to go back, and the horse was in such haste to get on, that he did not allow time to think. I threw the bridle upon his neck in perfect despair. How amazed was I to find myself completely delivered from the great danger in a matter of seconds by the sagacity of a mere beast! This incident was of great use to me afterwards, by inspiring in me perfect confidence in the horses reared in the forest here. Toward evening we came to the river Stewiacke, where there was a considerable clearing on the side of the river, and the soil very fertile. It was called interval [*sic*] in Nova Scotia, and haugh or dale in Scotland.[22]

Their prospects brightened after that, as a farmer paddled them across the river in a dugout while their horses swam. They stayed at his cabin that night, and James tasted frontier Nova Scotia hospitality, with bed-closets and a well-used Bible. But, "again we supped on bread, fish and tea, so that I began to conclude that there were no other eatables in Nova Scotia."[23] His host explained that meat would not last more than two days in the summer's heat – so much for the sub-Arctic!

The next day was Sunday, and MacGregor asked his guide to wait a day before completing the remaining 21 kilometres (14 miles) to Truro, but the frontier did not recognize such sabbatarian ways. How different this new land was – so much to learn, so much to accept. Arrived at Truro, he learned that Cock was away from home conducting a service, and with that, the rugged and devout MacGregor found himself "so fatigued as to be fit for nothing but rest."[24]

They met next morning, and later James somewhat loftily described Cock as "a man of warm piety, kind manners, and primitive simplicity."[25] Cock was happy in his coming, for he had recently formed a presbytery, the first in British North America, and he looked forward to recruiting another member. But he was chagrined when James declined the offer of the man who had drafted his invitation to Nova Scotia.

A lifetime of strict Anti-Burgher upbringing led MacGregor to decline, although he acknowledged how much he would miss clerical company. Less than a year before, Synod had censured those who "confessed with ministers of other denominations, on terms so loose and general as to open the door for the grossest latitudinaranism." Synod considered them guilty of "apostasy from their Reformation testimony and their witnessing profession."[26] Newly ordained, yet acknowledging that Burghers were not "another denomination," James was unsure of what to do. His hesitancy was also grounded in the discovery that along with several others in town – all Burgher Dissenters – Rev. Daniel Cock was a slaveholder.

He turned to John Buist for advice, but Buist's reply took nearly a year to arrive, and at best it was Delphic:

> As to supplying [at Truro] ... you can judge much better. We should engage in the Lord's service when the call is clear ... That is all I can say. I may also add, "Be ye wise as serpents, and harmless as doves." As to hearing Mr. C. [Cock], you are in an infant state and must come to our order by degrees. At the same time you may tell your mind as to such things as persons may be able to bear it.[27]

James concluded sadly that he must remain unattached: "This want of union was no small trial to me, as I was alone, and there were three of them."[28] Cock and Smith were two, and there was Rev. Hugh Graham at Horton, who would become a vital third several years later.

On the other hand, he recalled that Synod had sent him "not to make Seceders but Christians." He agreed to return in two weeks to preach and to discuss further his reservations.[29] He had refused a generous offer, but he was not inflexible; he would keep the dialogue open.

At sixty-nine, Daniel Cock was a man of great talent who had served at Glasgow and Stirling and had been Moderator of Synod at Edinburgh before turning to foreign missions.[30] He had arrived at Truro fourteen years earlier and had built up a large following. Cock was a considerate man, experienced in pioneering ways, a man of principle but willing to bend. For James, freshly ordained and burdened with the Old World's imprint and his father's precepts, it was a different matter. Although they had studied divinity under the same man, he and Cock trod different paths. James worried about their negotiations, but he was especially concerned over the slavery issue. He could not forget that he had come from the antislavery centre of Scotland, where John Buist was secretary of the antislavery society, and John Millar a militant leader; yet here in Nova Scotia, with the recent arrival of the Loyalists, slavery was widely accepted and practised. Further, he was deeply troubled to discover that even a clergyman like Daniel Cock and his ruling elder, Col. David Archibald, held slaves. For James considered that slavery was not just a deplorable custom but a sin.

Next day, Cock took James to Londonderry to meet Rev. David Smith. A graduate of St Andrews, Smith had come a year before Cock, but not

being assigned to Truro, had been sent on to this primitive Ulster settlement. Cock's people were experienced pioneers from New England;
Smith's were mostly raw Ulstermen. Smith had a good theological and
cultural background, but the Seceder historian James Robertson suggests that he had been given the lesser station because he possessed
a less "amiable and conciliatory disposition."[31] Yet Robertson also
describes him as "open, generous and affectionate."[32] He was probably
something of both, an able, frustrated man marooned on a demoralized frontier. Smith and James squared off from the outset, and some of
James's differences with Truro were eased only after Smith's death in
1795. But by then James, too, had learned some lessons. He recorded his
early impression of Smith:

> [Smith] was a man of more learning and penetration, but less amiable, than
> Mr. Cock. His untoward disposition had alienated a great many of his con-
> gregation from him. He proposed several judicious considerations to induce
> me to join the presbytery; but at that time they had no influence upon me.
> I believe that every honest Scottish emigrant that goes abroad, carries with
> him a conscientious attachment to the peculiarities of his profession, which
> nothing but time and a particular acquaintance with the country will enable
> him to lay aside. It may be so with more than Scotchmen: it was so with me.[33]

Those are the words of the mature MacGregor who had come to
terms with the New World. The recently ordained son of Jacob Drummond had not been so assured or flexible.

Two days later he left Truro for Pictou, travelling with two men
with business on the North Shore. They had to fight their way through
a'choille ghruamaich, the gloomy forest, for the distant blazes and narrow footpath were no reassurance. They lunched on "a ham of lamb
and a small flask full of rum," but by day's end were still 16 kilometres
(12 miles) from Squire Patterson's.

Fortunately, James received a hearty welcome at the home of one of
the lay signatories to the petition, an elder, William Smith. In Will Smith
he would find a steady supporter, lamenting later that "he didn't live
long, and his death was to me the death of half the congregation."[34]
MacGregor went to bed, snug in Highland fellowship and anticipating the amenities of town, "among them a barber, for I had never been
partial to the operation of shaving."[35]

Next morning, although Smith accompanied him on a cheerful progress past the cabins on the way, he was handed over to young Hugh

Fraser, who paddled him down the West River and harbour to Squire Robert Patterson's fine new log house. On the way he observed that most people lived in tiny clearings and low hovels, like the poorest Highland cottages, with turf over the ridge and smoke from a make-shift chimney-hole.

Still, it was a beautiful natural setting, and he was delighted at the prospect of Northumberland Strait that lay in the distance. Looking behind, he could see dominating the great inland basin the grand hill they had walked over on his arrival – a comforting hill, like Ben Fuith at home. It was a citadel of their commitment to the primitive community strung out along its lower flanks. The Mi'kmaq called it *Espakumegeh*, "High Land," but the newcomers called it "Green Hill."

He admired the "beautiful sheet of water, very much like one of the Highlands lakes in Scotland, about nine miles long and one broad."[36] It was a wonderful prospect, even to one who had seen the Highlands. Then he took another look:

> When I looked around the shores of the harbour, I was … cast down, for there was scarcely any thing to be seen but woods growing down to the water's edge. Here and there a mean timber hut was visible in a small clearing, which appeared no bigger than a garden compared to the woods. Nowhere could I see two houses without some wood between them. I asked Hugh Fraser, "Where is the town?" he replied, "There is no town but what you see."[37]

The petition had referred to a "Pictou township," but James now realized his mistake:

> I had foolishly inferred that there was a town … I had inferred also the existence of many comforts … My disappointments were immensely dis-couraging to me; for I looked on myself as an exile from the Church and from society. I saw that Nova Scotia, and especially Pictou, were very far behind the idea which I had formed of them. I renounced at once all idea of ever seeing a town in Pictou. Nothing but necessity kept me there; for I durst not think of encountering the dangerous road to Halifax again, and there was no vessel in Pictou to take me away. And even had there been one, I had no money to pay my Passage home.[38]

After a rough paddle over choppy waters, they reached Squire Patterson's home. His ten-week journey was over on this Saturday,

22 July 1786. Pulling the canoe up onto the beach and shucking "Jemmy" forever, the Rev. James MacGregor walked up the slope to meet his hosts.

He was warmly received by a devout family who welcomed his spiritual gifts. His mood brightened as he replied to all the questions put to him, and he was soon at ease. It was the beginning of a close friendship with the soft-spoken magistrate, a companionship central to his adjustment to the New World.[39]

Robert Patterson proudly displayed his new home, built in response to new immigration. The harbour's western shore had been empty while a speculator's claims had impeded development, but recently the land had been escheated to the crown, and Patterson was happy to add a resident minister and teacher to the short list of Pictou's amenities.

That evening James prepared for his first service in that exotic setting. It would take place in Squire Patterson's barn on the following morning. But he also listened carefully to accounts of Pictou's progress.

PART TWO

Adjusting

Chapter Six

Orienting

Pictou had long been an Indian site, with easy access to the sea, excellent places for curing fish and eels, and plenty of game along the three entering rivers. Later, it would develop one of the province's richest coal fields, manifested by tarry oils and gasps of methane that popped through the earth's surface. Hence, some claim, the Mi'kmaq "Piktook," place of explosions.[1] Although its name was spelled in the French manner, the French had not settled there in numbers, preferring Tatamagouche, well to the west. Pictou seems almost to have been reserved for the Scots.

The district was compact, defined, and secluded, lying between mountains and a broad waterfront extending for 80 kilometres (50 miles), which invited coastal commerce. From the coast the land rose south for 33 kilometres (20 miles), marking off a natural county, which was not officially recognized until 1835. Major streams carried logs from vast hillside stands down to the sea. The south-north course of the rivers offered two assets: as conduits for timber drives and saw- and grist-mills; and for carrying down rich alluvial soils that settled in broad farming "intervales." An old Melmerby man once observed, "God designed Pictou." He compared the hills to a half-saucer's rim, down which timber could be conducted by seven principal rivers – French, Sutherland's, and Barney's River on the east; River John on the west; and in the centre, the West, Middle, and East Rivers falling into the great crow's foot of Pictou Harbour that links Durham, Pictou, New Glasgow, and their hinterlands.

Along the coast were several fine ports: to the west, Caribou and River John; to the east, Little Harbour and Merigomish, which are sheltered by barrier islands and peninsulas. Facing Prince Edward Island and Cape Breton, Pictou invited a busy coastal trade.

The setting evoked, too, a broad development strategy and skilled, ambitious settlers, for it was an entrepreneur's dream. Pictou would raise farmers and woodsmen from "small patch plots and small mentalities" to success as agriculturalists, foresters, and in time, heavy industrialists,[2] and James had something to offer them.

Settlement had begun with Benjamin Franklin and several Pennsylvania settlers, America's agricultural leaders in the 1760s. At the end of the Seven Years' War, in 1763, the continental interior had been closed, and the land-hungry were diverted to New England and Nova Scotia. In 1767 a "Philadelphia Company" sent the brig *Hope* with Maryland families to Pictou. With ample money and provisions, and bringing indentured servants and black slaves, these Scottish southerners proposed to build a northern plantation. Dr. John Harris would serve as overseer, and Robert Patterson, as surveyor.[3]

But Patterson's wife was so intimidated by the shroud of surrounding forest that she leaned against a tree crying, "Oh, Robert, take me back." Help was at hand, however, for Samuel Archibald of Truro had led a welcoming party to offer assistance, but in the end several *Hope* families simply followed him back to Truro.[4] Others dug in.

Later, embarrassed by the Harrises' fervent support of the American colonists, the government appointed Robert a magistrate, thus committing the Philadelphia Company to development under the Crown. Dr. Harris removed to Truro, where American sympathies flourished. Few colonists ventured to Pictou, however, which led the proprietors to turn to Scotland for sound, skilled newcomers. To help them, they called on two associates: Rev. John Witherspoon of New Jersey, one of Scotland's ablest emigrants to America; and John Pagan, merchant-shipper of Greenock.

Witherspoon had led the Evangelical Party in the Church of Scotland, opposing the Moderates and their rationalist ways. In time he broke with the Kirk and became a leader of a group of Dissenters calling themselves the Relief Church. In 1767 he was called to America to preside over the Presbyterian College of New Jersey (later, Princeton University), where he set as the college's goal to produce "ornaments of the State as well as the Church." It was an ideal familiar to Glaswegians. Witherspoon, a congressman and the only minister to sign the Declaration of Independence,[5] was a lifelong friend of Dr. John Harris,[6] and it was hoped that with his help and reputation they could attract to Pictou able Scots, including a minister.

The company's new strategy bore mixed results. In 1773 two hundred settlers arrived at Pictou aboard Pagan's ship, *Hector*, but again most fled to more developed districts. Among the seventy-eight who remained were some able families, like the Frasers and MacKays, and especially a successful contractor from Paisley, John Patterson, no relation to Squire Robert.[7] John Patterson rose quickly in timber and construction in friendly rivalry with the squire. Both were active in church affairs, and to distinguish them, people called John, Deacon Patterson. Deacon and squire had much in common; they were forward-looking, had cheerful dispositions, showed good business instincts, and felt a strong sense of public duty. Both gained power and respect, even affection, working closely together until their deaths in the same year, 1808.

At twenty-seven, and still a bachelor, Deacon John seems to have taken the voyage almost as a lark. Still, with capital from cottages he had built and leased at home, he worked closely with the squire to foster Pictou's development. MacGregor would come under his wing.

Before the company could restart operations, however, the squire was obliged to dislodge "an aggressive and over-reaching ... land ... grabber."[8] Col. Alexander McNutt was, in the language of the day, "full of oily gammon," for although he was a company associate, he secretly had huge holdings encroaching on company lands. When the squire succeeded in ejecting him, development proceeded more confidently.

Not long before MacGregor's arrival, the deacon built a rough wharf and a substantial house, marking the beginning of Pictou town. The squire and another Harris, Matthew, settled there with more than twenty children between them. They alone could occupy James as preacher and teacher.

Perhaps the happiest couple to greet James, however, was Squire Robert and his wife. Their children had largely grown up and dispersed, and it would be pleasant to have fresh company, especially a young man with news of Scotland.

Among those attending MacGregor that Sunday morning were some diverse and interesting people. In 1775 fifteen destitute families had arrived from Prince Edward Island, the so-called Galloway Settlers, as weak and demoralized as the meanest immigrants.[9] Some were from Dumfries and Ayrshire, but most had come from Galloway, Kirkcudbright, and Wigton – centers of agricultural improvement. Some had been tenants, others the offspring of landholders; all were skilled at root crops, fodder, fruit cultivation, and animal husbandry, with fine cattle and the Galloway horse. But at Georgetown they had faced the "Years of the Mice," when even the seeds in the ground were eaten, and their supplies had been stolen by drunken American fishermen.

Totally dispirited and starving, they had no option but to leave, led by the sturdy Robert Marshall and others, and arriving at Pictou during a brutal winter.

Spring lasts half a summer in Nova Scotia, and in desperation they turned to an old Scottish soup prepared from the fresh shoots of nettles.[10] But survive they did, and slowly they began to show who they really were. With borrowed seed, replacing rough barley seed (bere) with improved varieties, sweetening the land, they became role models for the district's farmers. They were also well distributed to do so: seven families to West River, four to Middle River, and two to East River.[11] On his own arrival James immediately bonded with Robert Marshall, ensuring his welcome by these now-prospering Lowlanders who encouraged him to become an active Improver himself. He would not disappoint them.

After the Revolutionary War, fewer than three hundred people lived in the entire district, but soon new immigration commenced, auguring a stable pioneer community.[12] Soldiers with families mustered out,[13] the largest group being Lowlanders on the county's eastern edge. Pictou reflected Bernard Bailyn's distinction between "provincial emigration" and "metropolitan" in which single men follow only their economic interest.[14] Of these, a motley band of restless half-pays eked out a living near the harbour through an alcoholic haze. Most of the newcomers, however, had brought with them their families and the hope of reviving their Highland culture, which had been proscribed since Culloden. The 82nd Highlanders divided equally between Kirkmen at Pictou and Barra, and Catholics who moved eastward towards Antigonish.

The Second Battalion of the 84th, the Royal Highland Emigrants, out of Halifax, Quebec, and the American campaigns, were a different lot. Enterprising and ambitious, they had already been emigrating when war began, and they were offered Hobson's choice: debtor's prison or enlistment. Most "volunteered," leaving their families to live out the war in staging camps, many on Long Island. Now, they were coming to Hants County – hence MacGregor's later connection with Maitland and Nine Mile River in Douglas Township – and in greatest numbers to Pictou.

Several families noted for their sobriety and industry settled in West River, but most of the battalion settled along the lower East River. Known to the Mi'kmaq as "Duckland," it now became "The Soldiers' Grant," as they rallied along "The Great River." Other soldiers and some civilians arrived sporadically, as James's petitioners had forecast.[15]

There were probably five hundred residents in the district when MacGregor arrived in the summer of 1786.[16] A few fishing shallops worked the Northumberland Strait, and John Patterson and others had already begun a timber export trade. Those who could, cleared land and built log houses and simple barns. The Pattersons and Harrises, with money and slaves, soon expanded their fodder and crop farms. In 1779 the Deacon returned briefly to Paisley, and finding he had reaped a fortune in rentals, he invested in British trade goods and returned to Pictou to become the district's first general merchant.[17]

Most, however, lacked capital for such undertakings. No road connected the three river settlements;[18] travel was by footpath or dugout, although with rivers and harbour frozen over at least four months, the country opened up wonderfully. Heavy logs were moved across the ice to building sites or export wharves. Domestic visits were exchanged, reducing isolation. But progress was slow, there being fewer than a dozen horses in the county, and only a few *garrons*, the ponies of the Western Highlands.[19]

There were also no public buildings, for government was limited. Pictou was a company venture, but justice rendered as the squire's "fireside law" was backed by the Crown's satisfaction that he had the experience and insight to become a Justice of the Peace. Untrained in the law, he was wise in human nature. Nor were there schoolhouses, and little call for any. Life was work, the goal neither comfort nor culture but survival. Few felt regret for homes, furnishings, or books left behind, for in most cases there had been none. For the newcomers, game was plentiful, but if not, as in Strathspey, broths were flavoured with mugwort, beech leaves brewed in porcupine stew, and as at home, clams and mussels stockpiled in sandy mounds along the wintry beaches. In time they would learn from the Mi'kmaq how to bring down a moose, as they had once done a stag.

Many felt no less comfort or permanence, for life at home had been nomadic, with winter herders in the mountains, summer kelp burners on the coast. There had also been little striving for beauty, for the Scottish Presbyterian spurned frivolous decoration.

The Mi'kmaq seemed well disposed, however, probably more so to these "British" than anywhere else in Nova Scotia. Those near Halifax and Louisbourg had experienced much exploitation by European settlers and had often been pawns in the settlers' and Imperial soldiers' conflicts. But if Tatamagouche had once been a busy French entrepot centre, Pictou had lain at some remove from such frictions, and James found a close friend in Chief John Lulan, whose people were willing to share their skills. Fuel was plentiful, with abundant hardwoods, great oaks, and prized white pine for export. Cash was scarce, and the ready-made items of a more developed economy – tools, furniture, fabrics, clothing – could be fashioned at home. Barter in goods, skills, and labour sustained many, but that had been an ancient ritual to those who had long shared raisings, shearings, milling, and waulking songs (*Oran Luaidh*). Such "frolics" had been part of a close Highland communal life. An outdoors lifestyle and clannish support had been their way. Nor were shorter days in fall and winter any novelty to northern Highlanders, and while the chill might be deeper than in Brora, the delight of visiting neighbours over packed snow and ice helped offset the long winters. Their dangers, toil, and isolation should not be underestimated, but if they considered their prospects in the old country, they had gained a measure of freedom. Here, the land was one's own.

Meanwhile, those attending James must have savoured the prospect of new leadership. He was the only minister of the Gospel along the North Shore.

The Pattersons rose early on Sunday, 23 July 1786, and Robert dismissed himself soon after breakfast to direct the seating on slabs and planks. His barn was to be God's house this morning, and nothing must be amiss.

Inside, while the young minister scraped inexpertly at his bristle, he was also absorbed in reviewing his sermons. He would preach first in English, then in the auld tongue, which many had been starved for during Daniel Cock's visits. For some it meant understanding a service for the first time in years. James might say almost anything if it were in Gaelic.

After breakfast he excused himself politely and strolled down the clearing to the harbour-front. So much had happened in the last twenty-four hours that he had to call on huge reserves to face what lay before him. A few neighbours emerged shyly from the woods, passing by with eyes downcast, but most were arriving by boat. Voices and laughter came to James from across the water as the dugouts and canoes approached. Recalling yesterday's rough entry, he thought their passage risky, but standing aside discreetly, he listened with curiosity and mounting shock as they came near, "talking and laughing, singing and whistling,"[20] many shouting playful jibes at friends whom they seldom saw because of unceasing work and great distances. It sounded like a county fair, and disapproval was evident in his face as they, too, passed by with whispers and covert pointing. He chose not to reproach them then, however, resolving to win their respect by conducting the most proper service they had ever experienced.

He was rescued from his agitation by the Squire, freshly groomed after a morning of tiring preparations. James was edgy, and for a moment his eye lingered disapprovingly on the finishing touch that the squire had added to the fine suit he now wore: at his throat was a *ruche*, a gathering of lace, which James considered out of place, a show of vanity on the Sabbath. Then he was introduced to Matthew Harris and his wife, Sutia, and their many children. Matthew was forty-two, more temperamental than his brother, Dr. John, but less fervent in the Americans' cause. Today he was gracious and welcoming, and James replied amicably. His nephew, sixteen-year-old Thomas, born on the *Hope*, was visiting. A future surveyor and sheriff of Pictou, today he was a boy nodding shyly.

Matthew apologized that there would not be a full turnout, but that arranging the children on short notice and assembling sufficient dugouts had put them to the test. "However," James was assured, "West River will make a good showing."

Next, there appeared Deacon John and Ann Patterson, Thomas Harris's older sister. At forty, Patterson was an imposing figure with a sharp eye for business, and as a petitioner he inspected their investment carefully. MacGregor took his measure, too. John had first noticed Ann when she was nine and he twenty-seven. They had married when she turned eighteen, allying two strong families. Ann was only two years older than James and was already proving a major source of the colony's rapid growth.

At a lull in the introductions, James considered the contrast between Robert and John Patterson. John was hardly beyond medium height and breadth, but beside the squire, he appeared rangy and athletic. Someone described Robert as "short and thick-set, one of those men said to be broad as they are long," but his manner was "free and pleasant," and he was universally admired.

James's attention returned to his hostess and to Ann, for in succession he was being introduced to Ann's siblings and cousins: Thomas Harris's older brother, Robert, a doctor like his father and a farmer like his uncle; Ann's sister Margaret, married to William Lindsay, an educated Scot who proposed soon to open a tavern; another sister, Janet, whose husband, Simon Newcomb, would become MacGregor's colleague as schoolteacher and whose grandson, also Simon, would become one of the world's great astronomers.[21]

He was feeling better now, his mood improved in the presence of so many amiable people. Already he had met many whose support he would rely on for three generations. Then another petitioner came in sight, an epiphany had James known it – and perhaps he did, such was his nature. Donald MacKay was one of the Highland soldiers from The Soldiers' Grant, just upriver from the future site of New Glasgow. Ann Patterson introduced him as "Donald the Builder," and although he had little to say, James was drawn to him. But they had hardly begun when Donald's brusque smithy brother, Roderick, with his stocky wife, Christina, and their plain and sturdy daughter, Ann, came to greet him. Next came a third brother, William MacKay, but while he was courteous, he seemed, at first meeting, less forthcoming than his siblings.

When Ann Patterson brought the last of the petitioners, James noticed the respect she accorded the oddly dressed, shy little man. The introduction was brief, but Robert Marshall, reader at Middle River and a fine precentor, was of a rare nature. With his natural prescience, James may have recognized in him someone with whom he would work and worship intimately until death parted them.

Marshall had still not recovered from the grim sojourn on the Island; soon after, he had lost his wife and been left with several young children. He had not remarried, however, relying on his faith to get him through. His selflessness would often remind James of his father, Jacob, and his determined ways. Robert would guide him wisely, sponsoring him among the Galloway Settlers, who were all Kirkmen. Understanding would flow more readily while discussing choices in flax seed or the proper depth of shares. They became a dependable phalanx in his congregations, and on William Smith's death, Robert became James's faithful champion at West River.

MacGregor's reaction to MacKay and Marshall was not unusual. He was often subject to premonitions and forerunners, and sometimes in a dream was advised of decisive moments to come.[22] Donald and Robert left a mark, but at this moment he could not consider them further, for William Smith, the morning's precentor, was at hand to discuss the service and to introduce the afternoon's Gaelic-speaking precentor, Thomas Fraser.

Smith seemed a little distant today, and James wondered about it. The fact was that Smith had been disturbed by MacGregor's gloom and disappointment in the colony. Not taking sufficiently into account

James's exhausting journey, his difficult meeting with Cock and Smith, and the hard march over the hills from Truro, he had remarked to a friend, "I fear we have been disappointed in our minister; I don't think that he will do much good."[23]

Despite Smith's odd behaviour this morning, the general pleasure in James's coming was evident, and many sensed the gravity of the occasion. He was wrenched from further musing, however, as members of the congregation began to take their places. The service was about to begin.

The three Frasers – Thomas, Alexander, and Simon, already church elders in Scotland – accompanied the petitioners in procession while James walked slowly behind them all as they entered the big barn doors, like the "Great Doors" of some imposing cathedral, though he would not have welcomed such an image. Proceeding gravely past rows of men, women, and children who were straining curiously to see James, they reached the centre of the barn: an Anti-Burgher cleric preferred not to address his fellows from the front, as from "some papish altar." With great solemnity James approached a raised dais, rough but steady, from which he could command a view of those all around him. Atop it, one of the squire's best chairs had been set for him, and as he sat he nervously shuffled the papers of his sermon, which was fully written out – a practice frowned upon by the Scots. But perhaps today he would have little need of his script, for the looks of expectancy, joy, and wonder reassured him. The Lord was with him, and He was the Word.

Just below James, Will Smith stood at the precentor's chair, and later, when a provisional session had been constituted, there would be another row for the elders, so that all could keep a watchful eye on the congregation. The audience was variously dressed: a suit befitting a good grey Glasgow merchant, worn by William Kennedy, who had gained a fair living this year as a sawyer in the square timber trade; the homespun of those still struggling; here and there rags and patches desperately sewed or woven together; the faded red of an old uniform jacket. No matter, the shining faces told it all: they were ready.

The service was familiar to the Lowlanders as James moved through the "ordinary" – the careful examination of a biblical text – to the "lecture," which combined texts that spoke directly to personal behaviour. Few had ever seen a worship service so rigorously followed; some had not attended one for years; a few sat uncomprehending; all awaited the sermon.

Although James spoke simply, he always dealt with demanding material and ideas. Only in the sermon would he indulge the evangelical and strongly moralistic tone that marked Seceder services. Looks of puzzlement came from those who knew only Gaelic, but still they wept, whether because divine service was once more available to them or because they knew that shortly they would hear the wonderful words in the auld tongue.

He announced the first hymn, for in the Lowlands, hymns were beginning to creep into Dissenting services. Still, the early ones did not stray far from the psalms of David. Some Anti-Burghers balked at such "human composure"; many disapproved of "poetic paraphrasing" and the soft-hearted "Christianizing" in Isaac Watts's curious "hymns." They distrusted the trend from psalms to "unregulated" forms of worship. James was raised to that view, but his mind was open and he knew that many were Lowlanders. Like Henry IV, Paris was well worth a mass.

Like Covenanters, they sat while they sang, a few riffling through books but most relying on memory. James felt relief at having two experienced precentors "giving the line." For, no organ, chanter, or pitch pipe would be used, the human voice being considered a divine instrument needing no other.[24] Smith's rich tones and practised voice drew them into the wonderful lines from the doxology, "Praise God from Whom All Blessings Flow," sung to the familiar Genevan tune of "Old 100th." William was inspired, and covert smiles crept across many faces. Bands of sweat on white flesh shone from the brows of men who seldom removed their caps except to go to bed, and as they offered their cheerful praise, the sun broke through, sending down shafts of light through the dusty air. Brightness touched their heads and weary shoulders, until they were haloed in the mix of light and shifting motes – "diamond dust." So, the air itself glistened and spirits rose with the sounds of the grand old hymn reaching to the rafters. In their midst sat James, singing lustily in his slightly high-pitched voice. Although he may earlier have appeared troubled and strained, faith and joy now swelled his spirit. He had earlier felt the burden of his charge, but the certainty of his faith and his rising estimate of his flock lifted him up gloriously.

After further prayer, he announced Psalm 121, well suited to Pictou, which itself looked unto the hills. Smith led the unison reading in full-rounded tones, for the grandeur of the psalms was the soul of Highland worship. Then it was time for the sermon, and gathering his papers,

James rose and solemnly began to read. Preaching directly from head and heart would come later.

His English was touched by cadences of Gaelic, so that although Gaelic listeners could understand few of the words, they could sense from the rhythm and pitch of his voice when he meant to chasten, to exhort, to reassure, and to comfort. To many, this may have been their first sermon ever, for lengthy sermons were still uncommon in parts of the Highlands. But Seceders were noted for their evangelical preaching, and though James had much to learn as an orator, his earnestness and learning moved them deeply. Patterson remarks: "From the ignorance of the people, too he [sought] ... the greatest simplicity of speech ... For the purpose of rousing the careless ... [adding] a strong epithet, even though it might give offence."[25] Someone recalled years later, "He brought the prospect of heaven to earth so that we could all share in it in the language of ordinary men."[26] But his success also arose from his yoking of reason and strong belief.

This time the text was 1 Timothy 1:15, "That Christ Jesus came into the world to save sinners." He developed it carefully, with mounting fire and vivid imagery, growing more confident as he saw that they were coming to him. An hour went by, and he was like an oasis where all around were slaking their thirst after a drought. Then, casting off all restraint, he pictured the dark temptations around them – they stood in danger of being "shoveled into *ifrinn*, hell." Still appealing to their intellects, however, he assured them that their hope lay in Christ and in striving for personal piety, which they could buttress by uniting to build His kingdom on this frontier, and by renewing their communal faith in a true "congregation." It was the kind of rallying, of raising morale, that the petitioners had looked for, and they nodded to each other approvingly.

Smith closed with "When all thy mercies, O my God," sung to "Winchester Old." Then James came down, walked across the floor of the barn, and stood with the squire just inside the doors. He was weary from the mixture of remorse and hope he had conjured up, but with Patterson's help and a careful smile, he greeted everyone, especially the children, as the shy, admiring company shuffled past. Soon, the picnic groups, excitedly awaiting the Gaelic service, filled the air with sounds that, if not more reverent than before the service, suggested a more thoughtful cheerfulness.

But in the barn, several ne'er-do-well half-pays were milling about, and James's attention was distracted from those around him, hearing

MacGregor Driving the Noisy Half-Pays from a Service. (Frank Baird, *Rob Macnab: A Story of Old Pictou*. Halifax, Royal Print & Litho, 1923, opp. p. 35. Artist is C.W. Jefferys.)

"a gentleman of the army" calling, "Come, come let us go to the grog shop." But James observed, "Instead of going with him, they came toward me."[27] They addressed him politely enough, but in rough language that "had no savour of piety in it." He was tired and in no mood to discipline these disorderly baiters there and then. Acknowledging them politely, he retired to the companionship of the Patterson family, but it was a foretaste of troubles to come.

Perhaps it had been a shaky start, what with his unease over Smith and the soldiers, but as he walked out his eye fell on Smith, sitting with Thomas Fraser under a tall spruce. Smith remarked quietly to Thomas, "Ah, he is better than I thought; I think he will do yet."[28] James met his eye, and when Smith nodded slowly with a slight smile at the corner of his mouth, he knew that he had done well, and that he had won a valued friend and elder.

Picnics were taken outside on the grass, and this time he ate hungrily, rising when he had finished and working his way among the crowd, a word here, a smile there. Signs of shy respect came from all directions. Young women whispered at his fine bachelor appearance and splendid hat; others mumbled words of gratitude and regard. He looked to the shore, where dugouts, canoes, and rowboats lay in rows along the beach. It was an exotic scene for someone just arrived from Glasgow. His gaze swept across the harbour's sparkling waters to the distant shore, finding few breaks in the darkness of the virgin forest.

James was glad of the smiling picnickers and happy that the "gentlemen of the army" had no taste for the Gaelic today, for they were departing clumsily in their dugouts, bound to slake a keener thirst. The hot July sun burned down, and he withdrew among some mountain ash and moose maples to mop his brow and prepare his mind for the Gaelic service.

When all had reassembled, he mounted the dais, mindful that Thomas Fraser sat just below him. Through the ordinary, Thomas chanted encouragingly but they had little need of him. What a wonderful difference! For many, worship was at last in their own tongue! The psalms took on fresh meaning as the mournful minor tunes and breathiness of the Gaelic accented the sonority of their voices. Lowlanders sat fascinated by the strange sounds issuing from men and women with whom they had only exchanged polite greetings. "Oh," a Lowlander observed, "that Gaelic singing, there is grace in the very sough o' it."[29]

When James began to preach, there was excitement at the prospect of hearing the auld tongue from someone who had brought it to perfection. He had visited most of its reaches in Scotland, and if you were from Ross or Argyll, you could hear touches of your own tongue in this man from Perth. It would always be part of his attraction.

This time his text was Luke 1:10: "For the Son of man is come to seek and to save that which was lost." It might have seemed presumptuous, but they wept as he soughed, presenting alarming images of what it meant to be "lost," rejoicing as he sounded the note of hope for which they had waited so long. Weeks afterward, he discovered the incredible oral memory of those who were almost illiterate.[30] They recalled his words like some tribal tale of hoary vintage, quizzing him on the meaning of word and phrase, recalling whole biblical texts in the discussion. Now, his call to salvation reached its climax, and the emotions of his listeners poured out:

> It is well known that their mountain tongue has a peculiar influence upon this people ... the deep solemnity ... the earnestness of his [MacGregor's] address, the associations which it called up of their native land, and of similar gatherings there, rendered its tones still dearer and more impressive; and with tears streaming down their faces, they eagerly listened for hours to the words of eternal life, in language which fell on their ears like sweetest music, and awakened the most tender recollections.[31]

Then Thomas Fraser led them in the 102nd Psalm, "Thou shalt arise and mercy yet," and it was as though a hundred voices had been added to their number.

As the service closed, he was again exhausted, pouring down sweat. It had been a day of marathons, this second day in the settlement. He was stirred as he had stirred others, for the response to the morning service seemed almost restrained when compared with the tearful joy that now surrounded him. Everyone wanted to thank him, and in the auld tongue.

Later, as they straggled down to the beach, making their farewells and voicing their excitement, he regarded them with a dawning sense of pride. The young men took up their paddles and with sounds of quiet happiness, began the long return trip to their huts. Perhaps at that moment he felt the first traces of belonging, of conviction that God had meant him to be here.

Chapter Seven

Settling In and Broadening Out

Robert Patterson had wisely advised James to begin by visiting house by house the three widely dispersed and very different communities around the harbour.[1] Because it was the most Highland, he visited East River first. Many from the Soldiers' Grant had come to his first service – the blacksmith and armourer Roddie MacKay; his brother Donald the Builder; their brother Alex, limping since the Plains of Abraham; and a strong showing of Frasers. To succeed with East River's forthright settlers would advance his mission, for the Lower Settlement, rich in natural and human resources, was also the key to the interior's bounty in setting and souls.

Pastoral work was always James's best suit, the part of his mission in which he found greatest pleasure. At East River were former comrades-in-arms still willing to pull together on the same oar. Some were illiterate, but most had fared better. Thomas Fraser, his precentor, acquainted him with the other Frasers – Alexander, John, and Simon, two of them already elders. Alexander was a well-educated man, married to a woman of even higher station, and settled on the Middle River.[2] Captain John Fraser was a magistrate. No relation, Simon Fraser was the finest woodsman in the district. In them, James saw the makings of a session.

Having met the families on both sides of the river, he held his first service there that second Sunday. Again, there was "laughing and bawling," but this time he cautioned them against "the sin and danger of such conduct." Sunday was to be kept holy.

But he would encounter other problems, among them baptism, which was always controversial, raising questions of faith and order. As a student, he had studied the authority for child or adult baptism and had been attracted to the Baptists' adult baptism. Later, approaching the question more systematically, he had come down on the Church of Scotland side.[3] Even children could be brought to understanding. When someone suggested, "The Baptists think they are right," he replied, "Yes, but there is a great difference between thinking and being sure."[4] James was always the intellectual, all his life remaining sceptical of the evidences of "enthusiasm" he often saw in Baptists, Methodists, and especially New Lights. A balance between mind and spirit required judgment and vigilance, not unchecked emotionalism.

Beyond requiring them to pledge to raise their children as committed Christians, James was exceptional in requiring at baptism that the parents vow to provide their children with the best general education they could afford. J.P. MacPhie comments: "From the beginning ... he made the establishing of schools and the education of the people second only to the preaching of the Gospel."[5] Bruce MacDonald overestimates Thomas McCulloch's later role in advancing education at Pictou but concedes that MacGregor "sought to construct in the wilderness a community based upon the two pillars of intellect and integrity."[6] This solemn link between religious duty and the advancement of education would persist throughout James's ministry and is essential to understanding the groundswell of support for education that characterized Pictou and its presbytery.

Many early Pictonians, though intelligent and quick, were unlettered and barely schooled. James emphasized the importance of linking education and the baptismal oaths: only through the Word could one come fully to God.[7] "The priesthood of all [learned] believers" had been drummed into him by the old catechist Jacob. Under Cock and Smith, baptism may have seemed ceremonial, but James knit it into the family's educational life and development. Some might question the idea, but the list of applicants grew long.

He also linked a child's need for education to the parents' capacity to *provide* it, both in money and in spirit. Should he baptize an infant before the parents had the literacy and knowledge to ensure its proper upbringing?

> I was in great difficulty with some of them, ... and doubtless often erred, not knowing what to do with them, especially for their ignorance. To those whom I thought quite unfit, I advised delay ... till they got more knowledge, and to come and converse on the subject; telling them it was far safer for them to wait for it, than to receive it without the blessing of God.[8]

That was not enough for one East River listener, as James recorded:

[He] thought fit to stand up ... and say, in a loud and angry voice, that I was good for nothing, and did not deserve the name of a minister, and that he would never pay me a Shilling, as I refused to baptize his child. Some ... endeavoured to still him, but in vain, till he had got out his blast. I was sorry to hear him, but said nothing.[9]

Cooler heads prevailed, and faced with a fine by Session, the protester apologized. It was only because the protester had become heated and personal that he had been called short. Other, more temperate protests would appear from time to time.

Once, two East River soldiers, supported by John Fraser, asked that their children be baptized. MacGregor agreed, discovering later that both had wives in Scotland. Their deceit and his chagrin made him more cautious, but while East River would always breed controversy, he chose to live there, even when Pictou town and New Glasgow began to flourish.

Debate, reason, faith, and education remained his pole stars, as Patterson remarks:

He also laboured to promote the educational and social interests of the community ... He encouraged them in establishing schools, and when established, frequently visited them. And though for a length of time they were poor enough, they were the means of giving the young at least the elements of learning.[10]

Until the district grew, however, public schools could not be supported. James helped Peter Grant, John Fraser, and Simon Newcomb in their private "teaching rooms" and served as a trustee at East River.

The remaining part of his pastoral charge lay at Middle River, where he stayed a week with Alexander Fraser and his wife, holding his third service at their home. Fraser was a man of means and education, a relative of Lord Lovat, his wife a daughter of the laird of Skriegh, Inverness. There were only eleven original families at Middle River: four from Galloway, the rest Highlanders. Here, James came to value his precentor and later elder, Robert Marshall, of whom he wrote:

A man worthy of being had in everlasting remembrance. He and his family suffered every thing but death in Prince Edward Island, by hunger and nakedness ... Soon after he came to Pictou, he lost a most amiable

consort, and ... had a great struggle to bring up his family; but he was
filled with the joy and peace of believing ... For many a day he had to
go to hear sermon in an old red coat which an old soldier had given him,
and a weaver's apron to hide the holes and rags of his trousers. He had,
I believe, the poorest hut in Pictou; but many a happy night did I enjoy
in it. Robert Marshall was eminent for honesty and plainness, for charity, for liberality of sentiments, and public spirit. He was very useful to
the young generation, teaching, and warning, and directing them; and he
would reprove the greatest man in the province as readily as the least.[11]

Supported by men like Fraser and Marshall, James found the Soldiers'
Grant and West River generous and challenging charges.

After a month of settling in, he had earned the respect of many who
recognized his dedication and uncompromising standards. He had
given new direction and momentum to the community; he had proved
an asset to the company; he had shown independence from Burgher
Truro; he had earned the support of several community leaders; and
he had gained confidence. It was time to move to a broader and more
organized mission, for in the Presbyterian way it was not for the minister to be the driving force. As shepherd, teacher, and scholar, he was
involved in the community's general advance, but he also knew that he
must channel his energy, for the North Shore would fill and his responsibilities would increase. Organization would ensure stability and continuity. In the fall of 1786, he initiated that broadening process.

Immigrants were now moving into the Upper East River, but he had
ministered only to the lower river. Early in October he ascended to
Springville, Bridgeville, and Sunny Brae, agreeing to hold his first brae,
or outdoor meeting, on a sloping meadow at James McDonald's inter-
vale, near Bridgeville.[12] On a fine October Sunday, dozens – from as far
away as West River – made their way in single file up the East River
footpath to a wide field in mid-intervale. There, set back from the river,
the McDonalds and others had prepared a site under a tall elm that was
already over a century old. It is still remembered as "The MacGregor
Elm," with its dozen stout limbs called "The Twelve Apostles." As
James stood beneath the great tree for the first of many braes, the scene
was as fresh and inviting as the swift waters nearby, chuckling over the
pebbles in their dash to the sea. Here, he and many successors would
hold services until well into the twentieth century, with the great elm as
a rallying spot and an icon. With the scourge of Dutch elm disease there
remains only the stump, but the scene is hardly changed.[13]

The MacGregor Elm at Bridgeville. (Rev. J.P. McPhie, *Pictonians at Home and Abroad*. ... frontispiece. Boston, Pinkham Press, 1914.)

Under this towering tree, his listeners crowded in eagerly, sitting
before him in a natural theatre from which the voice is amplified as the
low hills throw it back, but James needed no help:

> But a few men could address large audiences in the open air as easily as
> he could. At distances of half a mile ... the words were distinguished. His
> voice was not indeed loud nor ... stentorian, but it was beautifully clear,
> and melodious as a woman's. There was not the least harshness about it,
> but its tones were rather plaintive and tender, yet such was its compass that
> he was easily heard over the largest assembly; and so clear ... that he was
> heard as distinctly at the outer edge of the crowd, as at the very centre.[14]

Nor had there been any "laughing and bawling," perhaps because
they had had to walk in single file and in any case it was too distant for
the "gentlemen of the army." The event became a legend, the first step
in broadening-out. Peter Grant, a fourth experienced precentor, was
a large man whose lungs were the bellows of an ox. James returned
home with only a single complaint: "They had very poor accommodation. I had to sleep on a little straw on the floor." It would not be the
last time.

His second venture was more ambitious. He was asked to visit a soldiers' settlement at Merigomish, where there also lived some *Hector*
originals, 21 kilometres (15 miles) east of Pictou. He acquitted himself so well that they urged him to come often, and the arrangement
stretched into thirty years. He was concerned, however, about "the lack
of piety" of some, and again baptism was the sticking-point: "[A] man
applied to baptize a child. Before consenting, the Doctor made some
enquiries. ... He received the most ample testimonials ... 'But,' said
the Doctor, 'does he not drink? I have heard that he sometimes takes a
spree.' 'Oh yes,' was the reply, 'but we all do that.'"[15]

As James's travels were extended, he reflected: "Indeed, I might be
called the minister of the north coast of Nova Scotia, rather than of
Pictou, for at that time there was no other minister along the whole
north coast."[16] His steady correspondent at Comrie, Rev. Sam Gilfillan,
who had succeeded James's old tutor, James Barlas, described him as
"*Apostolus primus* in that part of the world."[17]

Broadening-out of another kind occurred this first fall, marking a
signature moment in James's life, although it has been overlooked by
most historians. Old Jacob had drilled him in his sect's rigid closed-
communion principle, but in his new setting James turned his back on

his father and on the Old World.[18] Beyond his readiness to serve both Dissenters from the Kirk and Kirkmen, he was prepared to adopt a remarkable ecumenism.

> I resolved not to confine my visitations to Presbyterians, but to include all, of every denomination who would make me welcome; for I viewed them as sheep without a shepherd … I did not pass a house; and though I was not cordially welcomed by all, my visits were productive of more good than I expected; and I trust they were the means of bringing to Christ several who were not Presbyterians.[19]

Thus, he early recognized the ways of the frontier, both as apostle and evangelist, but could Jacob have believed possible such latitudinarianism in his Jemmy?

Yet, James never lost a basic prejudice against the Church of Rome, although he showed concern for Catholics who were not being supplied by their priests. Unlike Jacob and most Anti-Burgher clerics, he welcomed them to his friendship and to his worship services.[20] When indigent Catholic immigrants arrived at Pictou, en route to Antigonish or Prince Edward Island and needing help, he often led the relief effort.[21] Friendly with lay Catholics, he was on guard against their clergy, faulting them for their possessiveness towards the Mi'kmaq. Often frustrated in his concern for the natives, he wanted only to support the distressed Catholics.[22]

He particularly disliked Father (later Bishop) Angus McEachern of the Island, who was also charged with the mainland North Shore as far as Miramichi but seldom exercised that duty. MacGregor called him "priest McEachern" and grew annoyed when, after he had helped some group of needy Catholic immigrants, McEachern charged them to move on quickly to avoid corruption, threatening excommunication to those who did not. After a visit to the seventy Catholic communicants in the Pictou-Merigomish district, McEachern reported, "From the want of a pastor, and by the importunities of a *fanatical Dissenter of the Seceder faction* two or three have been perverted."[23]

Both men served their scattered parishes under similar circumstances; both spoke Gaelic, and both earned reputations as compassionate, enterprising leaders. Both were highly complicated beings who in other circumstances might have drawn close.

James eschewed sheep-stealing or poaching, being concerned only to serve souls and already having more than he could handle. He had no strategy of evangelism, preferring to reach out to individuals and families. But in succouring both, he showed a flexibility he had not been raised to. He was on mission as preacher and pastor, apostle and evangelist.

Broadening-out also meant church organization. Too much already depended on his personal enterprise, but as a Dissenter from the Church of Scotland, a teaching elder. Soon, the ruling elders would play a large part in guiding home congregations, especially when they realized how much James had an eye for extended missions. It was church law and polity to establish a session in each congregation, and as soon as possible to organize a presbytery of the district clergy, with a delegated elder representing each congregation.

Indeed, at this stage James's position remained hardly different from that of a travelling minister: he might preach and baptize, but by Presbyterian custom and law, elders must yet be ordained and inducted. Without a session there was no congregation, only a meeting, for as Norman Kennedy observes, "The Flock would have been shepherded but unfolded."[24] A presbytery comprised all the ministers and representative elders from congregations "within the bounds." At Pictou, however, one could not be brought together until James realized easier relations with Truro, or one could not be constituted until enough ministerial colleagues joined him to permit forming a new presbytery at Pictou.

He knew that cooperation with Cock and Smith could ease his load. "It was no small grief for me that I could not accept of the assistance of my brethren."[25] Still, nine years would pass before reinforcements arrived. Meanwhile, something had to be done, and perhaps with good laymen as elders to assist at services and undertake pastoral visits, it could be done. At Nigg he had seen how useful the catechists were (*Na Daoine*, The Men).[26] In time, at Pictou laymen would underwrite MacGregor's evangelical forays, although women in office were not included. It was not until 1966 that women were welcomed as elders in the Presbyterian Church in Canada.

Knowing that he held the power to constitute a *provisional* session and later to present new elders for ordination, James seized the initiative. He took the initiative, inducting only those who had served as elders in Scotland, ordination being for life. In the Frasers – Kenneth, Alexander, Simon, and Thomas – he found good men, requiring them first to draft a schedule of their visitations, to make plans for two churches, and to draw up a wider slate of prospective elders. His moves won swift support, and some of the new elders were among the colony's ablest men: Donald MacKay, Robert Marshall, James Fraser, and John Patterson. All that winter James trained them rigorously, and on 6 May 1787 the new elders were ordained.[27] His mission was now legitimized and made permanent.

Although a late spring delayed the groundbreaking for his meeting-houses, he could be satisfied with his early progress. But despite presenting a generally cheerful disposition James was always prone to depression, and he was soon weighed down by personal concerns. In June he received the first mail since his arrival nearly a year earlier, including the Delphic letter from John Buist that was so unhelpful with his relations with Truro. From his father he learned that his mother had died during the winter, and another letter told of the death of a young niece.[28] James's second sight manifested itself again, for on the night his mother died, he had dreamed of the house at Portmore being consumed by fire: "I really expected to hear by the first letter of the death of a near relation ... Reluctance to part with my mother was one of my objections to coming to Nova Scotia; and now I saw that staying at home would not have secured me from parting with her."[29] The news must have reminded him of his father's mortality and his helplessness to comfort him. He grieved, but the demands on him left little time to mourn.

His finances were also a worry, despite the generous promises made in the petition. He had stayed briefly and awkwardly with Donald MacKay's brother, William, but he had no security. He had received payments only in kind and often late, short, or in poor condition. It was his second November before he received a farthing in cash, and then only £27 of the £50 owed him for the first year. He owed his sister and others at home and was continually called on – and agreed – to assist distressed families. When Donald MacKay observed that some would never repay him, he replied, "Well, if they don't, I can want it."[30] He sold the surplus produce paid him, but if it arrived when he was away, he could not convert it to currency. Consequently, it was arranged for Deacon John to keep his accounts, which he did for ten years, receiving settlements in currency, selling payments-in-kind, and crediting James's account. The deacon, and on his death the town's other great merchant, Edward Mortimer, thus became "minister's brokers."[31]

James's purchases are interesting, for they include items such as "wheat for Widow Smithson," and they reveal the range of his needs: "feathers, rope, twist, snuff, buttons, pen knife, pipes, 1 gal. rum, blue cloth, magazines, thread, blue cloth for leggings, 3yds, Drab cloth, 1 qt. rum, leather for soles, red flannel."[32]

Some of his followers were late in paying; others, like the "gentlemen soldiers," were mean and withheld all support; and some who spoke only English whined that Highlanders who spoke both languages should pay a double share. Despite such pettiness, he recorded, "[My] mind was so knit to them, by the hope of doing good to their souls, that I resolved to be content with what they could give."[33]

Givings posed another problem. Many Kirkmen had not known voluntary offerings, only endowed livings or a session's check-off system.[34] When the Highlanders fell short, James would slip his own tithe onto the plate, confiding that he "did not like to see their collection far behind the English."[35]

In handling disputes among his flock, he was generous but canny. At East River, largely Highland, on Thomas Fraser's advice he began with the Gaelic service. Elsewhere, when asked to preach both sermons in one language, there being an overwhelming majority of that tongue, he agreed only if no one would fail to understand. If one were found, he would reply, "Oh, then he has a soul to be saved, – and who knows but this sermon might be the means."[36] Meanwhile, the tide of immigrants was rising, and as news of his services in Gaelic reached many parched believers who knew no other tongue, some moved to East River.[37]

In July 1787, after a late planting, the men began building two meeting-houses: one at Loch Broom between the West and Middle Rivers, the other on the East River. Gangs of volunteers appeared: cutters, haulers, hewers, boarders, shinglers, joiners, glaziers, "chinkers" – those who stuffed *fag*, moss, between the logs. There were no cabinetmakers, for the walls and ceiling would not be panelled. Split logs and planks served as rough benches. One was not expected to be comfortable at a worship service. A loft, reached by a ladder, was provided for the children. All was of white pine, sturdy and homely. There was no pulpit, for James preferred to stand surrounded by his listeners.[38]

That fall there were signs of an early winter, portents confirmed on 15 November when so much snow fell that it lasted until late April. It would prove the most severe in memory, and James recorded, "I was tired of winter before New Year's Day, but before March was over, I forgot that it should go away at all."[39] The harbour ice bore traffic before the end of November, but on Session's advice, James reduced his schedule:

> It was therefore agreed that I should preach two Sabbaths at the East River, two upon the Harbour, two upon the West River, and two upon the Middle River, and then renew the circle until the warm weather should return.

The Upper Settlement of the East River ... were excluded through the whole winter ... as effectually as if they had belonged to another world ... For six weeks in eight, I was from home almost totally deprived of my books and all accommodation for study, often changing my lodging and exposed to frequent and excessive cold. But it ... gave me an easier opportunity of visiting and examining the congregation, than I could otherwise have had, for I got these duties performed ... between the two Sabbaths on which I was there.[40]

Obviously using snowshoes was an essential skill that he quickly acquired from the Mi'kmaq.

But because James was unwilling to curtail his visits, his studies suffered, although his translations continued unabated and he corresponded regularly with Scottish ministers on ecclesiastical and theological matters.[41] Letters and articles were printed in *The Christian Magazine*, his Scottish church's journal, and he reviewed books in English.

His reference to "examining the congregation" raises again the subject of baptism. As was Kirk tradition, many had expected him to "do the children" quickly. But MacGregor's ways came as a shock: that winter, in fortnight-long visitations he rigorously prepared the candidates, even the children. He conducted two kinds of visitation (or "diets of examination," as they were called). When he could, he dealt with several families together: first, a social call to become acquainted; then, a second to get down to business.[42]

After asking each adult to review with him how they conducted their common prayer and their personal "closet" prayer, or contemplation, he gently explored the same questions with the children, commending those on the right path and exhorting the rest to improve their ways. To the adults he put questions about the "Shorter Catechism," scriptural passages, or points of doctrine, like original sin, fasting, justification, or good works. But he did so subtly and intimately, so that the visit became "a direct religious conversation with every individual," as he had experienced at home. These were learning experiences, not tests of memory, achieving a level of sharing that broke down barriers, as the best confessors can do. Finished with the adults, he would call out, "You young children, come around me," and he awakened inquiry and assurance in them.[43]

Little of his pastoral care centred on authority – least of all his own. He was intent on teaching, learning, and understanding, bypassing ritual for "kitchen visits," where he set a simple people at ease, as would

Fathers Jimmy Tompkins and Moses Coady in the twentieth-century cooperative movement in nearby Antigonish. To such believers, religious life and everyday living are yoked, and through understanding and knowledge they can be made to work together. His visits reflected the New Testament idea of "the church in thy house." Afterwards family and friends debated what had been said: "They traveled in groups homeward, when the conversation, led by one of the elders or some aged Christian, would be on spiritual subjects; but would chiefly turn upon the sermons of the day, and among the company, the greater part of what they heard would be repeated."[44] These were like scenes from James's boyhood, when Jacob led the family home from Kinkell. In 1886, celebrating the one-hundredth anniversary of James's arrival, Duncan Cameron Fraser of New Glasgow recalled that as a boy he had often sat "listening to aged Christians, when some passage of scripture came under discussion, referring to what '*Mhaighstir Seumas*' [Father James] said, long years after [his] ... death."[45]

In early Pictou, then, formal education being unavailable to most, visitations by MacGregor, Marshall, Donald MacKay, John Patterson, and others stirred young people to vie with their elders, developing memory, honing verbal skills, and teaching them to advance and counter argument. They did so in the only formal culture they knew: their religious life. MacGregor used scripture to elevate their religious and moral lives, but in another sense, he was engaged in teaching. Along with memory, logic, and dialectic, his diets and worship services aroused curiosity, competition, and pride in learning – something that challenged and bonded young and old. Daniel Harvey observes, "In studying the Bible ... they assimilated language and were saved from intellectual stagnation."[46]

For a long time, this was the only culture available to an isolated people, but the lessons of James and his colleagues prepared the ground for one of the most developed educational systems in the province or elsewhere in the British colonies. The roots of Pictou Academy ran deep into a rich and well-prepared soil.

Through the bitter winter of 1787, James tried to sustain his visitations, happy that the deep cold had discouraged the "gentlemen of the army." They had not forgotten him, however, perhaps blaming him because so many now spoke out against them.[47] Winter was their most mischievous season, and several half-pay officers organized a meeting to have him removed, even threatening his life. He faced their opposition like some biblical plague during seven of his nine loneliest years.

It was during this first fierce winter, travelling with Kenneth Fraser, that he experienced the terror of being lost in a snowstorm on open ice. With spring advancing, rot had set in, and they escaped by the narrowest of margins. Another time, after crossing a dangerously thin stretch to conduct a service, James was asked if he would return the same way. He replied, "No, we have no call to go." It was pointed out that it had been that way when he had appeared, and he replied, "Yes, but we had then a call to come, but it is not necessary for us to go back just now."[48] Legends grew among a superstitious people.[49] One old woman had such faith in him that she asked him to cure her ailing cow. When he demurred she persisted, and he took a rod that was at hand, dubbed the cow, and said, "If you live you live, and if you die you die." The cow recovered and, Patterson relates, "sometime after, the Doctor himself had a sore throat, and this old woman came to see him. As soon as she entered the room, she said, 'Ah, if you live you live, and if you die you die.' He immediately ... burst out laughing, which broke the abscess that had been forming, which discharged, and he soon got better."[50]

In the midst of such homely scenes, MacGregor tried to avoid controversy, but two issues arose which he could not ignore. One was thrust upon him; the other grew out of his own conscience. The first involved a central point of Dissenter principle. An Anti-Burgher from Colchester called his attention to an edict from the lieutenant governor at Halifax:

> I suppose you have ... received his Excellency's orders by proclamation to keep a fast upon that Holy day, dedicated to St. Mark, as also a copy of the Right Rev'd. Bishop's [Bishop Charles Inglis] prayer, which you are to read upon pain of being punished as the law directs, for disobedience to the lawful command of the best of Governments. Must they not be amazing strong and prevalent prayers, that they are sent up by the force of civil law?[51]

Similar civic proclamations in the old Puritan colonies, where the Church of England had not been "by law established," had brought alarm. In Nova Scotia, the Church was established, and some Dissenters, hearkening back to Old World ways, regarded such declarations as state interference in religious practice. They protested that they held their own regular fast days and "days of humiliation," but at Session's call, not at the state's command. Their occurrence is noted regularly in James's Session books.[52]

Those in the Burgher tradition, however, might not bridle at a lieutenant governor acting so: Burgher Seceders like Daniel Cock and
David Smith found no fault. James did not differ with them publicly,
but he refused to honour the state's call. The Anti-Burgher strain ran
deep in him, although he could now bend in many respects. His differences with official Halifax would not go away but merged with
Pictou's growing reputation as a chief critic of the capital, for he was
legitimately alarmed: what might be next? Would it be a resurrection
of the state's claim of the right to nominate clergy to their pulpits? A
repeat of the Scottish patronage controversy?

By contrast, he himself initiated another dispute, this time with Rev.
Daniel Cock. It was one that became more public and heated, and it
ranks as one of the most important moments in James's life and a significant one in African Canadian history, although blacks or historians
have seldom recognized it.

Chapter Eight

Letter to a Minister

Several of the original Philadelphia Company settlers, Squire Patterson among them, brought indentured servants and black slaves from their Maryland plantations. The practice was common among Loyalists newcomers, and the level of slavery in Nova Scotia rose sharply in the 1780s. At Pictou there is no evidence that slaves were treated differently from indentured or bonded convicts, with the critical difference that they could be sold as property and a stigma attached to them for the colour of their skin. They were personal property. Dr. Harris exchanged a slave, Sambo, as chattel for a private debt. Among Matthew Harris's slaves was a woman, Die Mingo, and a male mulatto, Martin, who figure in this story.[1]

In Scotland, attacks upon slavery had begun in the 1770s, and as we have seen, Glasgow was a leading centre of the antislavery movement during James's time there. His friend John Buist was prominent in the antislavery movement; John Millar, Glasgow's renowned professor, took an active part; and from Crieff, Rev. James Barlass reported approvingly the activities in Parliament of "a Mr. Wilberforce."[2]

In Nova Scotia, by confronting Truro Presbytery's Rev. Daniel Cock and his ruling elder, Col. David Archibald, James became a prescient pioneer in the antislavery cause.[3] Along with other large-scale farmers and townsmen, both Truro men were slaveholders, and to MacGregor this was sinful. His central objection centred upon religious principles and morality: further, as a clergyman, Cock was failing in his fiduciary duty. Here, as a radical social gospel evangelical, James was acting as a modern social activist.

Others – among them Samuel Salter Blowers, solicitor general, and Richard John Uniacke, attorney general – also opposed slavery but in sociolegal terms. They used their offices to judge and administer the laws of property in ways that must over time stifle slavery, but without rallying a frontal assault. Other religious leaders lent their voices to the debate, if less passionately or effectively than James – men like Henry Alline, the New Light leader, and William Black, the Methodist evangelist.

But it was MacGregor who took the most decisive action; in this respect, and because the doctrinal differences between the two Secessionist churches were of no great note, his radical actions defined the Burgher–Anti-Burgher split in Nova Scotia.

His efforts to undermine the legitimacy of slavery rested heavily in scriptural argument. He began at Pictou, first persuading Matthew Harris to sell him Die Mingo's freedom for £50, his first year's cash stipend. A year later, although he had received only £27 of his first year's stipend, he made a down payment of £20 and committed most of his receipts in kind over the next few years until Die was free.[4] Keeping up the pressure, he persuaded Harris to free Martin, and a few years later for £10, he bought the remaining term of an indentured woman, supporting her and providing her daughter with an education. Other cases followed, and in each he welcomed the freed slave to his congregation; he could not fully remove a prejudice against them, but perhaps their descendants would be treated with somewhat greater respect. James Cameron concludes too strongly, perhaps, that by his actions at Pictou James "ended slavery by example."[5]

Things did not go well in negotiations with Truro, however, for after consulting Colonel Archibald, Daniel Cock refused to release his young slave, Deal. Nor would he discuss the matter publicly, but that did not prevent his colleague, Smith, from taking on the defence. Cock, Smith argued, had earlier sold Deal's mother for being, "unruly, sullen, and stubborn, as to threaten ... her own life, in which case she forfeited her liberty, and so he disposed of her to [someone] more accustomed to the management of such, [but] she laid her new master under the necessity of confining her more than ever."[6] Deal was treated as a servant, Smith argued, free to come and go as she pleased, and she never complained of ill usage or indicated a desire to leave Cock – as if she had many options.

Deeply troubled, James remained aloof from the Truro Presbytery and on investigation was the more concerned to learn how widespread slaveholding was in Nova Scotia. He determined to write a powerful protest against Cock's practice, one that became the earliest published attack on the practice of slavery in British North America. It marks a decisive moment in the development of antislavery opinion and of black history in the province.

MacGregor had reason to be alarmed at slavery's common practice in Loyalist Nova Scotia, but he may also have been moved to oppose slavery by the appearance in Scotland two years earlier of James Ramsay's "Essay on the Treatment and Conversion of African Slaves in the British Sugar Colonies," even to adopting Ramsay's intemperate language.[7] He does not quote from or cite Ramsay's book, but his letter shows familiarity with it. Ramsay, surgeon and abolitionist, had studied at Aberdeen under the moral philosopher Thomas Reid, who was later elevated to the chair distinguished earlier at Glasgow by Adam Smith – and Reid had introduced MacGregor to moral philosophy, as John Millar had attacked slavery.

James's protest first appeared in an article in a Halifax newspaper. Entitled "A Letter to a Clergyman, Urging Him to Set Free a Black Girl he held in Slavery,"[8] it appeared again in 1788 as a pamphlet, published by John Howe, a Sandemanian Scottish Seceder who was already known for producing "seditious" literature critical of court and government. James knew well that he was challenging the sanctity of what was regarded as private property, and although he did not name Cock, it was plain whom he meant. Based largely on scripture, James was driven by a deep sense of caring – albeit the document is at times intemperate and likely to generate more heat than light. But it remains a landmark on the road to personal freedom in province and nation.

The letter opens with the ritual disclaimer that nothing personal is intended, but the style is declamatory and rhetorical, a polemic not a letter. He first informs the anonymous clergyman that he is troubled by "the concern you have in the most infamous and accursed of all commerce, the buying and selling of man." Since God has blessed him with more power or wealth than his slave, he should repay Him with liberality and compassion of his own, "particularly to exert yourself to the utmost for the redemption, protection and education of slaves." Urging compassion, he cited, as he often did, Hebrews 13:1–2: "Be ye not forgetful to entertain strangers: for thereby some may have entertained angels unawares."

Had you lived eighteen hundred years ago, you would not have scrupled to buy and sell … Jesus Christ, if at least he had been born black, and you had met with him before the fame of his miracles began to arise; for he

was not only made in the likeness of men, but took upon him the form of
a servant – and became obedient; Phil. ii. 77, 8; how could you have distinguished him, and such as you do enslave.[9]

If the clergyman had raised the girl a Christian, then "mystically,"
because those united to Christ in faith become "members of his body,
Rom. xii. 5 *Eph*. V. 30, he has enslaved Christ." Are they not one spirit
with the Lord, of "his flesh and of his bones?" James further quotes,
"Inasmuch as thou didst it unto the least, the very least of these, thou
didst it unto me."[10]

He dismisses the defence that slaves merit bondage because they are
deemed "ignorant, obstinate and wicked ... Yet may they be converted
from the error of their ways." This is the clergyman's job. MacGregor
links slaveholding with the trade in slaves as part of the chain of
bondage. Simon Magus had offered to buy the Holy Ghost, but the clergyman's sin "is greater ... as you have actually purchased and sold the
temple of the Holy Ghost wherein he dwells, and all that it contains."[11]

Relentlessly, he asserts that the clergyman knows that the slave trade
is wrong:

> but that avails you little while you help forward the affliction ... While
> you open the sluice, in vain do you cry out, Stop the stream ... Can you re-
> ally believe that any man will consider his property as his equal, and treat
> it accordingly? I defy all the world to prove it unlawful for me to kill and
> eat that man whom I may lawfully buy and sell, like my ox or my horse ...
> If you reply that you do not buy and sell their souls, I answer [that] as you
> cannot buy and sell their bodies without their souls, the Almighty Judge
> will account that done to the man which you do to the body ... The traders
> that deny the rationality of their slaves, act, at least, an open and consist-
> ent part ... Reverend Sir, let me ask you, Does not your practice in keeping
> a slave contradict your daily prayers?[12]

He then gives awful warning of where error may lead, for the slaves
will have their day:

> and at the great day of judgement, they shall stand at his right hand, and
> doom many of their masters to eternal slavery, torment and death. "Know
> ye not that these slaves shall judge the world?" 1 Cor. V. 2.; ... for as long
> as you believe slaves to be men, busy meddling conscience will not suf-
> fer you to keep quiet possession of your spoil ... O shame! O indelible

disgrace! That Protestants, Presbyterian ministers, who of all others, should keep farthest off from her, should be found publicly committing fornication with the Great Whore, drinking themselves drunk, and stupefying their conscience with their filthy wine! But blessed God, though hand join in hand, the Negroes shall be free. When the anti-Christian fabric shall tumble down, the slave merchants shall be covered with its ruins. It is hoped the period is not far distant.[13]

Here James checks his passion, appealing again to reason and conscience:

I would entreat you, Reverend Sir, to consider what baleful influence your example will have upon others ... Many will shield themselves against strong arguments with this: Surely when the Reverend Mr. – a good minister, does it, there cannot be any harm in it ... Therefore, set free your slave directly ... Sell her not; the price will be most cursed, and the Lord will not cease to have a controversy with your soul.[14]

In his peroration, he lists four "objections" to the defence of slavery: first, the belief that blacks are slaves because black is the colour of the devil; second, the notion that they are better for being enslaved because they are so different and have an "enslaved disposition"; third, the example of slavery among the Jews ; and fourth, the "seed of Canaan" argument from Genesis 9:25. Parenthetically, he asks why the clergyman would not himself prefer to be enslaved if slavery offers such protections.

His first objection is a deft, even amusing, quasi-anthropological argument that reveals his empathy with the blacks and addresses the "devil" theory:

Reverend Sir, being a white man, you are accustomed to having a black idea of the devil, and I doubt not but you would have taken the first Negro you ever saw to be him, if at least he had proceeded to torment you. But put yourself in the place of the Negro, and the thought will apply equally well to a white man ... The truth is, the devil is so contrary to man, that in the daytime, and among white people, you will always find him black; but in the nighttime, and among the Negroes, he is invariably white.[15]

He conjures up a scene in Africa in which the white "devils" seize Cock, put him in chains, and transport him through horrors to the

New World, where he finds more of his own people "toiling, sweating, fainting, dying under the severity of their drudgery, and the torments of the last waved by no gentle hand." Even if he encounters a few white people who show him kindness, "still you could not help being astonished that there was so striking a resemblance between them and the devil, as made you mistake the one for the other, and for so long a time."[16]

He concludes this first objection by observing that God has done the blacks a kindness in making them black in the tropics: "Reverend Sir, were you and I in Guinea, we would earnestly wish for a black skin." Therefore, he continues, "How strongly do men impose upon themselves, as if an imaginary connection between a black colour and unworthy deeds did really justify slavery!"[17]

Regarding the common assumption of the blacks' "slavish disposition," he spurns the idea that enslavement is kinder because "they thrive better bound than free."[18]

> How is it possible for that man to have anything manly in him, who is taught from his youth to consider himself as a beast of burden? How can any thing noble spring up where the very buds of sense or reason are crushed to death? ... but surely their slavish disposition will not be charged as a fault upon themselves, but upon those basest of wretches, who sink their minds in to that condition; and grievously will they answer it ... Were the Negroes free, and properly encouraged and instructed, they would in a few generations become as noble and free and high spirited as ourselves.[19]

The third objection examines the Jews' record as large-scale slaveholders. While Mosaic law "permitted slavery without limitation," Moses had been right to set rules for those, like the Gibeonites, who willingly sold themselves into slavery.[20] Without approving of slavery, it was right "to make laws to prevent cruel masters from abusing their slaves."[21] He then condescendingly suggests that Moses, like many who "came early had but little knowledge and experience ... and a very small portion of divine revelation" (presumably, such as appears in the New Testament). Therefore, "many things might be permitted, which cannot ... be suffered now in the fullness of time." As for the Jews, "the Lord severely chastised them" and saw them sold into the worst kinds of bondage. "Beware," he warns, "of forging chains for your children."[22]

In his final objection, citing the passage in Genesis 9:25, "Cursed be Canaan, a servant of servants shall he be unto his brethren," he opens ironically:

The connection and force of this argument must be as follows: – Slavery is entailed upon the seed of Canaan, therefore also upon every Negro. Reverend Sir, I hope there is no man quick-sighted enough to see the force of this reasoning, but will be able fully to refuse it by such arguments as this: – The Grand Turk wears a turban, and therefore ought to be held the sole author of all the hurricanes in the West Indies. If the seed of Canaan be doomed to slavery, what in the wide world is that to the inhabitants of Africa? What have they to do with Canaan, or his curse? You are more likely to be of the seed of Canaan than they.[23]

Barry Cahill observes that MacGregor mirrors Hume's warning that the slaveholder is inevitably enslaved himself.[24] MacGregor's evangelicalism sometimes had a populist, radical streak, probably stemming from his father's influence, but it was obviously too strong for many in early Nova Scotia. Here is the voice of the radical, reaching a pitch as his forebears had on the subject of clerical patronage.

MacGregor concludes with "the words of a fine writer," perhaps James Ramsay, one more temperate than he had been in his own letter: "Let avarice defend it as it will, there is an honest reluctance in humanity against considering our fellow creatures as a part of our possession."[25]

Robin Winks calls it "the sharpest attack to come from a Canadian pen even into the 1840s; he had also brought about a public debate which soon reached the courts."[26] But he had only begun it. The letter cannot be taken as the first step in the antislavery movement of Nova Scotia, for although it drew much attention, it remained for some time an isolated case. It was, however, the most direct assault, linking the practice to deadly sin – indeed, sin committed by a member of the clergy and therefore the more grave. It was a critical early step in what would become a broad social movement. MacGregor was prescient – he was a prophet, not leader, of a greater movement to come.

Daniel Cock was too mild-mannered to reply, but Smith did not hesitate, especially in view of MacGregor's statement that "he would rather burn at the stake than keep communion with" Cock and his kind.[27] Smith, however, relied on arguments already refuted in James's letter, insisting that well-treated slaves "had reason to esteem it a happy privilege that they ever came under the direction and protection of such masters." By his own lights, Smith charged, MacGregor was no better than Cock, for he had purchased Die Mingo – Smith overlooking the fact that MacGregor had done so only to liberate her.

MacGregor never mentioned his letter to his father or to church officials, not even to John Buist at Greenock, which led Buist to write:

> You were not so good as to tell me you had freed some slaves, but Mr. Fraser told me ... I thought such goodness should not be concealed, and sent to the Glasgow Advertiser ... the following, "Rev. James MacGregor ... [in] Pictou, Nova Scotia, has published in that country against the slave trade, and ... by a noble and disinterested philanthropy, ... [purchased] the liberty of some slaves. Such is [his] modesty that he has not given his friends in this country the pleasure of this news ... [But] he has purchased and liberated two young persons, ... and is in treaty for the liberty of an old woman, who may be very useful as a nurse for the sick ... It was copied in the newspapers through Britain, and your name is famous.[28]

James recorded on the face of Buist's letter that he had read the "account of the Advertisement with trembling and sweat." He may, however, have sent the letter to his student friend from Glasgow days, now Rev. John Jamieson, the distinguished etymologist, for in the following year Jamieson issued his first antislavery polemic, a poem, "The Sorrows of Slavery."

Throughout his life MacGregor defended and supported the province's blacks by calling for their freedom; by buying the freedom of several with his own small, uncertain stipend; and by supporting their claim to better education, greater opportunity, and a recognized dignity. His youngest son, Peter, also a minister, would do likewise. Ironically, although Daniel Cock's slave Deal may have been considered his property, custom was not followed and her surname was not Cock, but instead thereafter she was known in Truro as Deal MacGregor.

PART THREE

Missions

Chapter Nine

On the Road

With the new churches completed, MacGregor turned to other forms of building. He was determined to meet the extending North Shore's growing spiritual needs, but he must first guarantee that Pictou's own strength would endure. Like his father in his self-appointed task of bringing the Gospel to Strathearn, he was the driven evangelical, compelled to extend his ministry – but he could do it successfully only with Session's approval, authorization, and support.

In 1792 Pictou was freed of Truro's administration of customary law, Session having often, as among Dissenters in Scotland, performed the function in small communities. Until 1823 James kept its minutes, and over seventeen years he recorded twenty-three civil and domestic disputes that were mediated by Session; these included conflicting land claims, charges of theft, the passing of counterfeit money, cases of adultery, men being too free with the domestic help, and "ante-nuptial fornication."[1] Their scope was broad, their number small.

Consequently MacGregor's confidence in his people was growing rapidly, and he was ready to test them in the deepest testimony to their faith. For two years he had been criticized for his unwillingness to celebrate the church's most solemn service, while he maintained that education for the Lord's Supper was essential and that he would know the time. Because the ritual was unfamiliar to some northern Highlanders, he wanted their full understanding and commitment. With much help from the elders, he reviewed, prepared, and examined one hundred and thirty candidates, counselling and catechizing them during countless house visits.

He proposed two outdoor "Long Communion" services (as they were called) for July 1788, running five days and to be conducted in both languages. Huge resources of energy and organization, months of the elders' commitment, and days at the site were required. It was an awesome project in physical and spiritual energy, but after two winters of visitations he and Session considered them ready: "I had more reason to be content than to complain. People in general attended public ordinances diligently and attentively. There was much outward reformation; and I doubt not, some believers were added to the Lord."[2]

Renewals of this sort in North America were deeply ingrained in the Presbyterian tradition and, as Richard Sher observes, paralleled "a rich Scottish and Scots-Irish heritage of sacramental festivity."[3] Leigh Eric Schmidt cites the "sacramental meditations, advices, catechisms and directions that preceded these … distinctive eucharistic rituals."[4] In Robert Burns's satirical poem "The Holy Fair," in some mainstream Kirk circles, and in jibes from the "Moderate Literati" of the Enlightenment, such ceremonies were dismissed as mere revivalism, proof that "the fervour of conversionist piety … was incompatible with the solemnity of sacramental purity."[5]

But long communions were entrenched in the Highland Kirk tradition, especially those conducted in Gaelic, and a Dissenting minister like James might gain credibility by conducting them. Moreover, they were not aimed at conversion but served as an affirmation that the aspirant held a solemn and deeply instructed commitment. In part a folk tradition brought across the Atlantic, these were events of public witness in the church's most solemn sacrament. Schmidt remarks, "The Lord's Supper was the basis of renewal and evoked passionate, emotional responses."[6] But to James, passion must be wedded to strict discipline of mind and heart: learning and believing were yoked. He sought always to strike a balance between feeling and intellect, a hallmark of Glasgow's Enlightenment. Not for him the pietism and emotionalism of "revivals" taking place in the Americans' Second Great Awakening. There was a decorum, etiquette, and purpose at the heart of the church's greatest moment.

In this grand first renewal, then, the service would be held on the Middle River, "on a beautiful green … sheltered by a lofty wood and winding bank." Often referred to as "The Occasion," the service would reach a climax with the dispensing of Holy Communion on Sunday, 27 July 1788.

Although James would not condone "laughing and bawling" at Middle River, at these great meetings he would tolerate a lively excitement, for in time the prospect of communion and renewed friendships attracted hundreds from Amherst, Truro, Stewiacke, New Brunswick, and Prince Edward Island. Part holiday, but above all holy day, word went out five weeks before Communion, challenging families to prepare in mind and spirit by reading, through instruction by elders, and in prayer.

The logistics of preparing for such an event were formidable. Travel was by horse, canoe, boat, and footpath – the trip involving the provision of food and belongings for a family for a week. Few had horses, or those that could be spared, and many bore great packs of gear and food on their backs. Once arrived, some families stayed with friends, but most erected shelters, gathered firewood, and set up a large temporary village. Session had already worked prodigiously amassing fuel and other necessaries.

After the long build-up, people looked forward to seeing distant friends and family, comparing farm and lumbering practices, exchanging recipes and remedies, teaching natural dyeing techniques – the ways of wilderness life. The children, meeting new friends, were caught up in fresh games and excitement. These were times of rejoicing for James, too, for if their deepest purpose was worship, inclusion, and thanks, they were also an archetypal frontier ritual, helping to cement the bonds of the Pictou district and of the North Shore and beyond.

But James was unrelenting in guiding his charges to their spiritual ends. To some, the format was familiar, although accommodating two languages and Highland customs made it more complicated.[7] Thursday was a "Day of Public Humiliation and Prayer," praying in repentance all day, singing doleful psalms, and hearing two remonstrating sermons.

Friday was the "Day of the Men," or *Ceist*, when the *Na daoine*, or "old Christian enquirers," led in questioning and discussing and when, unrehearsed, many gave testimonials to the nature of grace and of their receiving it. The *Ceist* demonstrated their deep knowledge of scripture and their capacity for informed, passionate discussion.[8] In its lay-rootedness, *Ceist* Day was conducted almost entirely in Gaelic, but concessions were made for the many Lowlanders. Although women often joined in the discussions, *Ceist* Day was Men's Day.

Saturday was "Preparation Day," when MacGregor preached morning and evening, with song and prayer shifting from remorse to praise of the Lord. On such occasions James would often slip in a poem or song of his own.

The Sabbath brought the real climax, first with James's "action-sermons," his briefer, more plainly worded calls for renewal than regular sermons. Then the elders brought forth the candidates and dispensed Communion to the initiates and only to those already professing communicant members.

As in Cape Breton, Monday was "The Sad Day,"[9] when after two further sermons, James sent off his communicants charged to remain pure and to exhort others to follow.

At the close of his first celebration, he must have reflected on an exhilarating and exhausting week. During the whole time he had been in the limelight, his advice and aid constantly solicited, but he had resisted his elders' pleas to seek the help of the Burgher clergy. Frontier laymen might be more tractable than their minister, but James could not yet share with Cock and Smith the sacrament that lay at the heart of everything. Clinging to principle, he faced a decade of lonely, unremitting service on an ever-expanding frontier. He bore a heavy burden, but he also brought it on himself.

Sometime after his brushes with Cock and Smith had begun, James received a letter from the Kirk minister of Mather's (later St. Matthew's) Church in Halifax, appealing to him to heal his differences with Truro Presbytery. The writer was Rev. Andrew Brown, whom Bishop Charles Inglis described as "an ingenious young man from Scotland with amiable manners."[10] George Shepperson describes Brown as "precocious" (he graduated from university at thirteen) and states that he helped to heal the breach between Congregationals and Kirkmen in Nova Scotia.[11] But that accommodation had already been achieved at Mather's Church before Brown's arrival, staving off its designation as a Kirk for several more decades by agreeing that the minister might be Kirk but must follow Congregationalist practice. Those Kirkmen who Shepperson claims were reconciled were not distributed province-wide, but constituted the adherents at Halifax. For, there was no Kirk congregation anywhere except at Shelburne, a town quickly assembled a few years earlier as a Loyalist metropolis and as quickly deserted.

Although in time Brown worked very effectively to bring together his own congregation, the indifference of his Protestant Dissenting church towards other Dissenters across the province led eventually to talk of cooperating with MacGregor and with the clergy at Truro – even to leading Congregationalist ministers and Baptists. Brown was no diplomat.

After assuring James that he wrote "as a Christian Min'r ... with much meekness and humility," and although he was four years younger than James, Brown spoke in chastening terms:

From such Contests fanaticism gathers strength and its abettors always improve them to the Utmost ... Be admonished then My Dear Sir to make peace with all your brethren, and from this time forth to live with them in unity. You are yet but a young man, and in that view it may be graceful and comely on you to make the first advances. Tell Mr. Smith and Mr. Cock, that you are sorry if any part of your conduct ever offended them, and that on your part you heartily forgive whatever you may have thought uncandid or unkind in them toward you. I can see nothing mean in such conduct. By such a declaration you surrender no principle or truth, and sacrifice no article of Duty. Our lives are short, and our alienations embitter them ... This is strong argument to immediate reconciliation ... Far removed from the seat and the Subject of controversy, and having no connection with one side more than the other, I have ventured to suggest these things to you in the spirit of the Gospel of Christ. Peace is the characteristic of his religion, and Charity the badge of all his Disciples. I shall be happy if any efforts of mine are successful in establishing them.

Your sincere friend ...
Andrew Brown.[12]

George Shepperson faults MacGregor's failing to respond to this patronizing letter as proof of James's "uncompromising" nature, but for reasons of conscience and in deference to Synod – apart from his reaction to Brown's tone – MacGregor was unlikely to have bent to Brown's call.

Brown held no authority, beyond his perceived neutrality, had just been ordained in that year, and held his seat at Mather's Church at this early stage in a shaky compromise. In time he became a significant reconciler in his own flock and, as Shepperson notes, was "a leading figure in social and intellectual circles" at Halifax with a brilliant career ahead of him on his return to Scotland. But he was at the time still only a young placeman, installed by the lieutenant governor on the recommendation of his teacher, Rev. William Robertson, leader of the Scottish Moderates. It was Robertson who observed, "There can be no society where there is no subordination." Brown suited official Halifax.

By deferring to bishop and governor, Brown represented everything that Jacob Drummond and his church had opposed. James's alarm over Inglis's attempt to impose state-directed days of fasting was in accord with Seceder principles on patronage and establishmentarianism generally. Further, the class-based contempt of many Moderates for Seceder beliefs and practices was no less keen among Kirkmen in Halifax than in Scotland. By rejecting Brown's advice, James may also have helped fuel the outports' growing resentment of the petty little capital's lofty ways, but the letter of reprimand had come from one, whatever his later distinguished career, who had not yet proved himself. Brown entered comfortably into an accommodation with Halifax's establishment, where he was content to pursue the history of religion (very successfully) in his study, but hardly venturing outside the capital. James rejected his presumption, clung to principle, and thus sealed a further period of distancing himself from Halifax's patronizing ways.

MacGregor would not be diverted from his determination to respond to new souls, to encourage the building of churches, and to assist raw communities in need. He had travelled far, but Pictou was not the end of the road. He would embrace a more scattered and diverse flock than he could ever have imagined in Scotland.

After some difficulties with his testy first landlord, James moved in under Donald MacKay's roof, where Donald had built him a snug berth in a garret room in his recently completed log house. Donald the Builder held ten cattle on 450 acres, with ample woodland for his construction purposes. Thus, James could feel much at home with his built-in bookshelves and fireplace – a fine panelled retreat for quiet study when he was at home. But with a stable base and confident of Donald's friendship, he could travel with an easier mind while he was away on mission during much of the summer and even in winter. He always kept a little distance from his flock, as leaders must, but with Donald he was open and at ease.

Things were not always quiet at the MacKay household, however. Besides six sons, three daughters, a husband, and a boarder to care for, Donald's wife was subject to fits of violent insanity. Donald bore these painful episodes with patience, and when he was at home, James supported him. But he was often away during his eight years with the MacKays, when Donald had to carry his domestic burdens alone. Their closeness was important to them both, for they buttressed each other in their trials and loneliness.

MacGregor felt especially the pain of having neither fellow clergy nor wife, for his was what the Victorians called "an ardent temperament." Back in Scotland his passion for one woman had rivalled his dedication to spreading the Gospel. In 1785, anticipating his ordination, he had written an *Oran Gaoil*, "Love Song," to Anna Buchanan, whom he had met while assisting her father with his congregation at

Nigg in Ross-shire. But although she had been attracted to James, she had refused his offer.

James tried not to give up hope, setting his poem to the melody of Duncan Ban's *Mairi Bhan Og*. It comprised ten verses of eight lines each, and while it spoke clearly of Anna's fine character and many virtues, it also offers tantalizing descriptions of her "breast as pure as the breast of the swan … Rounded calf, jaunty, strongly buoyant, … so well trained in woman knowledge, … the gem of the heap, the rest are all stones, … the flower daintily wrapped, … the sapling that bends with honeyed apples," and more.[13] Written with fervour, it was filled with sadness, for it opens, "And I shall forever love the maiden / I've left behind for now."

In Pictou, believing he might compromise his mission by marrying a local woman, he tried several times to find someone to join him from Scotland. But he was no more successful in attracting a wife than a fellow minister. Ironically, the minister who came closest to joining him as an associate minister during these lonely years, the Rev. Aeneas MacBean, had married Anna Buchanan, raising intriguing questions about why MacBean abruptly withdrew his name. Meanwhile, with the help of Revs. John Buist, James Barlas, and Sam Gilfillan, other Scottish women were considered, but all proved too frail for the frontier or met with objections from their parents. "Providence," James was informed by one father, did not intend his daughter's "removal to the wilds of North America."[14]

From time to time he gave in to tiredness and despair. Once, after tumbling into a river in full spate, he arrived home soaked and low in spirits. The faithful Donald, older by nine years, asked what, beyond his soaking, was the source of his depressed state. James replied, "Oh, I am done out. I can do no more. I must go home … What is the use of my staying here? I am doing no good."[15] Donald replied calmly, "Go home? And what will you do with these sheep in the wilderness," chiding him gently. "But you are only sowing the seed." Despite James's rejoinder that "there is no appearance of any fruit," Donald listed his conversions, reformations, and successes until he was soothed and could contemplate the next day's toil.

Once, when Synod had still not sent James an associate minister, Donald found him lying on the floor and asked, "What's the matter with you now?"[16] On being told, he comforted him, and James revived quickly, saying, "I must go for assistance, where I have often gone before, and never have been disappointed yet." One must hope that in his gratitude he had Donald in mind as well as God.

Soon the pressures of duty and travel became so heavy that he could no longer write out his sermons, having also reduced his Gaelic researches. At Donald's urging, he sketched his headings and wrote out only the biblical texts.[17] He had remained the young lecturer, seldom straying far from his notes, but now Donald urged him to greater spontaneity. Arrived home late one week, James had no time to prepare for Sunday, but when he preached to much acclaim that Sabbath, Donald observed, "I think you got that sermon out of your sleeve." James began to apologize, but Donald replied, "Oh, I wish that you would always preach without study, if you would give us such sermons as that."[18] In time his wish was granted, and MacGregor came to hold hundreds spellbound at services throughout the region. "How do you like Mr. A.?" said a hearer to her friend. "Ah!" she replied, "I would rather listen to Dr. MacGregor's voice without words than Mr. A's preaching."[19]

Donald's insight and sustaining strength are summed up in his advice after another of James's depressions: "No, no, hold on while you can, and give up when you must."[20] Given his wife's illness and the demands made on him at home, it was hard-earned wisdom.

James was first asked to expand his mission beyond the North Shore when several men from west of Truro invited him to supply, which is to say, to provide spiritual service to a congregation. Largely Anti-Burghers, they were not attracted to Rev. David Smith. James knew that there was dissatisfaction with Smith, but he was wary of further friction with Truro. He declined, saying that he would welcome them to his Pictou services, and some moved.

In 1788, he received a petition from several families at Amherst, on the province's western boundary – all Ulster immigrants who had passed over Horton and Truro to settle in the Chignecto district. James asked Session for permission to preach at Amherst over three Sundays, and it was agreed.

It was his custom to start his journeys by stopping at Robert Marshall's hut to say, "I have just called in to ask you to pray for me when I am away."[21] Robert was a kind of talisman, and in his company James could reconcile his faith with simpler Highland beliefs and superstitions. A guide was sent from Amherst, and although James was courteous and grateful, during the last leg of the journey he became increasingly remote. In time, others noticed that on his travels he became totally absorbed as he neared the site of the visitation but would be garrulous and voluble all the way home. What his guides lost on the swings, they picked up on the shieses.

At Amherst he found fine farms on mixed upland and marsh, and a number of well-established families. From the many low rises of land that mark this "Beaubassin" of the old Acadians, he stared in wonder at its unique beauty:

> When I came fairly in sight of Amherst, I was charmed with the view, especially of its marshes, which are extensive, perfectly level, and, to appearance, extremely fertile. After a few days I crossed to the Westmorland [New Brunswick] side, here I saw the largest and most beautiful piece of level land which I ever saw, extending about six miles in breadth, and sixteen in length ... Little of it was yet mown, but I was told that after a few weeks it would be covered with thousands of hay ricks.[22]

He visited homes in the Amherst district, held midweek services, and was touched by their thirst for a minister. Knowing Synod's record, however, he could not promise a regular schedule but vowed to return from time to time. He fruitlessly forwarded their petition to Synod, but for many years he continued as one of their few lifelines to their Lord.

His relations with the native people were always cordial, for he had learned from Squire Patterson that the Mi'kmaq of the North Shore were a peaceful, often helpful people, for whom James and the squire felt great concern. Once, James encountered two Mi'kmaq dragging an old person on a sled. They had suffered a bad winter and were in need. James gave them a note addressed to two nearby parishioners asking them to give their annual share of his stipend to the Indians.[23] Such acts of kindness, however, were as far as he would go, for most native people were converts to Catholicism, and he was wary of offending their priests. Much later, he was more forthright in trying to persuade the lieutenant governor, Lord Dalhousie, to fund Indian benevolent societies, but Dalhousie scoffed, "Oh, they are just like the brutes; you can't do anything for them." James replied carefully, "Your Lordship should not say so," and he then attempted to picture what the Gospel could do for them. But his words were wasted.[24] As with his approach regarding blacks, he resisted mounting a full attack on the government for its lack of concern for the natives; instead, his sermons were usually directed to the individual conscience, motivated by considerations of theology and morality rather than of ideology or politics. Later, Walter Bromley would add his voice and "take myself into the wood among the Indians," but not until after 1815, a quarter-century after MacGregor.

For their part, the Mi'kmaq regarded James highly, partly because, like Simon Fraser, he followed their ways in the woods, becoming adept in the forest and on the rivers. He was often urged to buy a horse, but horses could become a burden in the snow, in swampy terrain, or along stump-choked trails. He bought one, but after a year concluded, "I had more pleasure in walking than riding, and therefore sold the horse and took to my feet again."[25] Patterson speaks of his "active, wiry frame" and describes his prowess:

> There were few [white] men equal to him in going through the woods. His very gait was peculiar. It was so fast that he kept others who were in company with him half on the run. The late Alexander Cameron, of Loch Broom, one of his elders, and a strong active man, used to say that he never saw a man, with whom it was so difficult to keep beside. By running he could outstrip him, but if he relapsed into a walk, the Doctor was sure to be soon away ahead of him. Though not a very strong man, yet he possessed such remarkable powers of endurance, that he travelled long distances with comparatively little fatigue, and out-did many, who were accustomed to labour and travelling in the forest.[26]

That, of course, is a description of the Indians' gait and pace, and of their capacity to cover long distances without tiring. It also recalls MacGregor's strenuous youth around Loch Earn. As his missions proved, he was tough as a heather root.

Winter required that he wear leather-thonged racquets (snowshoes) as the best means of travel. Those who could run "toes up and legs apart" could attain remarkable speed. With green hide for the shanks, moccasins ensured flexibility. His prowess was recognized, and the Mi'kmaq presented him with a handsomely ornamented pair of racquets. Patterson portrays him ready for a journey:

> We are describing not a modern, refined, kid-gloved, man-milliner of a preacher. We are describing a veritable man of labour, and one who bent himself to his work in the true spirit of endurance. His boots are taken off and deposited in his knapsack, which was generally carried by one of his companions, his feet are encased in … moccasins, over his legs are drawn what were called "Indian leggins," a sort of overall made of blue cloth, with a red stripe down each side, and fitting closely about the feet and strapped down, while the faithful racket (snow shoe) … is fastened to his feet by leathern thongs round the ancles; and whether you count him fit

for your drawing-rooms or not, he is fully equipped to go on his errand of mercy, to seek the solitary dweller in the wood.[27]

With the spring run-off came swollen rivers. To avoid a long inland march through spring slush to the first ford, James and his companions cut long poles as stilts and awkwardly crossed over or threw themselves onto a pan of ice being flushed downstream during break-up, poling across the river while anxiously scouting ahead for a safe berth on the other side. James became as adept at such winter and spring manoeuvres as he had in summer with a canoe.

He describes his adaptation to forest life: "I had to learn to walk on snowshoes in winter, and to paddle a canoe in summer, and to cross brooks and swamps upon trees overturned or broken by the wind, and to camp in the woods all night – for there is no travelling the woods at night, where there is no road."[28]

Rev. William McCulloch, Thomas's son, relates a story of James's daring in winter and at night, as told by a smithy near Mount Thom:

On a cold February evening, a person on snowshoes entered the smiddy, and asked leave to warm himself … Sweeping the ashes from the anvil, and spreading thereon his handkerchief, he took some food from his pocket, sat down, and having asked a blessing finished his repast and thanking the smith, he resumed his snowshoes and about 5 o'clock took his way to the East River. That man was Dr. MacGregor.[29]

Yet he often found beauty in the unforgiving wilderness that lay before him and was never so daunted as not to appreciate the glory of fall in Nova Scotia:

It is impossible to exaggerate the autumnal beauty of these forests; nothing under heaven can be compared to its effulgent grandeur. Two or three frosty nights … transform the boundless verdure of a whole empire into every possible tint of brilliant scarlet, rich violet, every shade of blue and brown, vivid crimson, and glittering yellow. The stern, inexorable fir tribes alone maintain their eternal sombre green. All others in mountains or in valleys burst into the most glorious vegetable beauty, and exhibit the most splendid and most enchanting panorama on earth.[30]

The journey to Amherst in 1789 marked the first of his extended missions, but he also preached along the North Shore at Tatamagouche

and beyond. On a few occasions, he spoke in Halifax, but he avoided
the capital. As his missions grew longer, his visits to Merigomish must
have seemed like a neighbourhood stroll.

On a hot day in July 1790, responding to another petition from
some of Rev. David Smith's disenchanted congregation, he appeared
at Onslow, near Truro. He had not wanted to incur Cock's or Smith's
displeasure, but considered it a courtesy to some very troubled men.
Smith considered it otherwise, for James found the church door locked,
and with difficulty succeeded in persuading his outraged listeners to
adjourn to a grassy knoll.[31]

When he had concluded, there appeared a New Light preacher,
Thomas Handley Chipman, one of Henry Alline's converts, who
announced that he would speak, too. MacGregor later confessed that
he immediately offered up an "ejaculatory prayer":

> I prayed in my heart, "Lord, confound him, that he may not prevent the
> springing of the good seed sown," for I knew that Mr. Chipman ... would
> teach the people the greatest errors. About five minutes after he began to
> preach, Mr. Chipman fainted and continued senseless about ten minutes,
> and though he recovered, yet he did not preach any that day. Therefore
> another New Light minister ... stood up to preach in his place, but after
> he had proceeded about five minutes, confounded, he gave it up, and the
> congregation dismissed.[32]

In August 1790, after a second trip to Amherst, on his return journey
he reached Kemptown, still far short of Pictou. He was wary of the
next leg of his journey on a thinly blazed trail over Mount Thom. At
the gristmill, he learned that two Pictou men were leaving in the morning when their flour was ready. His informant was the mill's owner,
David Archibald II, son of pioneers Samuel and Eleanor Archibald of
Truro, and nephew of James's earlier nemesis, the slaveholding Colonel
David. Yet he was warmly received, and gladly accepted the invitation
to supper and overnight lodging.

Knowing how few mills there were in Pictou, he spent the afternoon
sketching and measuring Archibald's extensive works. On returning
to Pictou, he gave his sketches to John Fraser, who had James's draw-
ings completed by an architect and then built an imposing mill. Not
long after, David Archibald moved from Kemptown to Middle River,
opened another large mill, and became a pillar of James's church,
remaining until his retirement.[33] Thus, James did not limit himself to

the care of souls: whenever new knowledge of a practical kind caught his attention, he found ways to apply it. Man's nature, welfare, and attachment to the land were all his concerns.

In 1791, he was asked to supply the inland frontier of Stewiacke and Musquodoboit. Thousands of Loyalists had appeared, and to forestall them, second sons of Truro's pioneers had hurriedly moved into these rich farmlands and forest stands. At Musquodoboit, an itinerant Ulster Presbyterian preacher, Rev. James Murdoch, proposed that they build a church and attract more regular supply. Most of the congregation were from Cock's flock, but age had hobbled him and they looked elsewhere, delegating the ruling elder, Robert Logan Archibald, to find a new man.

Robert, second son of Colonel David, was a cousin of David II, the miller, and a magistrate of some education and experience. In approaching MacGregor, he ignored the congregation's largely Burgher background, and like David II, overlooked the fact that James had once confronted his father as an erring slaveholder. It was a small world, and he sought supply. There followed a lively correspondence in which the sharp layman wrestled with the learned young minister.[34] A thorny point was the question of "Union" – that is, whether to exclude those who had not formally declared themselves Burgher or Anti-Burgher. It was one on which James's father had bolted from the Burghers. But by inviting James, Archibald had demonstrated his flexibility. Could James do the same?

He could, for ever since coming to Nova Scotia he had been learning to adapt. Or perhaps Archibald's disarming ways and poor spelling won him over:

Dear Sir:
You may see … what are my principals with respect to charity and church excommunication, although I cannot communicate my Ideas to my pen in a regular maner. Yet I hope your better understanding will enable you to … give me what evidence you have against what I have said … because neither my tallents or education are fit to engage in sophistical reasoning … I hope it may be the happy consequence of our correspondence … that we rather wish to establish truth than throw a stumbling block in each other's way – Dr. Sir, as you have more time and ability, I hope you will impartially examine and let me know, where and how far charity and church communion differ in there extent – for as yet I cannot persuade myself, that I am authorized by the word of god (which must be the rule) to … keep out of church communion, such as I am asured by the same rule, are members of

the church above ... many, if not all, that bear the christian name, if their
faults were known, would merit censure and rebuke. But that we can, or
ought, to exercise charity to such as refuse to manifest there repentance
on account of some open violation of God's holy law, appears to me a
contradiction in terms. I think therefore that charity and excommunication cannot long exist toward the same person. One must of course give
way to the other – "Let all bitterness and wrath and anger and clamour
and evil speaking be put away from you, with all malice – and be kind one
to another tenderhearted, forgiving one another even as God for Christ's
sake hath forgiven you endavouring to keep the unity of the spirit in the
cause of peace."

I am Dr. Sir your Humb. Servt.

Robert Archibald.[35]

After much agitation, MacGregor agreed: Musquodoboit would have
open communion, and for many years, by foot and by snowshoe across
the almost trackless hills dividing them, James would supply. He knew
when to bend and acted accordingly.

His next important mission also occurred in 1791 and marked the
most significant phase of his broadening-out program. This was the
first of ten visits to Prince Edward Island.[36] After Pictou, the Island
became his main mission until 1821. His role in the development of
Island Presbyterianism rivals his achievements at Pictou.

Chapter Ten

Years of Trial

When MacGregor agreed to serve at Pictou, nothing was said about his boundaries. Like Jacob he undertook extended missions on his own, for Daniel Cock was too old for lengthy visits and David Smith did well to get as far as Stewiacke once or twice a year. Even in the burgeoning neighbourhood of Pictou, supply soon became onerous, but there were souls to be tended and he would not ignore their appeals. Session backed him by assuming heavy duties of its own.

Many calls probably arose from word of his endurance, his commitment to missions, and his pastoral skills. Heavy Scottish immigration and his increasingly confident preaching, especially in Gaelic, also counted, while growing security and a rising birthrate contributed further. So, MacGregor and his Session soon faced a dilemma: whether to remain focused on a growing Pictou or to reach out and hope more ministerial help would come soon.

Session had approved Amherst's request for a minister, but Synod failed them again. Undaunted, Session asked for one, even two, associates at Pictou in order to release James for more distant missions, proposing that the second minister come at their cost. James pointed out that they could barely afford him, but Session argued that if he would agree to a 20 per cent reduction, fresh help would make possible an outreach program.[1] He agreed ruefully, knowing how irregularly his own payments appeared, especially in cash. Later, an old Highlander chortled, "Oh! 'Twas grand times, when Dr. McGregor ... lived, plenty of preaching and nothing to pay!"[2]

In fact, James had approached his Scottish friend Rev. Aeneas Mac-Bean, but his new wife, James's old love, Anna Buchanan, may have balked at the idea. No one else could be found, and for another four

years James worked alone. Renewing his commitment to Merigomish, Musquodoboit, and Amherst, he undertook a venture second only
to his coming to Pictou. Why he chose Prince Edward Island requires
explanation.[3]

The Island and Cape Breton Island were tiny, anomalous colonies.
In 1767, the Island of St. John, so-called until 1799, was divided into
sixty-seven private proprietories awarded by lot to some hundred non-
residents in recognition of civil or military service. That left no Crown
lands to produce revenue. Several Halifax notables were among the
proprietors, but most lived in Britain, a few sending agents to look
after their interests. However, without revenue from land sales, public services were limited. Government officers served without pay, a
tiny council ruled, and the coming of an assembly made little difference. Revenue and development rested with the proprietors who were
charged to pay quit-rents and ensure improvements – contracts honoured in the breach. Roads and bridges went unbuilt, and ferries lay
far in the future. A village at the mouth of the Hillsborough River was
designated the capital and named after the Queen, Charlotte Town. It
was bracketed by Princetown in the west and Georgetown in the east,
but no roads connected these royal burghs. Elsewhere, settlement was
scattered, dependent on a few committed landholders or the indifference of others to squatters. For a century, the "land issue" would breed
acrimony and confusion, undermining the morale of those arriving in
hope of owning land. Farming was slow to develop, and lumbering,
fishing, and shipbuilding appeared late. Highlanders lacked their traditional herds, and crop farming developed slowly, especially on alienated land. Some, with money and skills, fled to Cape Breton or Pictou.
The situation called for the consolations of rum or religion.

Soon, Acadians were returning from their sad dispersal, and mixed
groups of Scots appeared in large numbers. Loyalists gathered about
Bedeque in the northwest. Scots came from Argyllshire to Richmond
Bay, from Perthshire to Cove Head and St Peters, and from Moray to
Cavendish on the North Shore. There were in addition a few remaining ill-fated Galloway people at Georgetown. When Cove Head and
St Peters appealed to MacGregor for supply, in agreeing, Session may
also have considered the prospect of increased trade, for Pictou had an
incipient metropolitanism about it.

The Church of England benefited as the established church. A parish
and church were established at Charlotte Town, the rector paid by
London, parish costs being borne by local government. The Island came

then as now under the see of "Nova Scotia and its Dependencies," and Bishop Charles Inglis soon paid a pastoral visit. But Inglis's domain extended from Newfoundland to Detroit and Bermuda, and the Island would not be showered with episcopal attention. For a long time government and church served bureaucrats and the few land agents at Charlotte Town. The established church might only reflect the Island's petty class divisions and centralism, but doggedly it survived, enduring Halifax's benign neglect and nurtured at the gentle hand of Rev. Theophilus DesBrisay.

DesBrisay, a Low Churchman, was the lieutenant governor's brother. Like James, he had once been a Calvinist and was still an evangelical, ready to help others.[4] Although he served at Charlotte Town he lived outside it, ministering occasionally at baptisms and weddings to those outside the Church of England fold. James's coming would not threaten this useful accommodation, for MacGregor's mission lay among the rural Scots along the North Shore.

James arrived at Charlotte Town in the summer of 1791, meeting three men whose support would help secure his ministry. In Charlotte Town he rested briefly with a Scottish merchant, Mr. Rae, setting off next morning on horseback for Cove Head, where a New World John Millar, a ruling elder, awaited him. But he lost his way and happened upon an affable man who arranged for his horse to be ridden to Millar's home and then paddled him across the intervening water to his own home, where he provided tea and then escorted him to Millar's house. James's angel was Theophilus DesBrisay, and thereafter DesBrisay, born a Huguenot, was so welcoming that he offered his church at Charlotte Town for MacGregor's use.[5]

But another surprise was in store for MacGregor, for his host, John Millar, was "from the parish of Muthil, twelve miles from Loch Earne, where I was born."[6] Millar knew James's former teacher Rev. James Barlas, and in an evening crowded with reminiscence, Millar listed all his neighbours who had come to the Island from Strathearn. Years later, James told of encountering an old Kinkell schoolmate who failed to recognize him. He asked, "Do you not mind a little boy called Jemmy Drummond?" "Oh yes," was the reply, "and are you Jemmy Drummond?"[7]

Even on first meeting, however, controversy arose: for although ready for an Anti-Burgher clergyman, Millar allied with the Burghers in Scotland in upholding civil power. In the morning James – never adept at the job – was shaving when Millar tried to press the point, but

James cried out, "Stop, stop, you have made me cut myself. Let us talk of those things about Christ in which we agree till our hearts get warm, and then we will discuss these points afterwards."[8]

He preached two Sundays each at Cove Head and St Peters, 25 kilometres (16 miles) apart, filling the weeks with house visits. Asked to intercede with Synod for permanent supply, he warned them of how slim were their chances, and after a month of hard work he prepared to return home. But there appeared a delegate from a community of Argyll folk who, twenty years earlier, had settled on Malpeque Bay, 48 kilometres (30 miles) to the west. They had never been visited by a clergyman and begged his attendance. Recalling his good years in Argyll, James was well disposed to them and agreed to go, with confidence in his elders at home. Later, he recorded, "Indeed, the two weeks ... at Princetown, were the two most anxious which I ever passed in this world."[9]

The problem was familiar, baptism. In twenty years, even family prayer had gone by the board at Malpeque. Some sermons, house visits, a few baptisms, these would not be enough; what was needed was an intensive re-education program of the whole community, for over sixty people awaited the sacrament. At his first service James met more "laughing and bawling" than he had heard at Pictou, and he wondered anxiously how in less than two weeks he could prepare the parents to honour the pledges he would require at baptism.

As usual with MacGregor, the answer lay in hard work. With the help of his host, Donald Montgomery, he divided the district into two sections, further dividing each into five units, corresponding to the ten weekdays he would be with them. In the absence of elders, with Montgomery's help he visited and gathered the testimonials for each candidate. He had undertaken a gruelling marathon, the only relief being that everyone had the Gaelic.

However, he was then asked to face further risk by attending a large group quarantined with "Highland fever." In the end, he could warrant sixty baptisms under the strictest injunctions, for without continued visits, he knew how quickly the effort of missions could melt away: the community must have regular ministerial support. Leaving Princetown exhausted but encouraged, he hurried to Charlotte Town seeking swift passage home. He had been gone six weeks at the peak of the season for summer visits and services, sustained only in the knowledge that at Pictou he had a band of loyal, experienced elders. Encountering Mr. Rae again, he learned that a schooner was to have left ten minutes earlier, although it should have sailed the day before. Hurrying to the captain's lodgings, he found him still there, and ten minutes later they cast off.

A weary man stood beside Captain Worth as they broached the first swells of Northumberland Strait. James recounted his haste from Princetown but said that when he met Mr. Rae he had stopped worrying, the rest being perfectly natural.[10] Then he asked why the captain had not sailed the previous day. Worth thought a moment and replied: "Well, Mr. MacGregor, I was ready to sail yesterday at this time as I am now, and the wind has been fair all the time, and I could not go; but I know not what kept me ... I had nothing to do, and I wished to go; but it seems I could not."[11] MacGregor understood forerunners.

For the rest of the year, he spurned applications for distant supply. He had learned how desperately Island reinforcements were needed, but he knew how much he was also needed at home. Accordingly, Session boldly asked Synod for four men. But a familiar reply was returned; it had been five years.

The Island's other lesson, that he must not desert his home people by undertaking protracted summer missions, was driven home to him. He was not prepared to jeopardize the gains made at Pictou. To add the Island, then, two courses lay open: sending elders as catechists and conducting some Nova Scotia missions in winter. He adopted both.

Stewiacke lies beyond Truro on the road to Halifax. It began sparsely, but in prospect of the Loyalists' coming, the pace had quickened. Determined to forestall the newcomers, young Truro men with their families and possessions ascended the Shubenacadie and Stewiacke Rivers in flat boats, crossing trackless forest to the lush valley. These were second-generation settlers, experienced Scotch-Irish pioneers – Archibalds, Fultons, Logans, Creelmans, Johnsons – who looked to an orderly growth with worship in their own church.

Cock and Smith called a few times each year, but Stewiacke wanted more, and in 1794, as Smith lay dying and Cock ageing, Stewiacke turned to MacGregor.[12] Although most members of the community were Burghers, they were united in purpose, and after a late-summer reconnoitre James agreed to come. But his mission was delayed until winter, which proved unusually cold and snow-laden.

Patterson gives only a brief account of James's time spent at Stewiacke, probably because he thought the extraordinary journey warranted more attention. James had set off accompanied by two Pictou men, while a welcoming party would meet them halfway, beating a track through the unusually deep, wet snow. His account speaks for itself, and for many other winter trips:

Travelling on snow shoes is eligible only when the snow is neither very soft nor very hard; for when it is very hard the snow shoes are apt to slide, and when it is very soft they sink deep, and become wet, and so heavy as to clog the feet greatly. It was soft then, and though I had three or four men before me making the road more solid, yet I was quite faint by the time we had traveled eleven miles. One of the company had a little rum and bread and cheese, of which we all partook, and by which I was recruited more than by any meal of victuals which I remember. But I became faint again before I reached a house, which was four miles distant …

[At Stewiacke] I got through the usual course of examinations satisfied that the congregation was growing in knowledge and grace; but I was obliged to omit the visitation of a number of families …

On my way home … I was more hardly bestead, both by fatigue and hunger, than I ever was. I left … with four Pictou men – two belonging to the West River and two to the Middle River; but we took a little bread and cheese with us, as we expected to be hungry before we could reach a house. We had traveled only a short way when the weather changed, and the travelling became extremely heavy. We therefore resolved … to keep together, and steer a middle course between the two rivers … and so have less travelling after dividing.

By this plan we would have but one path to break, and each one's share of the fatigue in going foremost to break it would be less.

Thus we clung together till night, and then we judged ourselves only halfway to Pictou. With morning we … had good appetites but no provisions. We separated – one party squinting to the left, with intention to hit the West River at a considerable distance down from its source; the other, to which I belonged … to the right, with the same intention … We, however, missed our mark completely … and altered our course, and stuck to the left, assuring ourselves that we could not miss it again. Onwards we marched, till we again thought ourselves far past it; and not meeting it, we could not determine what was to be done. After consultation, we resolved to turn again to the right. By this time I was extremely wearied, and glad of any excuse for resting two or three minutes. We had not gone far when we met a blaze … crossing our path almost directly. We resolved to follow it, as it would lead us somewhere; but whether … to right or left we could not determine. By mere random we chose the left, and followed … about three miles, … when we began to fear it was leading us from home, and accordingly we came straight back ... and kept the direction for more than four miles ... and then stopped for another consultation. ... We now resolved to take a kind of random course till we could fall in with a brook, and then to follow it withersoever it went. This we did, shortening its windings as much as we could. It led us at length to burnt land, which gave us hope that a settlement was not far off, though the immense multitude of fallen trees ... oblig[ed] us to creep under them and climb over them with great difficulty ... but having got past, we soon arrived at a good path on the side of the Middle River, about four miles below the upmost settler. Here we took off our snow shoes, and being relieved of their weight, I felt as if I had no feet, and yet was so done out, that I could scarcely reach the next house. Here we were speedily supplied with plenty to eat and drink; but I could eat nothing until I had rested a while, when I felt an appetite for some boiled potatoes. Rest and sleep restored me to my usual appetite and strength.[13]

Instead of 130 kilometres (80 miles), return, they had travelled 160 (100 miles), and in the worst winter conditions.

While James was serving the Island, his Pictou elders kept up the momentum of stewardship, but Stewiacke confirmed winter's hazards. In the summer of 1793, Session declared Amherst to be his limit. The journey was no less arduous for being familiar, and he found Amherst's needs still unanswered.

He had reached a critical point in his ministry. His once-robust health was deteriorating, his breathing was laboured, and blood was showing in his sputum. Yet, desperate calls came from Amherst, the Island, Stewiacke, and even beyond, in Douglas Township, inland between Stewiacke and Windsor and along the Minas shore. Driven by concern, James determined to write his most ambitious letter ever, reaching beyond Synod to younger Scottish clergy who might take heart from his example. His "Letter of 1793" surpasses the "Letter to a Clergyman" in its compelling appeal. It was the *cri de coeur* of his life and would ripple well into the next century.[14]

In the letter, he described the specific needs of the mainland and Island, making the case for immigration to Nova Scotia and the duty of young ministers to undertake overseas missions. It was a powerful statement born of years of labour and lonely caring, a statement combining frustration, physical exhaustion, and a wrenching vision.

He spoke of specific needs at various posts, warning that false prophets were at hand: "If anyone call himself a preacher, and be able to blab out anything whatsoever, there he will get hearers, admirers and followers."[15] Passing over Synod's failure to provide assistance, he aimed his appeal at those who had been unwilling to answer the call. Moses's excuse is still in their mouth: "O milord, send, I pray thee, by the hand of him whom thou wilt send"; send another, and not me." [16]

Mixing the meritorious and the miscreant, he pictured "servants and officers of His Brittanic Majesty, … Worshippers of Mammon, … multitudes of emigrants, Pelagians, Socinians, Popish priests, and filthy dreamers," all crossing the Atlantic to their own purposes:

> [But those] engaged in the most precious and honourable of all employments … flatly refuse. It is astonishing that any servant of Christ can seriously think that his Divine Master will admit of such an excuse … Let them remember that there is a cup of fatherly chastisement, a filling-up for the disobedient children, as well as wrath for his enemies. No one can say how long his patience may last … I am not fond of using so much severity. I would much rather allure my brethren over, or rather I wish that they would of their own accord come cheerfully.[17]

In his peroration, he turned on the allure:

> My dear young brethren, let me recommend America to you. Whatever it be to others, it is the best place for Ministers that I know in the world. Only be prevailed upon to come. You will see that every thing that seemed against you will really be for you. The very ignorance of the people will be unspeakably in your favour; for there is every probability of your being more successful among such, [with] a far better opportunity of observing the success of your labour than if you were to enter into the labour of others, or build where the foundation is already laid … I have been here about six years, in as disadvantageous circumstances, I suppose, as any whom the Synod ever sent to this continent; and though indeed I have been in it, in weakness, in fear, in trembling, *yet I account it the happiest thing that ever befell me*, that I was sent to America. I had my reluctance, my struggle, ere I set off, but I have reason to bless God while I live, that I was not suffered to comply with the counsels of flesh and blood to stay at home. I am sure that all the world would not keep you out of America, if you only knew what it yields.[18]

This time, Synod took action. At John Buist's pleading, a committee was struck, and Synod authorized Buist and two others to prepare a report. One man was out of James's past; the other would share his future. Rev. James Robertson had preached at his ordination that "Great events have often small beginnings." Rev. Archibald Bruce, successor to William Moncrieff as Anti-Burgher Professor of Divinity, was located near Glasgow at Whitburn. In their report, they recommended that James's impassioned letter be published and read from every pulpit in the Church. Synod agreed. So, was a national mission forwarded, for while no one appeared immediately, the seed had been sown and in time would yield in abundance.

Many later affirmed that on hearing this powerful letter, they had then considered the mission field – especially James's mission – and after due training many journeyed to Pictou to serve with him. Encouraging them was Archibald Bruce, thirteen years older than James, another graduate of Glasgow and student of William Moncreiff. As colleague and correspondent, Bruce became a critical figure in the development of James's mission. They would remain correspondents and close colleagues until Bruce's death in 1816.

But until Bruce could send James's first assistants, he must struggle alone. Despite his perilous Stewiacke journey, in the winter of 1793 he made another pioneering journey, this time westward, along 80 kilometres (50 miles) of open shoreline, to River John and Tatamagouche.[19] With no established road, often confronted by a river, he had to bear inland far enough on snowshoes to reach the first ford, sometimes slashing a shortcut across some wooded peninsula. The weather was fierce, and he was often forced to walk the beaches, facing the wind-wracked coast. Only at the mouth of River John did he find any Mi'kmaq who could help him. But while he had gained confidence and learned the lessons of survival in the wilderness, such journeys would take their toll.

On arrival, his French may have helped, for his hosts were largely Montbeliardais, French-speaking Protestants from a German-Swiss principality. Often mistakenly described as French Huguenots, they had first come to Nova Scotia's South Shore as part of a large contingent of "His Majesty's Foreign Protestants."[20] Twenty families had then been lured to the North Shore by an engineer-surveyor and large-scale landholder, J.F.W. DesBarres, a Swiss who had served under Wolfe and was now a masterful hydrographic surveyor in the service of the British Admiralty.[21] Most of DesBarres's recruits spoke some English, and all were now second-stage pioneers, well suited to farm and forest. DesBarres, however, harboured a fantasy of creating a feudal barony in the

New World, and being more speculator than colonizer, he reneged –
now ready only to rent them their lands. Greatly frustrated, they had
abandoned his tract and begun again in isolation.

Their immediate troubles, however, were of a different nature. As
Calvinists, their peace had recently been disrupted by a visit from one
of Henry Alline's anti-Calvinist New Light associates. In the resulting
confusion, they had dispatched John Langille and George Patriquin to
ask James's help in calming the community. Despite the fearful weather
he had agreed to come, and he would succeed in rallying both communities. After he had conducted several baptisms, he agreed to supply
them from Pictou.

As at Malpeque, however, news of his coming had spread farther
west, to Ramsheg (Wallace), and at the pleading of twenty Loyalist
families he visited with similar success. Divine service on Wallace Bay
was now assured, providing a foundation for the many Highlanders
who would arrive not long after. Weary but satisfied, he fastened on his
racquets and turned east on the long trek home. The mission had lasted
nearly a month, but the North Shore was now linked from Pictou to
Amherst. A new regional awareness was emerging – one that, to some
degree, owes its beginnings to James.

At such times MacGregor recognized that in seven years he had given
and gained much and was no longer the frail vessel he had thought
himself at Greenock. But there persisted periods of doubt. Like other
dedicated ministers of the Gospel, he was a lonely man: he could never
put off the role of shepherd, which to some degree set him apart from his
flock. Many, however, also saw him in another light: He was respected
for his inspiration as conversationalist and teacher. They shared his
faith, but found him a stimulating mentor in other fields. For, he could
talk of many things with people of very different levels of education
and understanding: from poetry to farming methods, and the emergence of new sciences, like meteorology, geology, climatology, even to
explaining Copernicus.[22] Bruce MacDonald aptly remarks, "MacGregor
was an anomaly in eighteenth century Nova Scotia, a highly educated
man and an accomplished scholar."[23]

And he was always a proud Gael, reciting Gaelic poetry and singing the songs he had collected across Scotland. "Poet MacGregor" was
famous for his verse and song, and he often turned it to a Bible lesson.
When someone objected, "We can't always be talking religion," James
replied, "Oh, you should look at the example of the Saviour. When he
entered a house, he went slap dash in the subject of religion."[24]

But perhaps because he was teacher and preacher, he found himself at times lacking the comfort of ultimate closeness. He had the respect and gratitude of men, men like Donald MacKay, Robert Marshall, William Smith, Kenneth and Thomas Fraser, Squire Patterson, Deacon Patterson, Theophilus DesBrisay, John Millar, and now George Patriquin. And he kept up a large correspondence. But he had been gone from Scotland for seven years, and he was now thirty-four. Often he was in anguish over the apparent hopelessness of ever having fellow clergy to work with him, or of having a wife and family.

There is little evidence, however, that he kept in touch with his sisters. His communications with his father had passed regularly through Revs. James Barlas and Sam Gilfillan, but his memoirs seldom refer to other family members. His mission was all. Yet he was no longer the robust man who had arrived at Pictou. The years, the journeys, the strain of constant ministering, all had taken a toll. By 1793 he was serving over two hundred and forty in full membership, while five hundred were taking instruction. Too many years had been spent sleeping on straw on the floor of simple huts, as in the crofts at home, with heather arranged with the brush upwards and only a *maud*, a shepherd's plaid, and perhaps a dusting of snow, to cover him. His food was simple and scanty: gruel, boiled potatoes, a bit of bread, before a long snow-shoe tramp to the next settlement. By midsummer 1793, depression returned, and he began coughing blood again.[25] "Consumption" was wearing away his strength and spirit, and Jacob pleaded with him to "find a virtuous woman." Sam Gilfillan, always a stout friend, commiserated with him but could hardly have eased his mind in the following letter:

> We endured a most alarming earthquake shock this week, with many more these days. God is coming to this place to punish the inhabitants of the earth of all kindreds and ranks ... The clergy of the Established Church are insolent & careless & the generality of their hearers are prepared for any yoke. All kinds of sinners are becoming impudent.[26]

But James was not to be deterred. Once, after falling through the ice, he reached shore, walked a mile, and then preached two sermons before changing his clothing.[27] Constantly testing his strength, between 1793 and 1795 he reached his nadir. But then, quickly, his circumstances changed radically, and he began to regain the health that would not fail him again until his final years.

Relief came from several directions. First, news of war with Revolutionary France saw the half-pays fly off like a pack of hounds to the recruitment musters at Halifax. They had been worse than the mosquitos of Labrador. But Donald MacKay's and Robert Marshall's constancy had never wavered, and Donald was enough older than MacGregor to be beyond presumption when he urged and even chided James to spare himself. Between them, they sustained him.

The best relief, however, came with word that help was on the way. In June 1794, listing recent events, he noted: "The Lord granted me a happy confluence of favours ... I received letters giving an account of the Synod's appointing three ministers to Nova Scotia."[28] Two of the new men would arrive soon, easing the long stress and physical burden of his lonely mission.

PART FOUR

Partnering

Chapter Eleven

A Threefold Cord and a Wedding

A threefold cord is not easily broken.
Ecclesiastes 3:12

News that fresh colleagues were on the way opened a new chapter in James's life, and the closing of another helped. He rejoiced in having successfully "removed a trial which had been productive of much grief and sin."[1] Donald MacKay and Robert Marshall had been "overreached by the craft of an insidious enemy to the gospel, ... prevailed upon to subscribe a paper injurious to the character of one of their neighbours."[2] Acknowledging that they had been taken in by unfounded charges, they asked for public rebuke, as was the custom. But James sought to soften their censure:

> I stated to the congregation, as fairly as I could, both the fact and the state of the two elders' minds ... I exhorted the congregation highly to esteem the elders, and to profit by that example of submissive and cheerful acknowledgement of their fault which they had given. The feelings of all were excited in a very lively and affectionate manner, and the design of the enemy was completely frustrated. Besides, we had an opportunity of admiring the wisdom and propriety of Paul's direction to Timothy, "Rebuke not an elder, but entreat him as a father."[3]

This resolution restored him to a better frame of mind, and he turned his eye abroad again, answering a call from Douglas district – Maitland, Kennetcook, Noel, and the Minas Shore. Little had been done at Douglas by the much-nearer Truro Burgher Presbytery, perhaps because the huge, scattered district was too much for Daniel Cock at his age and for Smith's health. James's visit would mark the beginning of nearly twenty years of his supply.

Late in June 1795, Revs. John Brown and Duncan Ross arrived fresh from Archibald Bruce's hands, having been hurried through their last months of study in order to fulfil a mutual pact to join the man whose "Letter of 1793" had so moved them. Ross claimed that they had been "lectured for one season on heresy, and another on superstition, and then banished to America."[4] They had often been seen together in tiny Whitburn, scurrying after Rev. Archibald Bruce on his way to the printer with some new pamphlet.[5]

They arrived by different means: Ross on horseback from Halifax to Truro, where he first met James at Rev. Daniel Cock's home. Though Brown was a graduate of Glasgow and Ross of Edinburgh, they had become close friends at Whitburn. But Cox and James were taken aback at Ross's appearance, for he aped the *ton* at Edinburgh, his already portly frame in fine cloth and his hair nicely powdered. James had dressed as one must for travelling through the woods, in an ancient coat with a hole in the elbow – and the very forward Ross asked mischievously if he were a beggarman. Ross accepted Cock's invitation to stay over and preach a sermon, while James hurried home to greet the earnest Brown and his wife, who were travelling by boat from Halifax.

Back in Pictou, MacGregor's happiness at these reinforcements may be imagined. Soon after, they celebrated a joyful Lord's Supper, marked by sermons from both newcomers. James was pleased to find that both approached matters of belief and ritual much as he did, which confirmed Bruce's account of them. When Brown, a modest Perthshire man, demurred on being invited to preach, James cried out, "*Would you ask me to preach that has not heard a sermon for nine years?*"[6] Both preached, and in English, although Ross had been willing to test his shaky Gaelic. After Brown's sermon James was in tears, urging the congregation to give thanks for "a good gospel minister." On hearing Ross, however, he held him in a long embrace. The loneliest years were over.

Archibald Bruce had begun his ministry at Whitburn at the age of twenty-two in 1768. He remained there all his life, although it was an unlikely setting for a man of his broad interests and unorthodox views.[7] But because it offered limited pastoral cares, there was ample time for study and writing. His interests were wide and radical, as befitted a son of Glasgow's Enlightenment. An eccentric bachelor, he was attended by his orphaned niece, Janet Auld, as chatelaine and housekeeper. In the village of Whitburn he cut a striking figure, even turning heads in Edinburgh:

[He is] remarkably dignified and venerable. With a spare erect figure of the middle size, and a noble cast of countenance, resembling the Roman, dressed with scrupulous neatness, and wearing the full-bottomed, [powdered] wig, long cane with gold heart, [silk stockings], and large silver shoe-buckles of the olden time, he presented to the last the polite bearing of the gentleman with the sedateness of the scholar and minister.[8]

During five short fall semesters each class of students lodged in "The De'il's Barracks," attended by Janet Auld, who became acquainted with every student and every recruit for Pictou. On reading MacGregor's "Letter of 1793," she had been "vexed for the state of those poor people, and that no person goes to them." Bruce asked, "Would you go to them?" "Well," she replied, "if I thought I could do any good I think that I would."[9] She was a mature fourteen, and this was not the end of her story.

Bruce was a consummate correspondent and pamphleteer, his production so large that he kept a printer at Whitburn for twenty years. One historian observed, "The printing was bad, the paper was execrable, but the matter made amends."[10] Bruce admired Tom Paine's advanced views – his attacks on slavery, his support of republicanism, and his major work, *The Rights of Man*. James admired Paine, too, although he balked at his Deism.[11] Bruce's views might influence his choice of those he sent to MacGregor, but he was no firebrand: his deepest concerns were spiritual, but he joined spirit with society, supporting John Buist's campaign against slavery and his stewardship of church affairs in the liberal climate of Glasgow and its college. Although he lived almost as a recluse, Bruce had a wide acquaintance and earned much respect. Rev. Thomas M'Crie Sr called him "the most eminent ecclesiastical historian that Scotland has produced.[12] He and M'Crie were considered by Rev. David Brown at Aberdeen University to be "the most distinguished ornaments of the Secession Church"[13] "[His] literary attainments, and vast stores of knowledge ... made him deservedly looked up to ... For solidarity and perspicacity of judgment, joined with a lively imagination ... and guarding against extremes ... Mr. Bruce has been excelled by few."[14]

Like MacGregor, Bruce was a passionate evangelical, believing that salvation was open to all, not just to the elect but to the sinner, and that atonement rests in faith, whereby the church should pursue an active evangelicalism, including all classes and foreign missions. His ideal was a ministry based on great preaching, furthering religious and secular education, and encouraging public debate and ambitious domestic and foreign missions. Like that of John Buist, his advice and encouragement sustained MacGregor for many years.

MacGregor's antislavery activities and Bruce's pamphlets paralleled those of several of Glasgow's leading faculty members, among them John Millar. Millar and Bruce shared many ideas: on slavery, industrial labour relations, the worth of republicanism, and the need for constitutional government. Both were advocates of freedom of the press, Bruce so vividly that no newspaper would publish him. Both hailed the promise in the American and early French Revolutions.

Millar's liberal Whig ideas matched those of Bruce and MacGregor,[15] and through them, MacGregor maintained close ties with Glasgow's Secessionist and reform spirit. The elder Rev. Thomas M'Crie, himself an outstanding Secessionist minister, might have been speaking of Millar in his portrait of Bruce: "A genuine whig of the old school, yet with nothing of the virulence and vulgarity of the democrat, he was a thorough hater of all despotism and intolerance, civil or religious. He was a bold assertor of the right of private judgment and the liberty of the press."[16] One divine observed of Bruce's sermons: "[Bruce was] lecturing in the muffled tones of the 'Dead March in Saul' but uttering a depth of wisdom worthy of being listened to by a whole conclave of bishops."[17]

Bruce and MacGregor became the theological and intellectual masters to a growing cell of Secession missionaries gathered around MacGregor and Pictou with a passion for evangelicalism, a distaste for establishmentarianism, and a commitment to the links between religion and education as the principal means whereby people should govern their lives. Bruce was their first professor, MacGregor their field coordinator.

On 7 July 1795, a few days after Ross and Brown's arrival, ministers and elders gathered in Robert Marshall's barn to form the "Associate Presbytery of Nova Scotia."[18] The initiative was Synod's, but MacGregor has been accused of wilfulness and narrow-mindedness in rejecting Truro's invitation to join them. He was required, however, to follow Glasgow's directive, although he and his colleagues may have sought to send out a qualified signal, for they agreed not to bind themselves too strictly to the Westminster Confession, although at home it was still the prime subordinate standard. By this initiative, MacGregor and his associates moved closer to Truro's position and that of the Congregationalists, of whom there were many in Nova Scotia. Ross and Brown had hardly been there a week: could they have brought MacGregor around so swiftly, or did James use the occasion for a new beginning? There is nothing in the record to help us, but it's unlikely that MacGregor had been so hastily won over by two junior colleagues.

In fact, it was Truro Presbytery that took the exclusivist position this time. Until five days before the action taken in Robert Marshall's barn, Truro had continued to recognize James as a member of its presbytery, although he had not appeared at their meetings for years. Without waiting for news of the new Pictou Presbytery on 7 July, however, and recording no explanation for their action, on 2 July, Truro had declared James's association with them to be at an end.[19] Not much later, however, perhaps hearing of Pictou's reorganization, Truro changed direction again and renewed the proposal for union.

For James and his new colleagues it was all a little bewildering, but they were not yet prepared to take such a comprehensive step, for full union had many implications. For one, they could only make the move amicably with Synod's approval, which was unthinkable, and so Ross and Brown proved as unmoving as James in 1786. But with David Smith's death in the same year, 1795, further cooperation in specific matters became more likely. Daniel Cock was an accommodating man. He and Ross had hit it off well. The dialogue would continue.

With easier summer travelling, Presbytery agreed to temporary postings: Ross to the Island; Brown to Onslow, Belmont, and Londonderry, all near Truro; while James would continue up and down the East River, where his Gaelic remained essential. However, all did not go smoothly. In time Presbytery's meetings became a great delight to James but after the second one he was not so sure. For, despite urgent calls from the Island and Amherst, the first assignments were altered by Presbytery. Ross was recalled to West River, which nettled James because it left no one for the Island, and he considered it unwise to appoint the less adroit Brown to the contentious Londonderry, while Ross – more sophisticated and diplomatic, but with little Gaelic – was encountering criticism at West River. As a compromise, he and James agreed to exchange pulpits from time to time.

Not everyone at West River was placated, but Ross showed remarkable understanding: "What better encouragement could I wish, than to see people so unwilling to give up the man, who had laboured among them for nine years? When I have laboured so long among them, I hope they will be as unwilling to part with me."[20]

Presbytery then proceeded by lot, and James drew the East River. But West River cried foul, and following custom, two boys were commissioned to conduct a second draw, which overturned the first. James would not give in, however, and in deference got his wish. The town (called "The Harbour") would go to the next man to arrive, and James and Ross agreed to exchange pulpits periodically. Matters then eased, but Ross's congregation remained riven. Some simply missed James, but a righteous rump reacted against Ross's cheerful spirit and mischievous wit. In time he became noted for his "affability, harmless facetiousness and intelligence,"[21] but at first some took his informality amiss. Highland roots and frontier sensibility sometimes fostered a dour solemnity in church matters.

Still, the new arrangements held, albeit shakily, and calls for supply mounted. Clearly, another man was needed: Amherst had rejected the earnest Brown after the dynamic MacGregor, but John Brown proved an able incumbent at Londonderry, and his tenure would stretch to fifty quietly effective years.

Things seemed to be falling into place after Rev. David Smith died in 1795 and when Rev. Andrew Brown returned to Scotland and his successor, Rev. Archibald Gray, proved too sickly to be meddlesome. Ross was now becoming engagingly agreeable, too, as he visited Amherst from time to time and supplied Stewiacke for thirteen Sabbaths a year, although John Brown lived much nearer.

In fact, matters had been settled largely through the energy and good will of Ross and MacGregor, whose friendship steadily ripened. In 1801, Presbytery arranged a final and satisfactory division of the home congregations, led by the powerful elder and merchant-politician Edward Mortimer.[22] The bonds between the amusing, spirited Ross and the now more relaxed veteran, MacGregor, became firm. The new men's coming had raised problems, but James soon treasured the intimacy and satisfaction of working with fellow ministers. Patterson comments: "Their meetings were scenes of rich enjoyment. Business we fear was often a secondary matter … they settled what business they had to do sitting round the fire smoking their pipes until day began to break. At all events for five years they kept no minutes."[23]

The irrepressible Ross's adjustment was further marked by his buying a horse and a house lot, for he had set his eye for a wife. Before long he married Isabella, daughter of Samuel and Mary Creelman, leading pioneers at Stewiacke, which explains why he so cheerfully undertook thirteen annual visits to distant Stewiacke. He and Isabella would have nine sons and six daughters, with one son, James, becoming the first president of the restored Dalhousie University.

With Ross's example, James recalled, "I thought that I needed to do both these things too, and accordingly did them within a year."[24] He, too began by first buying a horse and then looking for a wife, which was not a new pursuit. Now, however, several women, whom Patterson dismisses as "local busy-bodies," set about to find a Nova Scotia woman. No one at Pictou seemed appropriate, but one name was well known: Ann MacKay, a resident of Halifax, the eldest child of Roderick and Christina (Grant) MacKay and Donald's niece.

Ann had been born in Inverness-shire, arrived on the *Hector*, and spent most of her early life in Halifax. Her father, described as "a thick-set strongly built Celt, distinguished for activity, determination and fertility of invention," was a skilled, Scottish smith and armourer.[25] Later, he was recognized for building a floating *slabbraidh*, a chain and log barrier, from "Chain Rock" across the harbour's Northwest Arm, to protect the town's rear flank from French and American marauders.[26] Christina, his wife, also called Ann and Nancy, shared Rod's grit and girth.

Ann MacKay was twenty-seven, James thirty-six. After receiving the best education Halifax offered young women, Ann had become a skilled seamstress, employed by the gentry. She was popular, spirited, clever, and orderly. But she and James had never met as adults. He wrote to her, setting out his eligibility and hopes, which probably sounded like a curriculum vitae, for he always spoke directly. His reputation might have given a more timid young woman pause, but Ann was her mother's girl and Robertson described James favourably: "His temperament was warm, inclining to the poetical, ... his general information extensive and varied, while his manners were exceedingly plain and affectionate."[27] Ann accepted James's proposal, and the marriage was set for 11 May 1796 from the bride's Halifax home.

Always the good shepherd, James conducted missions both coming and going to Halifax, reaching the capital late on Monday, where he was to be married on Tuesday evening. His groomsman, nineteen-year-old Alex MacKay, was a son of Donald MacKay's brother Alexander. With a large face and hands, he was not tall, but broad-shouldered and "somewhat colossal."[28]

Arrived late on Monday at his lodgings, James sent Alex to pick up his new suit and shoes, but they were not ready. James refused to meet his bride improperly dressed and dispatched Alex to explain his predicament. Ann was vexed, remarking wryly, "I suppose he thinks he has me." She waited all evening and all the next day until only min-utes before the ceremony, when they were introduced. But who would marry them? Barry Cahill has suggested an answer: James's grandson, George Patterson, either fudged his account of the wedding or may have been unaware of what took place.[29]

The MacKays had no connection with Truro, or Daniel Cock might have conducted the ceremony. In the absence of a Seceder minister in Halifax, it was unlikely that MacGregor would be married by Archibald Gray, Andrew Brown's Kirk successor. The MacKays were not mem-bers. Many people for whom denominational differences counted less than social recognition attended St. Paul's Church of England. St. Paul's and Mather's vied for the gentry. Further, it is possible that some Kirk-men, unhappy at attending Mather's, may have gravitated to St. Paul's.

In the event, Patterson resorted to the fiction that James was mar-ried "by the Rev. James Munro ... a travelling missionary" of the Kirk, a statement surely designed to forestall raised eyebrows.[30] In fact, MacGregor, inheritor of the Anti-Burgher distaste for a state church, was married by Robert Stanser, rector of the parish of St Paul's and in due course Charles Inglis's successor as bishop of the diocese of Nova Scotia in the Established Church of England.[31] Further, he was married by civil licence, one of many that the bishop was peddling to noncon-formists in a kind of ecclesiastical black market.

The scandal over James's marriage, then, was not that James was married under civil licence and without the proclamation of banns, but that he was married outside a Presbyterian church altogether. Yet, if as Judith Fingard suggests, Robert Stanser "maintained cordial relations with the non-Anglican ministers in the capital,"[32] he may have been a little too cordial for MacGregor's good, for James later reaped the wrath of some strict Pictou Seceders.

On the morning after the wedding, the bride "received" for several hours, followed by a grand dinner. Next morning Ann settled into an English saddle, James's very practical wedding gift, and with a train of friends they set off to the head of Bedford Basin, where they held a picnic. Then the newly-weds began the long journey to Pictou, which had so shaken James ten years earlier. This time, however, things were made easier, for at Gay's River they boarded a rowboat to enable James to preach and baptize along the river as they floated downstream to Minas Basin. Later, in Truro, they rested with Daniel Cock, who encoun-tered a remarkably relaxed James MacGregor.

On his return to Pictou, James was in such good spirits that from time to time he chuckled aloud, shocking "the old staid Highlanders, with whom a laugh was almost a mortal sin."[33] Some threatened to raise the matter of his marital arrangements with Session. How much they knew, we do not know, but it was a big secret to keep in a tiny society. James was called to account and apologized for failing to have the banns published, and for being married by civil licence. His assurance to his critics was disarming: "Well, my friends, I am very sorry that any person *should have taken offence*, and I promise that if you will forgive me this time *I will never do it again*."[34]

With gifts in cash and materials, he commissioned the district's first framed house, built on Rod MacKay's grant. In the end, however, Rod would not agree to sell the land on which the house stood. Stubbornly, James began again, this time on his own "Settler's land," importing an Old Country craftsman and the materials to erect the first brick house in eastern Nova Scotia. It stood on a knoll beside the East River, immediately up-river from the future New Glasgow. There Ann created an orderly household for her preoccupied husband, soon gracing it with a firstborn, Robert, born in the summer of 1797.

James enjoyed his new estate. He had always been drawn to the river and would end his days by its banks. He wrote to a friend, "We all live by the water-side, and boats are going always backwards and forwards."[35] Marriage and children gave him much delight and his days were crowded, for he was back at his studies, his translations, and his reviews of various journals.

But he was also in his garden, working with a hired hand, determined to develop new seeds and tools suited to the region, an improver's project he shared with Duncan Ross. So much domestication did not deter him, however, from planning new missions, and soon he turned his eye to a farther east and a farther west.

Chapter Twelve

East Side, West Side

MacGregor's missions lay in many directions during the next few years. Reinforced by new clergy and elders, he found new energy. Three of his journeys were among his longest and most ambitious.

In 1797, he travelled to New Brunswick's Miramichi River, where large-scale Scottish timber operators were opening an empire and Scottish Presbyterians sought spiritual support. On his return, he followed routine: a fruitless letter to Synod. A second trip to Miramichi earned him further good will, but again Synod could find no one for the mission field.

Although he had been summoned earlier to Cape Breton Island, it was not until 1798 that he answered the pleas of the Sutherland family at Sydney River. There were only about twenty Presbyterian families on the island, but his curiosity had been whetted by stories of its similarity to Scotland.[1]

After Cape Breton's recent separation from Nova Scotia, a tiny capital had been established at Sydney, where a fractious Loyalist elite fought over place in a Lilliputian government under Lieutenant Governor J.F.W. DesBarres – the man who had denied River John and Tatamagouche their lands. With no legislature, rural representation, or public income, Cape Breton showed little promise for his mission.

In August 1798, however, MacGregor hired a shallop, sailing first to St. Peter's at the lower end of the Bras d'Or Lakes, which divide the island in two. He was welcomed by Lawrence Kavanagh, later Nova Scotia's first Catholic member of the legislative assembly (MLA). Kavanagh assured him that the lake route to Sydney was shorter and safer, and he provided men and oxen to drag the boat across the portage. Soon after setting out along the lake, the party became lost, and in wading ahead to try to find the route and fighting his way through thick marsh, James was seized by old fears and hurried back to the boat in terror. At Glenlednock he had first heard of *Each Uisge*, the kelpie or water horse, "who lured people into the water that he haunted, and devoured them. He was sticky all over, and anyone who touched him could not withdraw and was inevitably dragged under."[2] Despite James's considerable adaptation to the New World, the Old World had not released him entirely.

At Sydney he had expected to make house visits and offer sermons, but to a tiny audience he lamented: "Oh! My dear hearers, how I have longed to visit you in this remote island: – and now I am come – But alas! What shall I say to you? Surely the fear of the Lord is not in this place. I can see little devotion of any kind here."[3] He had come four years too soon: in 1802 the Scottish invasion began and lasted for two decades. MacGregor withdrew discouraged, and not long after, the Sutherlands moved to Pictou. He would not visit Cape Breton again for another twenty years.

For a few years at the turn of the century, domestic life kept him closer to home, and improved roads made his regular visits to Merigomish and River John mere three-day absences. Family life took over as his eldest son, Robert, was followed in 1799 by James Jr and in 1802 by Roderick, and then Ann was pregnant again. In the midst of these joys, however, came fresh worries. In the spring of 1799, an old Portmore friend warned that Jacob's sight was threatened and that he needed money; that James's oldest sister, Jannet, now a widow, was in a bad way; and that his sister Elizabeth Donaldson wanted advice on migrating with her straitened family.[4] There is no record of his reply. Two years later, he learned that Jacob had died at eighty-four.

Jacob had been on mission until two nights before his death, meeting with a group who were reading an *Essay on the Duration and Character of the Millennial Age of the Church*, written by James and published in *The Christian Magazine*. Elizabeth reported that Jacob had died "unperceptibly and without the least appearance of agony and in the full belief of his profession."[5] Rev. Sam Gilfillan wrote that Jacob had considered it "his principal earthly comfort to hear of [James's] welfare, and of the success of the Gospel in those parts where you live. I cannot describe his joy to you."[6]

James may have paused then to reflect on his life and long separation from his father and others at home; he may even have resolved to become closer to his own family, but as Patterson concedes, "Returning home ... he would sometimes scarcely wait to warm himself, till he sat down to his reading or writing."[7] It may be that he saw little more even of his immediate family by being home. The hyperactive boy had become a driven scholar, intellectual, poet, and pastoral workaholic.

The prospect of a new century moved James to write a curious "Essay on the Millennial Age."[8] Reflecting Revelations and Old Testament prophecy, it was also based on current scientific accounts of such varied fields as pneumatics and climate change and on the works of one of the great naturalists of the day, the Comte de Buffon. Buffon's forty-four-volume *Histoire naturelle* was read by virtually every educated European and North American,[9] and his ideas on biological, anthropological, and environmental thinking led James to inquire into the new science of geology – with extraordinary results later on.[10]

Buffon, more ambitious and scientific than Montesquieu, startled a generation with his "Theory of American Degeneracy," arguing that North America's animals and native peoples were less developed physically and mentally than comparable European species. But Thomas Jefferson and Benjamin Franklin challenged him, Jefferson travelling to Paris with moose and panther hides and other "proofs" of the wrongness of Buffon's theories. By then, however, Buffon had moderated his position, conceding that North Americans could so alter the climate and landscape that a more favourable environment would encourage improvement in all North American species, including man.

This later, more optimistic view was incorporated in James's essay, where he also relied on Genesis 1:26 and 1:28: "Be fruitful and multiply, and replenish the earth, and subdue it ... Let us make man in our image, and let them have *dominion over all the earth*."[11] Buffon and MacGregor took literally the biblical promise, for, strange to our ears today, "to the ends of the earth" was taken by them to mean that recent changes in climate had rendered "dominion" possible. James welcomed global warming "so that the regions round the poles ... shall become mild and productive climates." Basing his ideas on "Scripture and facts," he argued that while the warming is God's gift, "human industry shall be the means." "The effect of cultivation in amelioriating a severe climate is surprising; slow indeed," he argued, "but sure ... In the United States, the climate is greatly altered since their population by Europeans ... Much the same is the case in the British dominions."[12]

Like Buffon, he advocated development through research, scientific education, and technological invention, even to draining the wetlands we so prize today:

Brute nature is hideous, and it is I, I alone, who am capable of rendering it agreeable. Let us dry up these marshes; let us open channels for all these stagnant waters; ... from them will they will obtain ... an ever renovating pasture. These new ideas let us still further employ, in order to complete our work; the ox subjected to the yoke shall exert all his strength in tilling the ground, which will become young again by our culture.[13]

Both men applied the lesson more widely than in this homely metaphor, and James closed with some perceptive predictions for North America's development, arguing that the new millennium had already begun,

in the revolution of nations, the progress of the arts and sciences; ... in the growth of commerce and the multiplicity of new inventions; in the discovering and peopling of new countries, and the civilization of barbarous nations; in the sending of the gospel ... and even in the horrors of war.[14]

The "Essay" is a typically optimistic product of the Glasgow Enlightenment, speaking to improvers of all sorts and affirming a bright future for the New World. Thus James's mind ranged from the East River to the cosmos, and as the ever competent Ann ran her household of increasing numbers of children, he prepared for further missions and causes.

In 1802–3, he was reinforced by the arrival of two more associates: Rev. Alexander Dick and Rev. Thomas McCulloch, both married men.[15] Dick, another Perthshire man, born in 1771, had been a weaver, a skilled carpenter, and a cabinet-maker when he had read James's "Letter of 1793" and resolved to join him. He came from "better than comfortable circumstances ... [and was] of more than ordinary mental ability."[16] His father, scion of a formerly Dutch Huguenot family ("Dyck"), was a linen manufacturer. Alex Dick had been much moved by James's letter, and after a crash course in Latin, he entered Glasgow University and later studied under Archibald Bruce at Whitburn.

Some recent writers have contended that McCulloch "almost single-handedly" brought science – along with the Academy – to Pictou.[17] But following Edinburgh and the example of his acclaimed astronomer/uncle, Rev. Thomas Dick, Alex Dick advocated mechanics' institutes and in the Enlightenment spirit the alignment of science and spirituality in the curriculum – a goal pursued no less by Dissenters than by Kirk Moderates.[18] The prospect of scientific education at Pictou did not await McCulloch's coming, for MacGregor had long been an advocate and had been engaged in it, Ross was an inventive agronomist, and Dick shared in it by training and family background. But for Dick's tragically early death he might have rivalled McCulloch as an advocate of the further development of education, science, and religion in Nova Scotia.

Chalmers Jack remarks that one of McCulloch's and Dick's greatest assets was that each was married to "one of a family ... destined to manse life."[19] The dedicated, energetic Ann Eadie Dick was one of three sisters in a distinguished Secessionist family, all of whom were married to Secessionist ministers, while their three brothers were all Anti-Burgher clergy. Like Alex, Ann came from comfort and education, and she and Dick appear to have enjoyed a modest independence, which relieved them of some of the anxieties common on a frontier stipend.

Dick was licensed to preach by Perth Presbytery in 1802 and at his own request was immediately appointed to Pictou. They sailed for Halifax in June, and after a brief stay in Halifax, Dick was ordained and inducted by MacGregor, Ross, and Brown at Maitland in the vast Douglas district – the first ordination in British North America by a properly constituted, permanent presbytery.

Dick threw himself into the mission, as Patterson attests, "brimful of his burning enthusiasm." Like the young James, his early sermons were fully written out, "terse in style, his illustrations fresh and striking, and his appeals personal and pointed."[20] Later, he came to preach as spontaneously as James, being filled with the Gospel spirit and recognized as the most eagerly followed preacher after James himself. With a "fervid temperament" like James's and a fine speaking voice, he drew throngs, his congregations expanding quickly. James observed, "He speaks as if he were in heaven already."

Heavy Scottish immigration to Douglas had led to Dick's appointment. Lying neglected beyond Truro and along the Minas Basin, it was a huge lumbering and farming territory, for as Dick observed, "Instead of a congregation it might ... be called a shire." He accepted the assignment cheerfully, however, pursuing a roving schedule like James's. So extensive were his missions that he and Ann often travelled together, with Ann mounted not on a palfrey of her own but behind Alex on a specially extended saddle.

Dick also put his carpentry skills to work by erecting a two-storey house that stood for ninety years and personally undertaking to build the first church in Maitland. He also created extensive kitchen gardens to provide for himself and Ann – and later for an adopted daughter. Like Ross and MacGregor, he was an ardent agricultural improver in the Glasgow tradition. Douglas, it seems, was in good hands, and MacGregor had a possible successor.

For although the other new man, Thomas McCulloch, complemented MacGregor and his mission-directed ministry in many respects, he was not suited to the larger charge: he was a town man, a political man, a volatile man, and no evangelical for the road. From their medical studies at Glasgow he and Dick brought new dimensions to the call for further developing educational and scientific training.

Of medium height, McCulloch had an athletic frame and limitless energy, and his wife was another indomitable daughter of the manse. Isabella Walker, albeit a Burgher, had been his sustaining partner in his ministry in Scotland, and she now joined the succession of Ann MacGregor, Ann Dick, and Isabella Ross in loyalty, talent, and spirit, affirming how essential were the wives to the success of early frontier missions.

McCulloch's background, MacGregor's preparations for over two decades, and the support of Dick and Ross (and soon, of the learned Rev. John Keir and his wife, Mary Burnett, who herself brought an interest in scientific enquiry) opened the prospect of greatly expanding educational facilities at Pictou and throughout presbytery, even to the Island. Accordingly, McCulloch proposed that at Pictou he might focus on advancing formal and scientific education.

This decision, however, was preceded by his assessment of the "religious destitution" of the Pictou district, seeming at a blow to dismiss the nine years of James's lonely and strenuous mission and the six years during which, with Ross and Brown's help, they had greatly extended and deepened Pictou's religious care. McCulloch had a penchant for translating causes into impassioned campaigns, and his grandiloquent portrait of Pictou was the backdrop to his single-minded determination to bring it into order.

Yet, in a not uncommon ambivalence that remains to be understood, McCulloch showed MacGregor great respect, even veneration:

Dr. MacGregor used to call me "his son." The Church of Nova Scotia may truly be said to be the work of his hands. God, I trust, will not forsake it, and as I, times innumerable called him "father," I must not desert a work [education] near his heart and the object of his daily prayers.[21]

In the Highland way and following New Testament and Protestant tradition, James encouraged people not to call him "father," but to use his Christian name, "*Seumas*." But most could not bring themselves to it, resorting to "*Mhaighstir Seumas*"(Father James).[22]

Because we have no portrait of MacGregor, McCulloch's description of his alter ego in his unpublished and thinly veiled fiction, "Morton," is of interest:

> In appearance he was a man of more sinew than muscle, and without that portly and commanding aspect which Morton had expected. His garb, too, was rather in accordance with the infancy of Pictou and the simplicity of primitive times ... When he arose and surveyed the assembly, there was in his features a beaming of kindness ... [and] the softening tones of [his] voice ... In the clergyman's sermon, there was neither display of learning nor abstruse disquisition: it was a plain statement of divine truth into which scriptural expression and allusion were aptly introduced. No artificial construction characterized its sentence, nor did the manner of the preacher indicate the tones and gestures had ever cost him a thought. Yet he spoke with an eloquence which fixed every eye; his audience drank in his voice and seemed to forget that he was there ... the effect was like the dew which descended from the mountain of Zion.[23]

With McCulloch, there was no jostling for position as there had been with Duncan Ross. McCulloch took the town pulpit comfortably and added teaching "to earn some much needed extra income." But his idea of what could be achieved in education began to grow, shored up by the strong support of MacGregor and Pictou Presbytery.

Change was afoot, and the coming of the new men coincided with significant growth and diversification in Pictou district. Fresh civic and religious facilities were needed to meet a rapidly expanded community.[24] The lumber trade was underway and a housing boom was at hand. Saw and grist mills, tanners, harness makers, and woodworkers were appearing, and with them, more people and problems. Law and liquor appeared as signs of progress. The administration of justice was extended, a jail was in the offing, and more businessmen, lawyers, and magistrates were appearing.

James worked closely with his East River Session to replace their original log church with a frame one at Irishtown.[25] East River added three elders, and Merigomish, which James still supplied, was shaken up and expanded. Baptisms and marriages mounted. In all, as James observed, Pictou was becoming "something of a town."

But while towns spur demand by concentrating attention and energy, they also enhance efficiency, making things possible that were inconceivable earlier. In this context, Thomas McCulloch had come at the right time. The home district was larger and better established, the pioneering era was waning, public resources were expanding, labour was becoming more specialized, and there was an incipient middle class. McCulloch may have accelerated the call for a college, but it lay in the logic and history of the town under MacGregor, for he had long advocated full educational development and the commencement of a divinity hall to offset the dearth of ministers from Scotland. For its part, Presbytery, the clergy all being Archibald Bruce's students, had long shared this view, for the union between secular education and the pursuit of studies in divinity had been recognized in the First Book of Discipline (1560), and it was a matter of principle with their common teachers, Archibald Bruce and James MacGregor. No Dissenter lost sight of that source, and McCulloch did not invent it.

Besides, sharp demographic changes were occurring: more people, more jobs, more children. Pictou had managed until now with privately run school "rooms," and if, earlier, MacGregor had had reservations about the settlers' commitment to religion, he had been even more shocked by a large-scale indifference to education:

> It was no little discouragement to me that I scarcely saw any books among the people ... Almost all of them had a Bible; and it was to be seen with some of the Highlanders who could not read. There was no school in the place ... Three of four [families] ... hired a teacher for a few months at different times; and this was a great exertion ... [But] I found it easier that I had thought to rouse the Highlanders to attend to the education of their children ... I made it a rule to inculcate this duty upon parents when speaking to them about baptism.[26]

In early Pictou, children had been needed for labour, not learning. McCulloch arrived in 1803, when conditions were much changed.

MacGregor had constantly expanded his own library and made it available to others. Since 1790, his chief supporters at his ordination, Revs. John Buist and James Robertson, had sent books,[27] and when Buist announced in Scotland the results of James's antislavery activism, Pictou benefited handsomely from one of Scotland's strongest antislavery leaders, David "Peasemeal" Dale, so named because he distributed free meals to the poor, declaring that he gave away in *gowpies*, handfuls, and received back from God in shovelfuls. In 1793 Dale sent a first shipment of sixty Bibles, sixty spelling books, and sixty primers.[28] More would follow. A Glasgow Seceder, Rev. James Watt – removed from the pulpit for his liberal views – was also engaged, probably by Deacon John Patterson, to choose and send books regularly.[29]

John MacKay came to Pictou in 1804 at nine and later remembered:

> Books were scarce ... yet I managed to get some good books anyway. – From the late Rev. Dr. MacGregor I borrowed many, among them an Encyclopedia in two large volumes. I read it all, and mastered a good deal of it, and made it my own. Any books that would be of service to me, if the Dr. had them they were all at my service.[30]

MacGregor also supported Peter Grant, his precentor, and Simon Newcomb in their teaching rooms.[31] Through letters to *The Christian Magazine*, he sought books for adults, reinforcing his call for greater literacy and broader learning as a duty to church and children. More than a decade before McCulloch's arrival, then, MacGregor had organized moves for literacy and for literary support.

By 1800 a burgeoning town was effecting great cultural change across the district, and after his arrival in 1803 McCulloch called on Pictou for a public subscription library, but it was not until 1822 that the town opened the province's fourth public library.[32] McCulloch's added burden of teaching was more formal and institutionalized than MacGregor's and Ross's, who appeared frequently in the local teaching "rooms," but Presbytery backed them all – and itself, elders and clergy, carried a heavier load in order to make that possible.

McCulloch acknowledged that in part he undertook teaching to supplement his income, and James was brought to farming for the same reason – and as a son of Glasgow, out of scientific curiosity. In 1799, with a growing family, he received not a penny in cash and only £50 in produce. Session was slow to correct the situation, and only after another crisis, in 1807, did it turn to voluntary payments,[33] which were not adopted officially until 1815.[34] Heavy financial pressure lay upon him. Ann had brought forth three sons, and in 1803 Christian ("Christy-Ann") arrived, followed the next year by Janet ("Hessie"), and the following year by Sarah. Challenged to feed, support, and educate them all, James renewed his interest in farming.

With the help of a hired hand, he experimented with fertilizers, making his land as fertile as his mind could conceive, for although he held rich bottom lands, he was not content with their size or fertility. In 1798 he received another 200 acres, and in 1810, another 450, experimenting with new crops and varieties and inventing tools to suit the local soils, like a double plough and a special harrow.[35] Lands were cheap, and his neighbours happily sold theirs to ensure that he and his experiments remained nearby.

Typically he linked the bringing of the gospel to fostering new farming methods and ideas. Duncan Ross matched him, and together they initiated a local agricultural improvement movement twenty years before Nova Scotia rallied to John Young ("Agricola").[36]

The potential of his new lands and especially of his inventiveness was not exhausted by his farming projects, however. William MacKay had received a license to mine coal on "The Big Seam" in 1790, but little had followed.[37] Curiously, coal was not widely used; but discovering it on his own land, James obtained a licence to operate a "home mine," and for two decades he met his needs and supplemented his income. The teacher complemented the entrepreneur, and at election time in 1799 he entertained the candidates before his coal fire, encouraging them to promote the district's richest resource after timber.[38] He would use his own coal to burn lime in preparation for sweetening his own lands.

But McCulloch's coming also made it possible to establish a pulpit for the growing town, and McCulloch was above all a town man. His educational initiatives would best thrive within the town, for he aimed almost exclusively at developing a single institution rather than the regional system that MacGregor and the rest had been labouring to build. In preparation for an academy, McCulloch sought town support as well as practical fundraising by two principals, Edward Mortimer and James MacGregor. McCulloch called James the academy's "warmest friend," and later McCulloch's granddaughter, Isabella McCulloch, cited him, never a modest man, as having acknowledged that "the Venerable Dr. MacGregor and others founded the Academy for the sake of the Gospel."[39]

Isabella McCulloch wisely added "and others," for while her grandfather and MacGregor were prominent advocates, Presbytery played an important part, and especially Rev. Duncan Ross and someone soon to arrive, the learned Rev. John Keir.[40] McCulloch's ministerial colleagues and the elders took on heavy pastoral and mission duties designed to leave McCulloch free to work on education.

At first McCulloch called only for a secondary school, assuming that the students would come prepared by private instruction, but if so, private tutors to prepare them had long been open largely to those living near the towns. As the colony slowly developed, MacGregor gave priority to teaching younger children and those across the whole district. By 1820 there were at least seven privately run elementary schools with over two hundred and fifty students.[41] He and Ross were trustees for three schools and regular visitors to the rest. But after 1800 the pace quickened as Pictou's role as metropolitan centre was accelerated. Still, Presbytery strove for a wide spectrum of pastoral and educational services at home and across the district and province, and it welcomed McCulloch's special talents.

As new ministers appeared, then, an increasingly complex and activist community was emerging, for which education and spiritual opportunity were joint priorities. Controversy often stemmed from Presbytery's antiestablishmentarian, liberal views on education, which reflected some of the most advanced ideas of the day – and may be traced in part to Archibald Bruce. As agricultural innovators and teachers, MacGregor and Ross broadened the meaning of education as an instrument of reform. Duncan Ross, John Keir, and later Ross's son, James, a future president of Dalhousie University, followed James's lead by actively promoting a divinity hall. All have suffered by comparison in the shadow of Thomas McCulloch's self-promotion and notoriety: McCulloch did not shun the limelight – and uncritical historians have kept the lamps fed.

Like MacGregor, McCulloch valued nondenominational, liberal education. James was himself an example of how access to higher education could benefit a mere weaver's son. In 1803, however, Halifax's Anglican establishment and members of the governing council agreed to exclude from the province's only college – King's College at Windsor – 80 per cent of the population, which is to say, all Catholics and Dissenters.

MacGregor, Ross, and McCulloch were outraged. In Scotland, Dissenters were not barred from the universities, but the blindsiding of King's College was fuelled by both class and denominational narrowness, as well as by a powerful Kirkman, Michael Wallace, who had joined the council in April 1803. Wallace gave enormous support to King's College, any establishmentarian model being preferred.

McCulloch urged Presbytery to make a countermove, proposing that under the circumstances the first step should be an advanced school.

James conceded the priority but insisted that the upper school be linked to plans for a divinity hall. No one knew better than James about Pictou's problem of ministerial supply, and he had long warned that Nova Scotia students sent to Scotland for training might be lured from Seceder ranks. Any strategy, Presbytery agreed, must be far-reaching and comprehensive. McCulloch was authorized to develop a plan that relied on the support of his colleagues, especially MacGregor, Ross, and Keir.[42]

The blueprint called first for a secondary school and undergraduate college as foundation for a divinity hall. It was also argued that by opening their doors to other Dissenter students, they might look for broad provincial support for free education outside Windsor. Pictou's proposal was two-edged: to ensure a well-trained, local clergy who would serve an educated public.

With Presbytery's blessing, McCulloch proceeded further, and James supported him, but his extensive parish and mission cares, his duties as moderator, and his faltering health prevented his leading the venture. Still, he felt confident in McCulloch, whom all believed to have the quickness of mind, sophistication, and grit to mount a firm challenge to Anglican exclusivism.

For Presbytery to find a balance between home and missions was difficult, but McCulloch's willingness to focus on developing schools and college eased that dilemma. Over the next twenty years, James regularly undertook approaches for financial aid,[43] for McCulloch had confessed, "I have tried many a trade, but begging is the worst … I would rather toil night and day at home than go begging." It was a wise distribution of talents and energy.

But MacGregor did not wait for McCulloch's proposed secondary school. With five children at home and a sixth on the way, he had a vested interest in elementary schooling. In 1805, working with Donald and Rod MacKay and Robert Culton, he signed an agreement to open a school on the East River, serving four families and up to twenty-four children, at £24 annually, half in cash and with costs shared in proportion to the number of each family's children. But they went further: if eight pupils signed up, a night school, also on shares, would be added. The project was designed as a model for places beyond the town where education was irregular.

Meanwhile, within three years McCulloch opened a high school in his own house. MacGregor and Ross assisted him by tutoring in Latin and Greek. Support came from subscription, which MacGregor courted, and in 1806 he was the first, pledging £20. But recalling 1799, when he had received no cash stipend all year, he added archly, "providing the Harbour [Pictou town] congregation pay me the £16 which they owe me."[44] The fund was generously subscribed, and then James turned to Sam Gilfillan and John Buist for further help:

> The increasing demand for ministers seems to intimate the necessity of raising them in this country ... Pictou people have subscribed about £1,000, a more liberal subscription than they are well able to pay. We expect some money from the Province Treasury if we give our seminary a little name, as not rivaling the University, which Government has established. We expect great assistance from Britain and Ireland. We intend to send Mr. McCulloch home to beg.[45]

Gilfillan replied that it might be hard to raise funds "for your seminary,"[46] hinting at resistance to the idea of the colonials' capacity to train their own ministers and making no commitment to other levels of support.

At Pictou a local society was formed to support the proposed academy, and Session adopted a 5s. levy, although it was criticized by the lieutenant governor. In 1811, however, Halifax adopted the principle of district grammar schools, and McCulloch petitioned successfully that Pictou's be so designated. It was agreed, an allotment was made, and construction of a log schoolhouse began on McCulloch's glebe lot, which he had been granted on application; for whereas Ross and MacGregor had been assigned glebes in the 1790s, neither had ever received an acre. It must be acknowledged that by his persistence, McCulloch often greased the squeaky wheel.

There, the plans for a Pictou Academy rested, awaiting a more flexible Halifax establishment and a more liberal council. McCulloch continued to exert pressure on the academy's behalf, and James wrote a friend in Scotland that McCulloch was "killing himself." But his grit in combining teaching with lobbying and his pulpit duties was no more than James and others had often done themselves.

Moreover, McCulloch was not alone. Isabella contributed heavily by offering advice and by preparing meals and managing the dormitory for sixteen resident students, as Janet Auld had done at "The De'il's Barracks" in Whitburn.

Thus, when Rev. John Keir arrived in 1808, Pictou boasted a large, stable presbytery, most of whose clergy had been drawn to Pictou by their admiration for MacGregor, urged on by Archibald Bruce. Most travelled regularly on mission, although McCulloch never did. He was backed by powerful business and political leaders, men like Edward Mortimer and Truro's powerful politician S.G.W. Archibald, who had long supported MacGregor and now supported McCulloch, too. In short, McCulloch's success resulted from a team effort. It is true that he often called the plays on the academy venture and drove himself, but Presbytery and others played important roles. One day, however briefly, they would realize much of their dream – and when it collapsed it was McCulloch, always limited by his temperament, and not they who bore the responsibility.

Chapter Thirteen

New Places, New Faces

MacGregor maintained an astonishing correspondence, but beyond writing to his father he seldom addressed his relatives at home in Scotland. In 1806, his nephew, Duncan Ferguson, complained of this neglect, asking about the new country, its mountains, what magazines were circulating – adding, "Elizabeth wished to know about Ann, and what is your children's names?" Eighteen years later, Duncan was still asking about the mountains and the children's names.[1] James's single-mindedness in his ministry consumed him: all his attention and energy were focused on his new family, nuclear and extended, overseas. Whatever his merits or circumstances, the Gospel must be fulfilled.

In 1805, he resumed his ambitious visits to new fields. Called again to Miramichi and to the St John River valley,[2] he undertook his longest journey yet, this time travelling on horseback in response to a call to Sheffield, downriver from Fredericton. One night, weary and despairing of finding a place to sleep, he dropped the reins, allowing his horse to take its head. The forest trail was narrow, the animal unlikely to stray, and James too exhausted to care. He stirred once at the sound of water rushing behind but thought little of it, learning next day that the horse had crossed a powerful millstream by skilfully treading the narrow top of a dam.[3] This was the journey of a consumptive man of forty-six, who had nearly burned himself out.

At Sheffield he found a settlement of pre-Loyalist New Englanders – composed of Congregationalists, Baptists, Methodists, and Anti-Calvinist New Lights – but few Presbyterians. Still, he preached to all on two Sabbaths, visited their homes, and commended them for putting worship before denomination. He was delighted to meet several families from Perthshire. One woman remarked, "Well, I never saw a

Presbyterian minister before, but my mother used to tell me that they were the very best in the world. But what do you hold to?[4] He declared that he did not understand, and she asked whether he "held to conversion." He replied that surely all churches held to that, but she replied, "Now, the Methodists and the New Lights hold to it but the Church of England hold against it."

Travelling the beautiful river valley, he saw scenes that have changed little:

> It appeared extremely large and grand. [The] spring freshet overflows all its banks, and covers the whole intervale, two miles broad, in some places two or three feet deep [and] ... every house and barn is an island; the potatoes and other things ... must be carried up to the garret. Every house has a canoe for sailing into the barn or byre, or neighbour's house ... The use of the beautiful row of trees along the riverside was to prevent the ice from spreading over the intervale and destroying houses, cattle, etc. ... The resistless fury of a thousand streams, and the ice carried with them, drive before them the ice of the great river ... with reiterated and irresistible crashes.[5]

James was greatly moved and felt compelled to travel farther upstream to a demoralized settlement of Highland veterans squatting at Nashwaak, just above Fredericton. He recorded, "They had been miserably abused in their settlement. The officers got large lots of the best land; the men ... all length and no breadth ... One-half of the men had to leave ... and shift for themselves ... stray sheep in the wilderness."[6]

In their need, he recounted, some had become Methodists and Baptists, but "the best and the worst of them had continued Presbyterians."[7] Back in Pictou, on their behalf he sent off another urgent letter to Synod, observing, "They would accept a Presbyterian minister, if he were not very rigid."[8] Nothing came of it, but it was another beginning, and he proudly tallied the cost of his trip at only 20s.[9]

In 1806, his twentieth year of ministry, he returned to Prince Edward Island for a six-week marathon of thirty-seven sermons and five addresses in twenty-seven days.[10] To the east, at Murray Harbour and Guernsey Cove, there lived Scottish Presbyterians and Channel Island Huguenots[11] – good Calvinists all. There, with careful preparation, he opened an important new mission. The Island was always a challenge to the traveller, but after Pictou it was his favourite field. He would continue for another fifteen years before leaving it to others to build on his foundations.

For, MacGregor's "Letter of 1793" was still working its wonder: in the autumn of 1805 there appeared Rev. Peter Gordon.[12] Like Jacob, he had been a weaver, but at James's call he had turned to divinity, studying so hard under Archibald Bruce that he probably undermined his own health. By now Bruce was one of Pictou's great colonizers, having helped to make Pictou Presbytery the largest number of Seceder ministers on the continent.

Sam Gilfillan wrote that he did not "know Mr. Gordon very much, but I hear that he is an ingenious, pious lad."[13] On his arrival Gordon embraced James, crying out, "Oh, father you have brought me to this country."[14] But he had brought a wife equally devoted to MacGregor, for it will be recalled that at fourteen, Janet Auld, Archibald Bruce's niece and chatelaine, had been "vexed" that no one was coming to James. Her strong evangelical conviction had prepared her for this new life, and as keeper of Bruce's home and "The De'il's Barracks," she had known all the men who had come from Bruce to MacGregor. Recently jilted for a lady of higher station, she had then accepted Gordon's invitation to marriage and accompanied him to Nova Scotia. His love did much to restore her confidence.

With their firstborn, Elisabeth, they arrived in Halifax in the summer of 1806. Janet was twenty-seven, Gordon, thirty-three. He had been assigned to Halifax, but being needed urgently on the Island, he was posted to St Peters on the exposed North Shore just as winter set in. The question then arose as to who should preach at his ordination in Theophilus DesBrisay's church in Charlotte Town. James would preside as moderator, and Duncan Ross was considered, but although he was a fine writer of sermons, Ross's delivery was considered "more heavy than popular." James suggested mischievously, "I would make Mr. Ross to prepare the sermon and Mr. Dick to preach it!"[15] Dick won the toss, and Gordon then threw himself into his mission with great passion, quickly recommending himself to all.

Sending Gordon to the Island, however, proved unfortunate, for the North Shore receives all the winter storms out of Labrador, and Gordon was not a well man. St Peters was an arduous mission, and the conscientious Gordon was quickly worn down. In October 1807, however, further confirming the existing links between Pictou and Truro, he made the long journey to preach at Daniel Cock's church, now under the jurisdiction of Rev. Hugh Graham.[16] Like James, Gordon was often on the road for weeks, his letters full of longing for Janet and Elisabeth, told in fervent love poems of an indifferent quality. But the letters also affirm his worsening consumption. On his return to the Island, and during the worst winter in thirty years, his condition grew grave.[17] Indeed, in April 1809, he died while he was away from home, leaving Janet alone with Elisabeth and a newborn, Mary, until MacGregor could hurry over to assist her to Pictou and find a replacement for Gordon.

In 1808 there arrived a fifth and very promising graduate of Glasgow and of Archibald Bruce's seminary. Rev. John Keir was thirty-eight, a native of Stirlingshire, even coming from the parish of MacGregor's friend and correspondent Rev. Sam Gilfillan at Comrie. Gilfillan declared him "sober, steady and intelligent."[18] Like James, Keir had taught for five years during his probation, and like MacGregor and McCulloch, he and his wife were well prepared to further literary and scientific education. He and Peter Gordon had been friends at Whitburn, and he, too, had been sent to·Halifax first. With Gordon's collapse, however, he was the obvious replacement.[19] Settling in the west at Princetown (Malpeque), he would serve for fifty years, at first also supplying the distant, grieving St Peters.

Only days before his departure Keir had married a capable bride, Mary Burnet – a distinguished name in Scottish Secessionist. clerical circles. With her help, he organized Sabbath schools, an elementary school, and an Island literary and scientific society, with Mary as treasurer. As at Pictou, their school became the district grammar school, and both developed a curriculum reflecting their considerable learning. In many respects, the Keirs made a great addition to the Pictou Presbytery and when John succeeded McCulloch as professor of divinity. MacGregor's correspondence with him makes clear his great regard for another able administrator and teacher. There is deference in James's letters to Keir, suggesting how much he appreciated the worth of these further well-matched newcomers.

For, Keir's coming rescued Pictou Presbytery from the Gordon crisis and significantly reinforced it in other respects. He was another graduate of Glasgow and Whitburn, clever, well trained, and well suited to advance the cause of education in Nova Scotia and on the Island. Now, as was Douglas, it seemed, James's beloved Island was in good hands. Ross, Dick, Keir, and McCulloch were treasured peers.

A formidable team, based at Pictou and arising from MacGregor's liaison with Bruce, was paying handsome dividends. Bruce's commitment to Seceder principles and his liberal ideas suited James's needs and temperament. Moreover, in the face of Janet Gordon's recent widowhood and of her cares as a single parent, James and Bruce would grow even closer during Bruce's last ten years.[20]

Archibald Bruce and John Buist had served Pictou and MacGregor well, helping to assemble a lively group of like-minded clergy and educators who reflected the values and aspirations of Glasgow's Enlightenment and the strength of Seceder evangelicalism. In dealing with official Halifax, they also reflected the views of Bruce and John Millar on the need for carefully defined relations between church and state, for equal rights for Dissenters, and for constitutional government. The looming conflict over Pictou Academy would bring Pictou Presbytery to an intense focus, but the colony's cultural and intellectual energy had taken root much earlier. Thomas McCulloch and John Keir would help to advance MacGregor's dreams and those of Presbytery, lay and clerical, to new levels.

Ann MacKay MacGregor had filled her own house, but she was concerned for Janet Gordon and anxious to help; in the event, in a way that boded ill. Presbytery proposed to send Janet to assist Alex and Ann Dick in Douglas, the sprawling, demanding district that called Dick away frequently. But Ann MacGregor opposed this plan, perhaps considering it too menial or simply improper. If the latter, she did not solve matters by insisting that James put up a dwelling for the straitened family at Pictou in a corner of their own lot.[21] Not long after Janet and her children had moved in, idle tongues began to wag.

Ann was indifferent to such busybodies and probably pleased to have Janet's company. At forty-one she was in her seventh pregnancy, and Janet's help and company eased her load as she neared the end of her term. James was happy, too, considering the Island crisis resolved and that things were generally improving. Besides, he had hardly been home again before a sixth colleague appeared.

Rev. John Mitchell, an English Presbyterian, was an experienced, robust frontier missionary who had stayed briefly with Duncan Ross in 1803.[22] In 1804 he moved his family to Amherst, where James billeted with them on his journey to Sheffield. Mitchell was drawn to Ross and MacGregor and asked to join Pictou Presbytery, which cordially welcomed him, partly because he offered an answer to the perennial problem of Amherst. Patterson characterizes him as only a worthy yeoman, but a healthy yeoman would do at this juncture, and Mitchell was more than that. He willingly undertook Amherst and a huge district to the east, extending to Wallace, Tatamagouche, and River John. In 1809, he was moved again, this time to River John, to serve a new wave of Highlanders settling the North Shore.[23]

James found relief in these promising developments, and in the summer of 1810 undertook a successful mission over the mountains to the south, into the St Marys valley, to Glenelg at the forks of the East River St Marys. Truro timbermen had been moving into the valley's oak and pine stands, and although many came from Burgher backgrounds, most were indifferent to the shade of Presbyterianism they found at St Marys. To them, Cock's and MacGregor's differences were ancient history, the stuff of parental gossip. When Truro could not send a man, James filled the gap and was warmly welcomed, soon bringing together a lively congregation. A local historian concludes, "This was the beginning of Presbyterianism in Glenelg."[24]

With another salient opened up, these seemed indeed to be halcyon days: all the pieces were coming together.

But suddenly, they blew apart.

On 6 November 1810 Ann was delivered of a fourth son, but through "unskillfulness" she lapsed into excruciating pain and died within hours.[25] The baby died as well, striking a terrible double blow to James's always-vulnerable spirit – for depression was never far from him. After twenty-four years he finally missed a service, and in the following weeks it was noticed that his sermons were following a morbid track. Ann's intelligence, independent spirit, and support had been integral to his success as father and shepherd, and he was struck low by her sudden passing. In deep grief he composed a fitting epitaph and not long after, raised a monument to her beside his beloved East River:

> Bu dhean phosda bha tlathi
> Bu mbathair bha caoin
> Bha creidimh le gradh aic
> Us gnath nach robh faoin.

> She was a wife most affectionate
> A mother most tender,
> She had faith with love
> And a conduct consistent.[26]

Through the winter he probably often visited the cottage at the back of the property, sharing his bereavement with the woman still nursing her own. Soon, however, the idle talk was rekindled.

Thoughtful people wondered at James's failure to come to terms with his grief. Had he not always carried them through such crises with a strengthening of their faith? The gentle Donald MacKay asked for them all, "James, where is all the strength and support you have been giving us in our trouble?" To which he replied, "Ah Donald. I was then *in the spirit, now I am in the flesh.*"[27]

The following two years were difficult as he tried to ease the grief of his own six children while comforting Janet Gordon and her two little girls. His income was hardly up to the challenge either, for it still rested on the sporadic payment of dues, and now past fifty, his pastoral cares were again challenging his once-sound health. He and Janet began to take stock, and in November 1812 James wrote archly to John Keir: "There is talk, and I suppose upon good authority, that Mrs. Gordon and I are to be married in a week or two."[28]

Over twenty years divided them, but it was a sensible arrangement, ensuring the care and education of eight children, although Robert and James had already left home. But it also grew into a loving attachment, and Janet Auld Gordon MacGregor rejoiced that she could at last "do some good" for the man she had so long admired and to whom she was so recently indebted for support.

This happy ending was marred, however, by several developments: first, word reached him of the sudden death of his most beloved and ablest clerical colleague, Alex Dick; second, his concern was deepening over Christy-Ann, his oldest daughter, who was still in mourning and obviously not adjusting well to having a stepmother; third, alarm arose over developments at Pictou.

In May 1812, the popular and energetic Alex Dick was caught in a storm and died from a severe chill. Like Ann MacGregor, he was only forty-one. He had carried a huge territory, bringing efficiency and cheerfulness to his mission, while his wife, Ann Eadie, was as worthy as Ann MacGregor, Isabella McCulloch, Isabella Ross, or Janet Gordon. He was buried under the church that he would never complete.

Patterson reports of Dick, "In the view of his contemporaries, Dr. MacGregor was the only one of all of the Presbyterian ministers … who excelled him."[29] Dick had combined pastoral, administrative, and educational skills that rivalled James's own, and his charisma reminded many of James.

Alex Dick would be hard to replace, but James set about repairing the damage done in Noel-Maitland, which often meant being away from home while his own family was adjusting to its great crisis. Ann's loss had come as a terrible shock to the children, most of all to nine-year-old Christy-Ann. Her Grandmother MacKay, who had known happy times in Halifax, shared James's concern and sought to help the troubled child. In March 1813, James recognized that Christy-Ann could not yet adjust to a substitute mother. Besides, Janet was pregnant, which probably added further distress. James bowed to Christina MacKay's proposal that the girl should move to the capital for a little, where, like her mother, she might find new opportunities and friends.

James's troubled reservations come through in a letter addressed to Alexander Fraser, his old West River elder, now living in Halifax:

Pictou, March 5, 1813

Dear Sir:

I have sent my Daughter Christian, to remain a little time with you ... Her grandmother wanted her to go in, partly that she might get a little education; and partly [to] be useful to Mrs. Fraser ... [But] my family is so large, and my stipend so ill paid that I cannot let her stay long in Halifax. A quarter of a year is the longest ... I hope that Mrs. Fraser will take care to keep her from vain and bad company, from idleness, and from buying foolish things, in the way of dress, or other ways. Also that she shall stir her up to read the bible and other good books, & to pray to God at least morning and evening ... And that she will not let her spend her time in reading useless books, or going abroad by herself; and in short that she will prove a pious mother to her while she stays there. I would not let her to town at all if it were not for the trust that I have in you and Mrs. Fraser ... [G]et for her ... nothing above necessaries. I will endeavour to pay you sometime for these; but I cannot say when. As long as she stays about your house accustom her to do any thing needful for the family; it will be for her good, and I hope she will not be unwilling ... [C]onsider what is reasonable between man and man and charge accordingly. Mrs. MacGregor & her grandmother want her to learn only plain sewing; any other being of little use to her through life ... Robert has got a Daughter. Mrs. MacGregor joins in best love to you and your family. I am Dear Sir.

Yours etc.
James MacGregor.[30]

When Janet's first MacGregor baby, Annabella, arrived, she brought great joy to her parents. Christy-Ann was then with the Frasers, who were well suited to help her, and she would return in better spirits.

In the following year, James's own spirits suffered again, however, when Janet lost a child. Archibald Bruce wrote to thank James for his sensitive care of his bereaved niece,[31] but within months, Bruce, too, would be gone.

Meanwhile, further trouble was brewing: Dick's loss was still deeply felt, McCulloch's feisty push for an academy was stirring up opposition, and several serious social issues were arising at Pictou. There were bumps ahead in the road. James continued to support McCulloch, but he and Duncan Ross were more immediately alarmed over the district's social stability in the face of sharply increased economic activity. When war was declared in 1812, these threats took on new dimensions, with alarming results for a once-isolated, stable frontier.

PART FIVE

Community and Union

Chapter Fourteen

Pictou and Progress

In the first two decades of the nineteenth century, Pictou developed new industry and trade while the town grew prodigiously.[1] In 1806 ferry service began across the harbour.[2] Clannishness spurred rivalry between the town and other coastal centres. New Glasgow, 14 kilometres (9 miles) up the East River, thrived in a productive cycle beginning with James Carmichael's general store and soaring to tradesmen's, craftsmen's, and industrial operations – tinkers, farriers, coopers, masons, saddlers, tanners, and shipbuilders.[3] Competition was a driving force. Saw- and gristmills appeared everywhere, and "John the Collier" MacKay put new vigour into his father's dormant coaling licence. Spurred after 1808 by Napoleon's closure of the Baltic timber ports, upriver and along the coast lumbering and shipping advanced. Britain's desperate need for timber became Pictou's opportunity.[4]

But there were limitations to this success. Although heavy logging was complemented by ambitious shipbuilding for the same market, even at its height, lumbering remained a raw staples exchange, only squared logs being exported. Thus, Pictou's timber profits rested not in manufacture but in export volume, which prompted careless exploitation of the forests, leaving clear-cut land unfit for farming or useful regrowth. British trade became Pictou's obsession. Fifty vessels loaded annually, and as early at 1805, £100,000 in value went to Britain. At its peak, timber realized more than £100,000 a year,[5] the most successful trader being Edward Mortimer, who assumed the mantles of both Pattersons, squire and deacon, at their deaths in 1808.[6]

Mortimer married the squire's daughter, erected a grand house and two wharves, and became the richest man in Nova Scotia, worth over £100,000 from timber and land. Once, in seven successive weeks, he shipped to the value of £5,000 a week.[7] In business dealings he was uncompromising, blacklisting those who dealt with competitors, and by truck and trade (bartering supplies for labour) keeping lumber and shipping gangs in peonage.[8]

Yet, he was generous in good causes and earned wide respect. As magistrate, he delighted in presiding over weddings. He liked to command but was a welcome ally. Recognizing that Pictou's interests and his own needed political support, he won a seat in the legislature, where he became Pictou's tireless booster. As ruling elder, he was accorded the privilege of conducting a restored Christy-Ann MacGregor's marriage to Abram Patterson, the deacon's fourth son, himself a major trader in timber and fish. Pictou's leaders were close-knit.

With MacGregor and Ross, Mortimer supported progressive farming and the church, becoming the district's most prominent lay promoter of education in all of its aspects. In the legislature he allied with Truro's powerful S.G.W. Archibald, who later served as solicitor and attorney general and had many ties with Pictou.

Yet Mortimer contributed to two major problems that alarmed both Presbytery and Session: the first derived from the timber boom; the second centred on plans for an academy at Pictou. In both, his support proved a two-edged sword.

Mortimer shrewdly played off against the Council and worked with other rural assemblymen to reduce Halifax's stranglehold on trade and customs revenue, as he strove to elevate Pictou's and rural Nova Scotians' educational prospects. In doing so, he readily locked horns with centrally minded lieutenant governors like Sir John Wentworth and Lord Dalhousie.[9] For two decades he used his wealth to Pictou's advantage, guaranteeing the district direct representation. By contrast, travel and lodging costs forced Yarmouth and, Guysborough to elect Halifax men to sit for them as "virtual representatives." But Mortimer maintained a Halifax residence from which he lobbied strenuously in his and Pictou's interests. In Mortimer's first (1799) election, MacGregor supported his campaign,[10] but when a "Country Party" was formed under the feisty William Cottnam Tonge,[11] James withdrew from playing too overt a role. Tonge apologized for trying to enlist him,[12] and although James supported Mortimer, he approved parts of Tonge's platform.

But Mortimer's victory brought down upon Pictou the wrath of a powerful Kirkman, Michael Wallace ("King Michael"), who had lost the election to Mortimer. With private interests along the North Shore,

Wallace became a thorn in the side of MacGregor and Pictou for thirty years, especially in the battle over Pictou Academy.[13]

The great contest at the time, however, lay in timber, and there Mortimer and MacGregor were deeply involved in very different ways. The short-term benefits of big timber were huge. Empires arose from the forest's bounty, but for hundreds working in the woods there were only trickle-down benefits, and the negative impacts on the community were enormous. Economic diversity and flexibility declined; pioneer farming was neglected. But when, with the coming of peace, Britain abruptly reduced her overseas timber imports, Pictou's risky dependence on a single market and easy timber profits along with the weaknesses of its attendant credit system were exposed. A crisis loomed.[14]

MacGregor viewed these contradictions in moral and social terms, listing the dangers from excessive reliance on consumer goods and the abuse of alcohol:

> But the grand cause of our deprivation is the shutting of the Baltic. If the Devil contrived it for the ruin of our morals, he is a master in politics, ... that all the vices in the world would have done so much damage in Pictou, as I have seen drunkenness alone do ... [S]quared timber came to be in demand; and ... might have been turned to profit had we known to make it in moderation, ... but the love of money did not allow us to stop there. The farmer neglected his farm and went to square timber; he had to go to the merchant to buy provisions, and the merchant persuaded him that he needed many other things besides provisions. If the farmer scrupled ... he would ask him, Why do you hesitate? You know that a stick of timber will pay for it ... This answered well enough for a time, but after a few years the price of timber fell, and the taste continued and could not be gratified ... The merchants, partly owing to the system of credit, and ... to the changes ... in the lumber market, nearly all failed. Scarcely one of them died wealthy, ... and the country came out of a season of commercial prosperity, ... with exhausted resources.[15]

Ross and McCulloch shared his alarm, and McCulloch launched a series of satirical sketches, "The Stepsure Letters," in the *Acadian Recorder*, where he deftly traced the dangers of "a quick buck" made in a fleeting trade. His humour was broad and clever as he joined James in urging the stability and permanence of managed farming and balanced commerce. Calling for a return to landed ways and strengths, they advanced the old Calvinist virtues of frugality, self-sufficiency, and sobriety,[16] arguing in a spirit of moderate liberalism that along with individual fulfilment the interconnectedness and stability of the community should be preserved. Progressive, methodical agriculture in the improving mould, they argued, would reward initiative and invention, and be linked to sound commerce. James repudiated unchecked commercialism and materialism:[17]

> There is an incredible change in Pictou in my time. There were not much above 400 souls … whereas we are now 4000, if not more. When people increase, sin multiplies. We have suffered from emigrants … from different parts of the Highlands; but more from merchants and traders from England, and the south of Scotland. The ignorance and superstition of the former have not done us so much evil, as the avarice, the luxury, the show, and the glittering toys of the latter.[18]

Trying to rekindle the rural, agrarian ideal, however, was not welcome when commerce and industry were in the saddle: to many, great profits still seemed within their grasp. Presbytery's warnings were swallowed up in the chimera of timber.[19]

But first, in 1815 the district suffered what the Galloway men had experienced on Prince Edward Island: a "Year of the Mice," followed in 1816 by "The Summer-less Year." Farmers were hard hit, and James despaired: "Our farmers … scourge the land most unmercifully with white crops," pursuing fodder and cereal crops over root and vegetable production.[20] Duncan Ross set up a model threshing mill on his farm, and in 1817 he became president of the West River Farming Society, the first agricultural society in the province. Edward Mortimer held a ploughing match in his field, another provincial first.[21] MacGregor continued experimenting with fertilizers and manuring techniques and initiated a parallel East River Agricultural Society, filling every office himself by default. The societies often worked as one, cooperating with distant Stewiacke, where Rev. Hugh Graham had helped found another district society.

The movement spread quickly across the province, encouraged by Lieutenant Governor Dalhousie, and Ross and James began corresponding with another Scot in Halifax, John Young, whose serialized "Letters of Agricola" in the *Acadian Recorder* promoted agricultural reform. Dalhousie appointed Young secretary of a new Central Board of Agriculture, and Joseph Howe claimed it had become de rigueur to "hire an acre of land and plant wurtzels."[22]

By the 1820s MacGregor was spreading 300 bushels of lime and much ash on 2 acres of land, developing a stable system of manuring. With his own coal, he burned lime to sweeten the fields, and with coal ash tested varying depths of tillage. Importing and inventing new farm tools, he also learned scientific fruit farming from the Galloway men. From 1820 to 1824, what Graeme calls "MacGregor's handsome harvests" won him nearly a third of the cash prizes for best ram and best wheat, oats, barley, turnips, and potatoes. By 1826, however, Wynn remarks, MacGregor's reports to Young had grown "dolorous, dour and rueful."[23]

His fresh depression arose from two sources. One was his gloomy assessment of recent East River immigrant farmers, "an ignorant lot." He observed to Young that they had come "from the mountainous parts of Scotland, where their fathers were little occupied with either plough- ing or reading ... Very few of them could read and understand the let- ters of Agricola."[24] His Highland pride was being tested. Ross reported that on James's farm he "saw the first roller and the only plough with double mould boards, and turnips in raised drills. Unfortunately none of his neighbours followed the example."[25]

But MacGregor also had harsh words for Young, complaining about the board's "miserable seed," charging him with taking credit for mills built privately, without a board subsidy, and condemning the clover provided as fit only for England's milder climate. He scolded Coun- cil for denying access to the abundant surface coal to burn lime and observed bitterly, "Some think the whole bustle about agriculture is a contrivance to pick poor people's pockets." Some, he charged, were already abandoning the movement because it was for "gentlemen, not the farmer." In frustration, he challenged Young to "use your superior mind" to put things right and ended with the most telling grievance: Young had sent a bull that "produced nothing." Ray MacLean con- cludes that his criticisms were on the mark.[26]

Graeme Wynn considers "shrewd" James's view that only their neighbour's profit would nudge some to undertake improvement,[27] but James had a long experience of human nature. In 1824 the East River Society failed for want of a quorum, and later, Ross's organization barely outlived him. Agrarian reform awaited a later decade.[28] Wynn concludes, however, that it had been a useful start in a land of inter- vales, rocks, and clear-cut forestry, where farming must be uneven. As early "ag-reps" to the North Shore, MacGregor and Ross were success- ful, holding to their shared conviction that such extended education was integral to the cure of souls and the community's well-being.

In decrying big timber's negative effects, they also argued that it would attract a poorer class of immigrants – profiteers, not farmers. Many took to the woods soon after seeding, leaving planting and harvesting unmatched by tilling and manuring. Soil exhaustion meant smaller yields and poorer crops, weakening the county's agricultural reputation. Such neglect, James argued, would lead to the collapse of the credit system as merchants tied to farming and logging failed – a prediction soon borne out.

Timber was governed by huge external forces, like Britain's postwar depression, which the big operators in Lower Canada and New Brunswick could survive, but which hit Pictou hard. The credit system collapsed, and Edward Mortimer, once the province's richest man, left a widow dependent on private charity. [29] John Patterson had already left barely enough to maintain his wife.[30] Both had been rich in lands and poor in cash, and truck and trade had tied so many people to the fluctuations of trade that first it brought down the deacon, and after its grand collapse in 1816, even Edward Mortimer. Pictou entered the 1820s in a perilous condition.

Meanwhile, at Douglas, the trade in timber also affected Alex Dick's old followers. Dick had finally been succeeded by Rev. Thomas Crowe, another minister from James's old Perthshire neighbourhood. After over three years without a resident minister, Douglas was in need, but the nimble Crowe married Dick's daughter, won Ann Eadie Dick's blessing, and tripled the congregation. His quarrel with timber was over its association with excessive drink, and his attacks on its purveyors were described as being "snappish as a mink." He had cause.

The first casualty of timber was sobriety. Under truck and trade a man often emerged from the woods with nothing to show for his winter's work, his wages having gone to rum. Work stoppages over rum were common. It took a gallon of poor rum at 8s to the company to cut and carry each ton of timber to the docks, where, with less added water, it cost 25s.[31] At home the social consequences were often severe: neglect of the farm, isolation, loneliness, and cruelly hard work for wives and young children. For those who succumbed to rum, their absence might be considered no great loss.

Perhaps James felt especially troubled by these developments because he knew so much joy in his own stable family. The children of both marriages passed successfully through their teens, and in 1815 Janet presented him with another daughter, Mary. Two years later came Peter Gordon MacGregor, James's last child and close successor. James spoke of "God's generosity with my family life," but he remained deeply concerned for the district's social condition.

Presbytery pressed for strict liquor regulations, but it would be hard to deny a Highlander the moderate use of strong spirits. An average family consumed annually five gallons of rum at 20s a gallon, or about $200 a year in buying power, a large sum for those struggling in town or on the farm.[32] Ross and MacGregor became so alarmed that Ross founded the West River Temperance Society, another first in the province. McCulloch's town congregation took a little longer, and James's East River Highlanders were like Will Rogers's Alabamans who would "vote for prohibition, as long as they could stagger to the polls." But by 1832 a *district* temperance organization was in place and to some effect: a notice appeared in the *Colonial Patriot*: "On Friday last, the frame of a large dwelling house ... was erected without the use of *rum*."[33] Yet, with the first spring ship from the West Indies bearing rum, flags were unfurled, crowds rushed to the docks, and even Pictou Academy was dismissed.[34]

But from his pulpit at Maitland, Thomas Crowe outdid both Ross and MacGregor, campaigning so fiercely for temperance that soon it was said, "Douglas is dry."

With Edward Mortimer's death in 1819 the spectre of Michael Wallace loomed larger, for he wielded incredible political weight. A Virginia Loyalist, he had made a fortune at Halifax as a military contractor, judge of the Vice-Admiralty Court, and later Provincial Treasurer. He was a fervent supporter of the Halifax oligarchy and in 1803 joined the Council of Twelve. Advancing his North Shore interests by hovering about successive lieutenant governors, he was rewarded with five stints as administrator in their absence.

Wallace's quarrels with Mortimer and Pictou were economic and political, but they also reflected his religious and educational interests. An intensely ambitious and wealthy placeman, he maintained a richly prejudiced loyalty to the Church of Scotland, albeit the Kirk would not establish a single presbytery in the province until 1823. He sent his sons to King's College and curried favour with whatever bishop of the Church of England was in office. In his conservatism he wished for a shared establishment between Church and Kirk, if the Kirk ever achieved a foothold in Nova Scotia.

Wallace opposed Mortimer, but McCulloch he held in contempt. He shared the view of Lieutenant Governors Wentworth and Dalhousie, who sought a non-sectarian, centralized college. Anything that served as an academy at Pictou was a threat to King's College at Windsor. Wallace represented the polarity between Halifax and Pictou: the one, Loyalist, counter-revolutionary, deeply conservative, and establish-mentarian; the other, a centre of political and social liberalism, and sometimes of radical Dissenting Presbyterianism.

Until Lord Dalhousie, a Kirkman, saw at firsthand the troubled state of King's College, he had toyed with the idea that his preferred non-sectarian college might be brought about by bringing an altered King's to Halifax. But finding nothing to recommend King's, he turned single-mindedly to his own plan, strengthened in his resolve against its possible rival in what he dismissed as "that distant corner," Pictou. Thus, secular and religious issues, mixed motives, and forceful men tangled in the struggle over the prospect of a Pictou academy and college.

Edward Mortimer had been one of those men, generously support-ing Presbytery and McCulloch's school, and figuring prominently in gaining a charter for the academy. Although the building would not open for two years, the first class assembled in the fall of 1817. But it seemed almost a pyrrhic victory, for it intensified and distorted Pictou's spectrum of grievances and ambitions.

Encouraged by the charter, however, McCulloch expanded even more sharply his own ambitions for the Pictou Academy, openly and none too adroitly challenging King's College's exclusivism. The acad-emy might be denied the power to grant a degree – a painful conces-sion in return for political recognition, but MacGregor had long been determined that it would be open to all denominations. Wallace and his colleagues bridled, fearing a Dissenter coalition that would outnumber them by more than three to one. This, and prospects of a Secession-ist in 1816–17, tipped the scales. First, Union gained momentum, and then controversy over the academy blazed higher. MacGregor would be caught up in both issues.

Chapter Fifteen

Onward Christian Soldiers

Michael Wallace's fear of the Seceders' initiatives was well founded. Cooperation had been building between Pictou and Truro. Duncan Campbell later observed, "[There] was a keen and long-continued controversy, in which there was a good deal of Highland ardor exhibited, but which ended in the combatants being very good friends."[1] MacGregor had come to hold Cock in great respect, and relations with Truro were put on an even more promising footing on Cock's death in 1805, when he was succeeded as senior minister by an irenic figure, Rev. Hugh Graham. Graham had been serving since 1799 at Stewiacke and Musquodoboit, where he reported his dislike of administration and squabbling. A quiet man of stamina and purpose, like James he moved about on mission as often as he could manage.[2] Their mutual interests and regard would deepen.

Graham's disjointed musings to his home family (they could not be called letters) suggest a troubled, unhappy man, questioning his role in "this distant and destitute corner of the vineyard." Yet he had served well and by 1810 was an experienced frontier preacher of MacGregor's age and length of service. If he lacked James's brilliance and boldness, he showed a dogged tenacity and great conscientiousness in fulfilling his ministry. Patterson describes him as "a man of kindred spirit," although at first he had been sceptical of James – until he saw that it was compassion not aggression that drove MacGregor. For some time Graham played an almost disinterested part in his presbytery's affairs,[3] but as relations with James and his colleagues warmed in the move towards Union, he became more content, for he had always deplored the province's sectarian bickering. In time he played an active, mediating role as Truro and Pictou shadow-boxed their way towards Union.

Thomas McCulloch and Graham, however, had little contact, for McCulloch was not an itinerant. During the three and one-half years it took to replace Alex Dick, with John Brown's help from time to time, MacGregor and Graham worked as a team to supply Douglas. Together they eclipsed territorial rivalry, carrying Douglas through a difficult adjustment in a spirit of cooperation that portended well for Seceder Union. They also shared a commitment to education: Since 1808 they had jointly imported books from the British and Foreign Bible Society, and both had long worked in their respective private school "rooms." Both were also initiators of their agricultural societies, sharing ideas on experimentation. Later, Graham brought great support to Pictou Academy, after working amicably with James and his colleagues in the move to Seceder Union.[4]

However, their connections ran closer and deeper. Graham had grown up on a farm in the Bathgate district, and his married sister, Margaret Hamilton, lived in nearby Whitburn, where her husband, William, was a leader in the Burgher church. Margaret and Janet Gordon MacGregor had been friends in this village that was notable for the lack of friction between Burghers and Anti-Burghers at a time when Seceder differences were unresolved in other parts of Scotland. Hugh Graham corresponded with Margaret's husband, William Hamilton, who was a senior lay aide to Whitburn's engaging Burgher minister, Rev. John Brown (grandson of the renowned Rev. John Brown of Haddington). Indeed, Whitburn's John Brown and Archibald Bruce dealt with each other almost as colleagues – so close that Bruce directed that Brown and MacGregor should be joint executors of his will, which included a bequest to his niece, Janet Auld Gordon MacGregor. During this period Brown wrote to James expressing his regard for Hugh Graham, his "dear worthy friend," and observing that at Whitburn the Secessionists were already "in a fair way of coalescing into one body."[5]

Thus, circumstances, common friendships, and shared goals brought Graham and MacGregor together as their churches broadened out at home in Scotland and in Nova Scotia. Talk of Union would progress more amicably, smoothed by sharing stories of the charming Brown, the eccentric Bruce, and life in West Lothian, stories in which Janet could engage with an intimate knowledge and a lively interest.[6]

Hugh Graham's coming to Stewiacke and Musquodoboit also reduced James's burden as they ministered in harmony. Thus, it was not by chance that as Cock's successor, Graham took the lead among the Burghers in closing the gap between Truro and what he called

"Mr. McGregor's church," Pictou Presbytery.[7] John Keir affirmed Graham's critical role in seeking Union.[8]

But softening took place in other respects. Hugh Graham's appearance at Stewiacke might have alarmed Duncan Ross, who had supplied his wife's village for thirteen Sabbaths a year, ordaining elders and dispensing the sacrament. Still, a large Burgher wing of his flock – probably those baptized by Daniel Cock – now indicated respectfully that they wanted to return to the nearby and highly regarded Hugh Graham. In the event, determined to do nothing to reopen the past, Pictou Presbytery and Ross agreed that he should step aside graciously, even to urging the balance to go over to Graham. The gesture was not lost on Graham, and his willingness to work with Pictou increased accordingly.

By 1816, as John Keir reported, Pictou was ready to explore a union with Truro, centred on their respective senior clergy, MacGregor and Graham. Accordingly, MacGregor and his associates invited the attendance of Burgher, Anti-Burgher, and Congregationalist clergy at the ordination of an Anti-Burgher minister, Rev. John Cassilis, at Windsor – directly under the nose of King's College – the more so because some considered Cassilis to be Kirk or even Church of England! Their other purpose while attending the ceremony was to explore the prospects for Seceder Union and for cooperation with the Congregationalists.

But powerful lay support also drove them together. For example, one Truro layman, James Kent, who had been in at Halifax's founding and later moved to Truro to become the justice of the peace and an activist, rallied to the ecumenical spirit and to the prospect of the liberalization of education. This familiarity was no doubt fostered by his sharing with MacGregor reminiscences of his birthplace, Alloa, which James and his father had known so well. Thus, in various ways, a consensus was developing that would forward the prospects in Nova Scotia for broader Dissenter education and a more generous Seceder Presbyterianism.[9]

At Windsor it had been agreed to advance Union quickly, but progress was slowed at Pictou by the effects of current Highland Kirk immigration. In James's Lower River church his authority was being undermined by hostility from Kirkmen and ministers, his high profile attracting attention and opposition. Donald MacKay and Robert Marshall urged him to wait for the congregation to return to their senses, but instead he brought his foes to account in an impassioned sermon, one that left him and his audience in tears. Some later wrote apologetically for "our being unfectionate [*sic*],"[10] but although James was forgiving, he remained cautious, preaching in English but writing his text in Gaelic to confound those who would misquote him. Ironically, these confrontations probably advanced Union by rallying supporters to the founder, who was becoming the more resolved to work towards achieving Union and establishing the academy.

He reported to John Keir that a committee struck at Windsor had produced "the best plan for extending and perpetuating the Church here; and especially a Gospel Ministry." Ross and McCulloch were two of three on the committee, reflecting the respect accorded Pictou – or its force of numbers. Peter Waite claims that McCulloch "drew adrenalin from the vitality of his hatreds." But he usually regretted his abrasive temperament, and Ross's and James's affable ways often softened him. When, however, he recklessly proposed that all Dissenters, not just Presbyterians, should join the Academy movement, wiser heads, including James, knowing conservative rural Nova Scotia, counselled one step at a time.

Then, in 1817, under Graham's leadership, at Truro they debated an eleven-point plan for Union that Graham had drafted. Ten points emerged, Union was accepted, and a first synod was proposed for Truro on 13 July 1817.

Pictou negotiated a few small changes, and on 3 August in Truro the first synod of the "Presbyterian Church of Nova Scotia" (PCNS) assembled, consisting of three presbyteries: Halifax, Truro, and Pictou, although Halifax was largely nominal. New boundaries were drawn to include Brown's Londonderry and Crowe's Douglas in Truro Presbytery, which thus relieved the overextended Pictou. In 1821 a presbytery would be announced for Prince Edward Island, with John Keir as founding moderator. Keir maintained close ties with the PCNS and with MacGregor, replacing McCulloch as professor of divinity on McCulloch's death in 1843. Links to the PCNS remained strong. Not much later, New Brunswick formed a presbytery of its own. Union, it seemed, was everywhere in the air.

Twenty ministers and elders joined the new Nova Scotia synod, although from Halifax, where the church was imploding , only a single Halifax delegate appeared. Elsewhere, a few individuals and congregations entered grudgingly or not at all. But most had agreed – and with that, Pictou's worst problems of supply were eased. Union had been launched, the ship was underway, albeit the pumps were working hard.

Hugh Graham had played a key role in negotiations leading up to Union, but MacGregor was chosen unanimously as first moderator. Graham was not drawn to administration and had often deferred to James Robson, minister at Halifax until Robson moved to Truro to carry a heavy administrative load as clerk of Synod. Still, Graham brought steady support to Union and to the Academy at Pictou.

When Synod struck a committee to study how to advance Union, however, its members were all Pictou men – MacGregor, McCulloch, Ross, and the ruling elder, John MacLean. McCulloch drafted the report, from which several proposals familiar to Pictonians emerged: seminars at Presbytery meetings, better-organized visitations and examinations, ministerial teams in poorer regions, a synodical press, and a Presbyterian college at Pictou. It was almost a test of how far the Union principle could be carried under Pictou's colours.

MacGregor had already written to Scotland for cost estimates and to solicit support for a printing press.[11] Now he even wrote to Gaelic-speaking Highland Kirk ministers, inviting them to send missionaries into all corners of the province, even into his own domain.[12] This bold proposal was probably his own, for he had already posted several letters on the progress of the Union negotiations, suggesting that they join this broad movement. His letters were directed among others to Dr. Macdonald of Ferintosh, who ten years earlier had been associated with a great revival at Muthill in James's old parish and who would later join the Disruption in 1843; to Rev. MacIntosh, of Tain, a prominent evangelical; Dr. John Kennedy, of Killearnan and Dingwall; and Mr Stewart, also of Dingwall (both of the latter being Highland evangelical preachers of great renown). Synod's agreement to support this initiative probably reflects James's generosity, his broad influence, and his euphoria over Union. But a proposal to include Kirkmen would come to haunt them all. They were welcoming a Trojan horse.

In the end, Pictou's initiative and Hugh Graham's support had carried the day, and MacGregor wrote to Keir urging that Island contributions would help ensure that both press and an academy came to Pictou: "[The Island] might be the first to reap the benefit of the Ministers we raise." His vision of Union was clearly centred on Pictou.[13]

Hugh Graham was happy, too, describing the synod of 1819 "a comfortable one," rejoicing that Truro had "joined our church to Mr. McGregor's" and that "the Breach in the Secession Church is in so far repaired and Peace restored."[14] Synod then appointed Graham and MacGregor to prepare plans for consolidating future missions. They proposed a "Domestic Missionary Society," an idea presaging Home Missions and one that James had been developing for some time.[15]

Incidentally, Hugh Graham's goodwill may have been further enhanced in 1818 when his brother, William, emigrating with his family to Stewiacke, through misadventure landed destitute at Pictou. Until forwarding arrangements could be made, they must remain at Pictou, and one whom Hugh Graham later described as "a truly good man" invited William and his family to stay with him while he arranged their transport. The Good Samaritan was Robert Marshall, James's old and beloved elder, and it may be assumed that William relayed to his brother a tribute to the saintly Robert Marshall and an account of Robert's veneration of MacGregor.[16] In 1824 MacGregor was re-elected moderator. The man often accused of being "divisive" was reaffirmed by his peers as the symbol of their unity.[17]

To cement their cooperative spirit, both presbyteries proposed to share new mission fields, and the leaders set the example: MacGregor and Rev. John Waddell took Sherbrooke; Hugh Graham and Rev. John Laidlaw, Sheet Harbour. In 1818, although James had founded the congregation at Glenelg and The Forks, he yielded to the former Burgher Rev. Alexander Lewis, now PCNS. Many recent St Marys emigrants were Kirkmen, and receiving no assistance from their church, they came over to Lewis.[18]

In Synod's first two years, although Archibald Bruce had died in 1816, five more ministers came to Pictou Presbytery from Scottish universities and divinity schools. In August 1817 Keir and MacGregor attended an installation at Miramichi,[19] but New Brunswick was on the brink of its own presbyterial and synodical system. In 1817, Rev. John Liddell arrived at Amherst; Rev. Andrew Kerr assumed the Fundy shore at Economy, east of Parrsboro; and Rev. John MacKinlay joined McCulloch at Pictou Academy, later succeeding him in the Pictou pulpit. Meanwhile, James heralded the ordination of Cassilis at Windsor as "an extension of the bounds of our church … into the Western part of the Province,"[20] although Rev. Matthew Dripps had been serving for some time at St. John's Presbyterian in Shelburne. But for MacGregor, there were always new fields, and now with fifteen colleagues and many new elders, his vision would not falter.

Kirkmen saw matters in a very different light. Confronted by Pictou-writ-large, a Western bridgehead at Windsor, and continued Secessionist and Dissenter reinforcements, the Kirk picked up the glove, throwing able clergy into Pictou and raising new opposition to the academy.

Like the clergy reserves in Upper Canada, the academy became the magnet for old resentments and aggressive new strategies.

The activities of the Church of Scotland in the next decade leave little doubt of how uneasy Kirkmen felt in the face of recent Seceder initiatives, but there would be no Kirk Presbytery until 1823, and it was not until 1825 that a "Glasgow Colonial Society" was founded to inaugurate Kirk missions to British North America. Meanwhile, in Nova Scotia, ultramontane Kirkmen urged the Scottish Kirk to open its own missions, especially at the Dissenting citadel of Pictou.[21]

After fifty years of ignoring Pictou and of neglecting its responsibilities to Nova Scotia, Scotland's Kirk reopened an ancient war in the New World. In 1817, a determined Kirk minister, Rev. Donald A. Fraser, had arrived at Pictou, and others would follow. The exception was Rev. John Martin, who appeared at Halifax in 1821: no Moderate or fanatic, he was an evangelical Kirk minister who in time became the Kirk's James MacGregor.

In 1823, the Kirk finally established its first provincial presbytery, at Pictou, and four years later Rev. Robert Burns, secretary of the Glasgow Colonial Society, sent in its first collared troops. It was James's forty-third year on the scene, and Ross and Brown's thirty-second.

It has been suggested that MacGregor refused "to associate with ministers of other Presbyterian denominations,"[22] which we have seen was not the case either personally or officially. His matured cooperation with Cock and Graham – and with Congregationalist leaders and the Baptist clerics Manning and Chipman – belies it. And now MacGregor was straining credulity by challenging his colleagues to welcome Highland Kirk ministers to join their missions and even their presbytery. If James did not consort with many Kirk ministers before 1823, it was because there were next to none. Further, Kirk ministers like Rev. George Gillmore of Horton and Rev. James Munro, who was largely an itinerant, drew close to the PCNS, for both were firm evangelicals, and Gillmore, a friend and associate of Hugh Graham, as Elizabeth Chard reminds us, emphasized that Protestant dissenters should join together in "this time of common danger." Even including only nominal Kirk lay adherents, they were outnumbered by PCNS laymen by more than three to one, and there were at most only two or three Kirk ministers. Indeed, the Kirk made "virtually no effort to serve its members in the New World until moved by the new missionary spirit, which produced the Glasgow Colonial Society in 1825," and the motives behind its secretary, Rev. Robert Burns, in advancing that "missionary spirit" should be carefully considered.[23]

By contrast with the Kirk's unilateral expansionism in the late 1820s, even before Seceder Union in 1817, Seceders on both sides had opened dialogue and earned the support of other Dissenters. Talks with the Congregationalists had been encouraging, and in 1816 a Baptist, William Allen Chipman, backed by Truro's Burgher leader, S.G.W. Archibald, brought to the Legislative Assembly an enabling bill for Pictou Academy, which proposed opening its doors to all denominations.[24]

Council, which acted as the upper house of a bicameral legislature, tried to block the move by requiring that new trustees must be Church of England or Kirkmen, but the assembly rejected the proposal and legitimized Pictou Academy. In 1820, the new PCNS confirmed MacGregor's and McCulloch's hopes that a divinity hall would be opened, although they recklessly located it within the academy itself, presenting a bold target to its opponents.

While MacGregor had long recognized the need to train new clergy at home, founding and devising curricula for academy and divinity hall is generally attributed to Thomas McCulloch. Anne Wood demonstrates how closely they followed Glasgow, which most ministers in the Pictou Presbytery, including McCulloch, had attended.[25] They were not conceived by McCulloch out of whole cloth but had a long history at Glasgow and now a promising one at Pictou.

Nor, as we have seen with MacGregor, Dick, Ross, and Keir, had the Enlightenment interest in science gone unnoticed until McCulloch's appearance. MacGregor followed scientific development in agriculture, geology, astronomy, meteorology, metallurgy, anthropology, and environmentalism; Dick was born into the scientific spirit; thus both men reflected the spirit of Glasgow in both the natural and social sciences – and the city of Glasgow's culture still pervaded Pictou town. So many members of Pictou Presbytery were Glasgow graduates that it is not surprising that science was included in Pictou Academy's liberal curriculum.

Further, like most of the Pictou-based clergy, McCulloch was a graduate of Whitburn, and accordingly Pictou's divinity curriculum was modelled on that of Archibald Bruce. McCulloch did not invent these things: he *impelled* them, as he impelled the Academy movement, once begun. Far from McCulloch's giving the "leadership" to Pictou Presbytery or to the PCNS, his single-minded pursuit of college status for Pictou Academy led him to resign his pulpit, and his forthrightness often proved divisive. Notoriety and leadership are not the same thing. Thomas McCulloch did not lead the Seceder church, before or after

Union, but in his zeal he set it on a course that could result in great achievement and a tragic impasse.

But in 1817 support for the academy was still pouring in: Mortimer gave £100; Ross, MacGregor, and McCulloch each pledged £50; and James again carried the burden of "the begging," raising over £600 in the district. Plans were afoot for expansion, when Union blew the matter into dangerous new dimensions. For the next decade, what appeared as a division over education tore Pictou asunder, but it was aided and abetted by opponents across the province; in truth, it became a cultural, almost a social war.

Many recent immigrants were true Kirkmen, supplemented by a small commando of Kirk ministers aimed at Pictou. Their attacks on the PCNS and its academy far outstripped the opposition of the past. The 1820s would be a decade of turmoil, and they would mark James's declining years. Wider missions and administrative matters fell increasingly into the hands of others, particularly to Rev. John Keir and to the underestimated Rev. Duncan Ross. The specific battle to support the academy was spearheaded by the zealous McCulloch, who, while given much provocation, had a flair for stirring up and inviting acrimony. He was fortunate to have such strong back-up as he went about his task, although his were often Pyrrhic victories of his own making.

In the midst of these alarums, in the summer of 1817 there appeared at West River the ultimate dissident, an autocratic Old Testament prophet, Rev. Norman McLeod, who had broken with every form of Presbyterianism and attracted a huge and fanatical following dubbed the "Normanites." Norman once boasted, "I am so full of the Holy Ghost, that my coat won't button on me."[26]

But his emotionally driven evangelism repelled MacGregor, who spoke of his "making merchandise of souls." He wrote to John Keir: "He is not licensed, but he has the Call of the Spirit ... I do think him pious, but I fear he is enthusiastic. If he be not he may be useful."[27] "Enthusiasm," or great displays of emotional preaching without long study and sound biblical grounding – whether in Henry Alline, Norman McLeod, or some Calvinistic Methodist – was anathema to a rationalist like MacGregor. On hearing that McLeod was to visit the Island, he warned Keir to prepare for "a great speaker ... He will get three hearers to [the Kirk's] Mr. Fraser's one."[28]

James also wrote anxiously a "Letter to the Friends of the Glasgow Society (In Connection with the Established Church of Scotland) ... " deploring the divisiveness among Presbyterians:

The Academy, Pictou, N.S.

Pictou Academy. (Postcard, ca. 1905, author's collection.)

There is a four-fold zeal in Pictou: 1st, zeal for the Established Church of Scotland; in some this zeal is wonderfully strong. Secondly, zeal for the Presbyterian Church of Nova Scotia. Thirdly, zeal for lukewarmness; and this party are so earnestly set upon it, that neither of the foregoing parties have been able to move them. Fourthly, zeal for Norman McLeod ... [whom] people will go much farther to hear ... than any minister in Pictou. And who is Norman? A self-made preacher, who declares that there is not a Minister of Christ in all the Church of Scotland.[29]

But, the Glasgow Colonial Society ignored James's invitation to cooperate in combatting "lukewarmness" or Norman McLeod. Happily, Norman shortly set sail in his "Ark," followed by hundreds of others, establishing a theocracy at St. Ann, Cape Breton, lasting thirty years before their ultimate hejira to New Zealand.[30]

Meanwhile, with failing health and knowing that he could no longer be the warrior-leader, MacGregor rested great confidence in McCulloch, Ross, and Keir, shifting his focus and showing few signs of slowing down as he picked up the pace of his studies, his charitable activities, and his missions.

Chapter Sixteen

Last Calls

New ministers had been joining Pictou Presbytery for some time. In 1811 Rev. Edward Pidgeon, a Yarmouth Congregationalist, having served on the Island with the London Missionary Society and married a local girl, was admitted to Presbytery and joined John Keir in the Island mission field.[1] Pidgeon promised continuity, for MacGregor's visits to the Island would be interrupted by American privateer attacks in the coming war with the United States.

In 1815 there arrived Rev. William Patrick of Stirling. At forty-four, Patrick had served several years at Lockerby,[2] and Ross and MacGregor welcomed him as another agricultural Improver. He was the seventh Bruce alumnus, a strong Unionist in Scotland , and in Nova Scotia, he would promote Union and relieve James from thirty years of serving Merigomish.

In the following year, three more ministers appeared, the ablest being Rev. John McKinlay, a scholarly graduate of Glasgow and of Archibald Bruce (who died in this year, 1816). Working with McCulloch in classics and mathematics, McKinlay would succeed him in the pulpit in 1824. Thus, Presbytery continued to grow despite the transfer of Londonderry and Douglas to Truro. Further, the first locally trained young men were beginning to emerge from the divinity school.

James's health had been restored, and despite a growing family at home,[3] he returned to his lengthy missions, visiting Pidgeon and Keir in 1815 and in four of the next six years opening new missions in the east of the Island. From the 1815 mission he returned so invigorated that he set out immediately on his longest journey ever, six weeks to Passamaquoddy Bay on the undefined border with Maine. There, a body of Highlanders at Scoodic (St Stephen), many with only the Gaelic, had been begging his attention. Ignored by government, they had seldom seen a minister.[4] James sailed from Windsor to Saint John and then travelled to his destination on horseback.

Presbytery had indulged its founder in agreeing to the trip, but it could not agree to incorporate a place so distant. Still, the old shepherd would seek the lost lamb, and these sheep preferred to remain 100 per cent British wool. The border went undefined until 1848, and they probably saw in James's visit an affirmation of the British connection. On the return journey, he visited several of the other "Saint ports'" along the Fundy – St Andrew's, St George, Saint John, but not St Martins – feeding his dream that the Maritimes could be supplied from or centred on Pictou, but it would be hard to bring off. He made no further visits to Scoodic, but he had given them hope. Presbytery remained in contact, but in 1820 the prospect of a New Brunswick presbytery offered a nearer alternative.

In 1818 he visited Cape Breton again when it was about to be reabsorbed into Nova Scotia.[5] Travelling up the west coast, he served a rush of post-war immigrants: most in the district were Scots Catholics, but there were Presbyterians at Mabou, Port Hood, and Margaree. Many had come with some means, for the collapse of the kelp trade and of the cottars' last hope was still a decade off. Travelling up the glens, he preached and baptized, "making straight the way for Presbyterianism in Cape Breton,"[6] but Catholic families welcomed and billeted him, too, in the Highland way. The west coast, Lake Ainslie and Margaree districts were being settled and becoming proud, as one Presbyterian minister declaimed:

> Above all, O Lord, do we thank Thee for the Gut of Canso, thine own body of water, which separateth us from the wickedness that lies beyond![7]

Then travelling southeast, he visited St Peter's, West River, and River Inhabitants, where he found great changes everywhere, but after Douglas he must have known that Pictou would overreach itself trying to absorb Cape Breton. He had grown too old to undertake the mission himself, and Presbytery was swamped by pressures arising from the struggle over the academy. Nonetheless, acting through his good offices, Mabou and Port Hood attracted a Scottish licentiate and the academy sent two of its first divinity graduates: Hugh Dunbar and Hugh Ross[8] to his assistance.

Elsewhere, although James noted that most immigrants went "to Canada – so distant and disconnected," natives and immigrants were moving across the interior hills into the St Marys valley to tidewater. There, they began filling the Garden of Eden, Glenelg, and the vale of Lochaber, which had once been called "College Lake," a reserve to endow King's College. Sherbrooke village was entering its great logging and shipbuilding years,[9] and in ten years Pictou's frontier would be closed.

Many of the newcomers were Gaelic-speaking northern Highlanders, others from parts of Scotland least touched by the Secession or even by Protestantism. The Kirkmen among them challenged the PCNS, and James acknowledged that events were catching up with him:

> Great are the changes taking place in the Highlands. Different denominations, not excepting the Baptists, find a footing in some of the wildest parts of them. But that dispensation of Providence which scatters the Highlanders over the face of the earth, as it did the Jews, is to me strange and mysterious.[10]

James laboured hard in the backcountry, cooperating with Truro, even ready to work with Kirk missionaries, had there been any. The Truro-Pictou alliance, however, could not mollify some of those who looked insistently for Kirk ministers. For James, the wheel had come full circle: he was fighting again his early battles – and his father's.

But the Kirk's shadow was mitigated by local circumstances. Pioneers have much to learn from native people and experienced settlers, and many in St Marys were sons and daughters of Truro, Musquodoboit, and East River. The Pictonians had left home following timber as the prospects of farming were undermined by clear-cutting. Those from Truro followed their town's restless, ambitious path.

MacGregor's connection with St Marys had begun in 1809, when he had conducted the wedding of the first couple recorded in the St Marys Register of Marriages.[11] In 1815 he appeared again and might have hesitated in approaching the district's most powerful landholder, David Archibald III, "Clerk David," son of Colonel David, the leading Truro slaveholder whom James had once opposed so fiercely.[12] Now young David was opening a 7,000-acre tract, including most of today's Sherbrooke and much land upstream. His support of James's mission would be invaluable, and in truth they got on cordially.[13] For by 1815, Union was the watchword and old jars had been forgotten. On this new frontier squabbles over truth and turf seemed remote. Clerk David welcomed James as he had been received by other Archibalds at

Kemptown and Musquodoboit,[14] and as Clerk David would host Joe Howe a decade later.[15] Besides, for long stretches men like James and Howe were often the only visitors, and both were always entertaining guests.

Wading across the St Marys River sixteen times on a primitive trail was not easy for a man of James's years, however, but his zeal made it hard for him to accept the waning of his powers. His spirit was with these pioneers in a replay of his earliest adventures.[16] Seemingly often worn down by a life of taxing missions, he would rally at St Marys as he always did.

One of his firmest upriver advocates in the St Marys district was Alex MacKay, the first post-war farmer and lumberer to settle the valley from East River. Alex was Donald's nephew, which must recommend him. A man bursting with energy, he had brought his wife, seven children, and all their possessions on four horses to the upper valley, where he soon became an outstanding timber man. But he was also a legend as "The Strongest Man in Nova Scotia," having once run down and corralled a young caribou, an achievement hailed even by the Mi'kmaq.[17] Further, Alex had a unique place in James's heart, for at nineteen he had been the young groomsman and diplomat who had accompanied him to Halifax on his marriage to Ann MacKay. Their reunion brought MacGregor powerful support on the flourishing St Marys–Sherbrooke frontier. Meanwhile, he found similar support in another mission district.

After 1810, James regularly visited Chedabucto, noted for farming, fishing, lumbering, and shipping out of Loyalist Guysborough, east of Antigonish. Its founders had served under Sir Guy Carleton, commander-in-chief of retiring British forces and Loyalists at New York, after the Revolutionary War. One late officer, Thomas Cutler, had received a huge river grant and extensive waterfront property.[18] Cutler (Yale '71) had become magistrate, town clerk, judge of the Inferior Court of Common Pleas, lieutenant-colonel of militia and MLA. His thriving legal practice and success as general merchant and shipper earned him the title "King Cutler," and he was described as "a man of great force and domineering."[19] Friendship with local leaders was invaluable to James until he could assign a "homespun," a permanent minister.[20]

As vice-president of the Guysborough and Manchester Farmer Society, Cutler had much in common with James. His son, Robert, now MLA, brought other useful connections, for his fellow MLA for Guysborough was a progressive Pictou lawyer, Thomas Dickson of the powerful Onslow clan, near Truro. Dickson was a brother-in-law of S.G.W. Archibald, Truro's improver-politician and Pictou Academy's staunch supporter. At Pictou, Dickson attended McCulloch's church and married Sarah Ann Patterson. Back in Onslow, his brothers were also assemblymen, improvers, and protégés of Archibald. In short, as missionary and reformer, James drew advantage from these complex social and economic links.

Although a practising lawyer and politician, Thomas Dickson had kept his Onslow holdings, opening the first oatmeal flour mill in Nova Scotia. Soon eighteen such mills were begun across the North Shore, and Lord Dalhousie declared proudly that the "whole east half of the province uses mills for oatmeal cake and porridge instead of fine American flour bread." The Cutlers and Dickson made James's path easier.[21]

For James, however, the central figure at Guysborough was Duncan McColl, who had married King Cutler's daughter, Caroline.[22] McColl, a bright young man from Argyllshire, had profited from his older brother's connections as aide-de-camp to the lieutenant governor in Halifax and won the Guysborough Customs Office. The McColls' imposing house stood just above Duncan's wharves, where Caroline raised fifteen children, home-teaching them and several others in the big kitchen while spinning, cooking, and baking bread in an outdoor oven.

McColl was a shrewd man with a fine sense of politics. Whatever his Old Country affiliation, he attended the Church of England. He and James shared memories of Argyle, and Duncan must have enjoyed James's reaction when, on first entering the McColl drawing room, he found between the tall windows facing the harbour a life-size wall painting of Rob Roy MacGregor in full Highland dress. Despite his attachment to the Church of England, Duncan McColl contributed generously to MacGregor's mission.

Years later, James's youngest son, Peter Gordon MacGregor, began his ministry in Guysborough, marrying McColl's daughter, Caroline. They were married by Rev. John Campbell, who had succeeded James at Sherbrooke after marrying Isabella MacGregor, James's oldest daughter with Janet Gordon. Circles within circles. If there was a family compact at Halifax associated with the Church of England and its establishmentarian allies, its Dissenter parallel in eastern Nova Scotia was growing at St Marys, Guysborough, Pictou, and Truro. The Truro-Onslow connection with the Archibalds and the Dicksons reinforced this cooperation and eventually contributed to an early liberal reformist political movement. The eastern compact centred on the PCNS, having in common: blood, intermarriage, and an interest in education, scientific agriculture, and improved public service like transportation and farm support. In all of these, James's voice was heard, for he was not afraid to enter politics behind the scenes, as he had done for Edward Mortimer. Networking was food and drink to him, and it was a short step from talk of cabbages to talk of kings.

These contacts between the eastern agrarian reformers were further advanced in 1824 when John Young, "Agricola," became co-MLA for Guysborough. To James, allying with those with such mutual interests and activities was a natural extension of the minister's role in bringing together applied science, education, and the community.

In 1821, MacGregor made his last visit to Prince Edward Island, presiding at three official functions. The first was the ordination of yet another Perthshire man, Rev. William MacGregor, no relation but a Bruce alumnus with fourteen years of missions behind him.[23] Second was the bittersweet task of easing in a successor to the "erratic" Edward Pidgeon. The third was the establishment of an Island presbytery under John Keir. Ties with Pictou remained strong, however, for as Duncan Campbell observed, "Dr. MacGregor planted; Keir watered; and others reaped."[24]

The Island mission had found its feet just as James's were beginning to falter. The 1821 visit marked the end of his thirty-five years of distant missions. Henceforth he confined himself to Pictou and St Marys.[25] Apart from John Wentworth as surveyor general and governor, J.F.W. DesBarres as marine surveyor, and Henry Alline as itinerant evangelist, it is unlikely that anyone in his lifetime was so widely travelled across the region as MacGregor, or by such diverse means. His goal had remained the same: not conversion but affirmation of one's faith, to provide pastoral care and encourage faith, to serve souls and save sinners; and to advance education and improvement in society and the individual. Although he could be eloquent, his message was usually plain, his sermons unadorned. He spoke from the Book and the heart.

Chapter Seventeen

Erring Shepherds

Seceder Union alarmed Kirkmen, making worse the conflict at Pictou
between them and the Seceders. The central issue was Pictou Academy,
but the roots of the social war were religious and cultural. Campbell
and MacLean suggest that the friction "was in some ways beneficial,
for the tension was creative, new ideas did develop, discussion flowed
and the intellectual tone was raised to a high standard."[1] Perhaps, but
as in modern Belfast, streets were divided by fences, and as Joe Howe
satirized,

> But mercy preserve us, we are riding into Pictou with as much ease and
> as little ceremony as we would into Chezetcook [*sic*], or the Dutch Village.
> Into Pictou! That seat of disaffection and bad government – that abode of
> patriots and den of radicalism – that nook where the spirit of party sits,
> nursing her wrath to keep it warm, during ten months of the year, in order
> to disturb the Legislature all the other two. Into Pictou, that cradle of lib-
> erty – from whence, after strangling the serpents that would have crushed
> her, she is to walk abroad over the four quarters of the globe, regenerating
> and disenthralling mankind. Into Pictou, where it is a mortal offence to …
> take a pinch of another's mull – and where, as the Yankees have it, it is
> impossible to live upon the fence; or in fact to live at all, without "going
> the whole Hog" with one of the parties into which its society is divided.
> The Lord only knows whether we may ever live to come out, but here we
> go merrily in – we may be burned by the Antiburghers, or eaten without
> salt by the Highlanders, but our "foot is in our native soil, and our name
> is –" no matter what; having got to the threshold of Pictou. We are not to
> be frightened out of a peep, by all the hobgoblins that the diseased imagi-
> nations of the timid and uproarious have conjured upon our path.[2]

In rural areas, sectarian issues were less intense, perhaps because there was less concern about the academy and because the frontier called for cooperation.

Synod had earned respect well beyond Pictou; Pictou's relations with Truro were cordial; Cobequid and Prince Edward Island were well served; Douglas was calm; and the PCNS was reaching out to Congregationalists and Baptists. But the academy issue clouded Secessionist strategy, for their potential allies – Congregationalists, Baptists, and Methodists – were wary of a divided Presbyterian educational initiative, and the arrival of a firebrand Kirk minister younger than MacGregor himself had been on his arrival thirty years before deepened divisions. McCulloch was well matched by the Rev. Donald A Fraser, and the academy was open to annual attack in the Legislative Assembly as each year the members debated government support.

In nineteenth-century Nova Scotia, after the passage of the 1811 Grammar Schools Act, having an established local grammar school was acknowledged as a symbol of a town's or district's sense of progress and of its achievement. Moreover, as Pictou Academy was conceived and had been authorized by the legislature in 1816 in the Pictou Academy Act, it could become a unique unifying factor for the North Shore and an encouragement to Dissenters throughout the province. It was a bold plan, and its foundation in the established tradition of Scottish education raised its profile, challenging the hegemony of the faltering King's College. Indeed, so carefully were plans developed for the nature and scope of its teaching – with an uncommon attention to science – that it had every chance of displacing King's College's enfeoffment. Even Rev. Archibald Gray, Andrew Brown's successor at Mather's Church, defying Michael Wallace and other lay Kirkmen at Halifax, supported Pictou's plans for an academy and was a member of the original Board. But like the Clergy Reserves of Upper Canada, the academy also stood in danger of becoming a kind of Aunt Sally against which any kind of attack might be mounted. Certainly it would enflame passions.

Resentment and recrimination festered steadily, especially in the ranks of Church of England and Kirk adherents in the capital. In a submission to Glasgow in May 1819, MacGregor, McCulloch, and Ross complained to Synod of Anglican support for the Kirk: "While the Church of Scotland is recognized as the bride, the Secession Church is denominated a harlot."[3]

MacGregor was torn: with more time now, he might look forward to a return to his studies and his poetry, and to finding less direct ways of promoting church, academy, and community. But he must also support McCulloch, who was facing a war of which as late as May 1819 he seems hardly to have been aware. Writing to Rev. John Buist's successor, Dr. John Mitchell of Anderston, he observed, "The established Church [of England] here now hate me with all their might, but they act only by private intrigue."[4]

But not long after, the Kirk's new Glasgow Colonial Society launched an all-out campaign that was no "private intrigue." The Kirk had determined to become a real presence in Nova Scotia, directing its ablest clergy to Pictou, where, as Anne Wood has set out so vividly, their accusations and encroachments became bolder and increasingly irresponsible.[5]

Whether by the society's design or his own, Rev. Donald A. Fraser stepped up his attacks, acting as an enforcer, ready to unseat James in his own church. Fearing that such tactics would bring down the academy, Presbytery resolved to send McCulloch home to raise funds and try to mend fences over issues such as missions and the academy with the society's irascible secretary, Rev. Robert Burns. But McCulloch was hardly fitted by temperament to succeed in either assignment.

Meanwhile, the Glasgow Society offered supplementary stipends of £50 to "needy parishes," and James feared that wavering or indigent congregations might be tempted. The Kirk had never supported voluntarism, he observed, "To make a poor enough mouth was all that was thought requisite to ensure the Society's bounty."[6] By contrast, "The Seceder ministers have the alms by the will of their hearers."[7] Raising the oldest Seceder issue, patronage, he pictured the Kirk as a threat to local autonomy because its subventions were governed by distant Scottish patrons. But his voice was lost in the storm, and as the decade drew to an end, further friction developed.

In a remarkably conciliatory gesture, however – perhaps through James's influence, certainly not McCulloch's – the Seceder churches in the Upper Settlement offered to share their church building with the local Kirkmen, who had not yet built their own. In 1824, partly from concern over James's health, Presbytery sent a brave young graduate, Angus McGillivray, to supply the Upper congregation. Trouble erupted immediately, however, for McGillivray was one of the earliest divinity graduates, and ardent Kirkmen saw in him the threat of a growing cadre of seminary reinforcements. Questioning his credentials, they threatened a lawsuit, claiming that his coming infringed on their rights, although they were using the church by invitation. James prepared a broadside, and when McCulloch asked if he had sent "one of your soft, slippery answers," he began to read it until McCulloch broke in with a laugh, "That's enough!"

Still, at McGillivray's induction, although the suit had been abandoned, one Kirkman shouted, "I protest in the name of the Church of Scotland against your marrying that man to this church!" James rose and this time replied softly, "Oh, we do not marry him to the walls of the church, it is to the people."[8]

He would not live to endure the turmoil of the 1830 "Brandy" election or the formation in 1833 of the Kirk Synod.[9] Both confirmed a vicious Kulturkampf, with men from both sides pouring into Pictou for days of brawling and killing, both sides carrying cudgels. Overzealous Kirk supporters wore bonnets and chanted the old slogan: "Fear God, vote Tory, and hate the Anti-Burghers." For, Kirkmen saw in Union the triumph by one branch of the secession over the other, a Seceder secession. And by that time, James was gone.

His worst battle had been in his own congregation in 1816, when he had confounded his critics with his emotional rhetoric, restoring order and winning the admiration of moderate Kirkmen. One of these was James Fraser, who had come to Upper East River as schoolteacher and Kirk catechist. MacGregor was a trustee of Fraser's school. Long after, writing from London, Upper Canada,[10] Fraser left a remarkably detached memoir:

> [We] had no minister ... I would ... lead them [at the schoolhouse] ... for Dr. MacGregor was to preach to them one Sabbath in every month ... [A] great division came between the people ... for they were all, before they left Scotland of the Established Church of Scotland, and never saw seceders ... [S]ome of the people liked [MacGregor] well, for he ... laboured very faithfully ... [They] began a College in Pictou, and was doing well, and the Government of Halifax gave 400 pounds to help them, and all was going on cute and quiet for years. But ... a minister or two came from the Established church [Revs. D.A. Fraser and K.J. Mackenzie] and preached boldly, and showed the people that they were ... made into seceders unknown to themselves ... and some of them put the question [to MacGregor], "why did you not tell us that you were a seceder?" He answered, "Would it not be time enough when you would ask me of it?"[11]

Fraser continues:

> I felt sorry ... for the people who were all Highland Scotch were divided, almost every second family ... Although I never saw any seceder in

Scotland, still I could like Dr. MacGregor and went regular to hear him ...
some of them would like that I would keep meeting at the school house
when he would be in the church, but I never yielded to that, for I was
striving to give ... the example of love and peace. Although I could not
join or take Sacrament with the secession ... I went the round of Catechist
... and was accepted in every Seceder's house, so I was socially in friendly
acquaintanceship with [MacGregor] and his people for the ten years I was
in Nova Scotia.[12]

Fraser's distress led him to consider moving, but two men – a Seceder
and a Kirkman – offered him some good farmland close by the schoolhouse if he would stay. He agreed, joining James as a catechist along the
St Marys River. Soon, however, another determined Kirk minister, Rev.
John McRae, tested his patience too far:

Some ... were [out] ... to destroy the secession College ... [Two of our
ministers] went into Halifax to watch and plead ... Mr. McRae pitched
on me to ... search [support] for the Established Party ... On the road at
night I met my opponent of the secession party, a good man I believe,
but we stood a long time, and both smart enough for argument. Law was
on my side, but I believed right was on his ... But when I parted from
Duncan Cameron, I could not quench my own conscience and had a bitter night of it, and a new light upon the matter. On Sabbath morning ... I
gave my papers to Rev. McRae, and ... he called us together for money to
help the [lobbyists] ... I arose immediately ... took out a quarter and told
him, "Although this shilling would pay the whole sum, you will not get it
from me. Why destroy their college, why don't you make a college of your
own?" Under great astonishment he said "I thought you would be the last
man to speak that way." I told him I took the honour of being the first ...
And after that he had to dismiss the people without getting a copper ...
[W]e made up our minds to go to [Upper Canada].[13]

An English soldier-engineer, William Scarth Moorsom, passed
through Pictou in this period and sniffed less generously:

I believe all the feuds of all the Macs from A to Z ... have emigrated from
their ancient soil in order to concentrate their violence within the precincts
of Pictou ... Pity it is, that a little population which has plenty of fish to
pickle outside of its harbour's mouth, and plenty of forest to clear, and
of land to cultivate ... should distract its brain with political arguments

upon abstract questions of privilege and party squabbles for sectarian aggrandizement.[14]

Susan Buggey blames McCulloch for his "total commitment to the [academy's] promotion and defence by whatever means … [It] lay at the root of the inflexibility which dominated the parties in the Pictou Academy dispute,"[15] but Anne Wood instances more tellingly the Kirk Presbytery's extraordinarily provocative measures.[16] And the overriding issue was the status of the new school: academy or college?

In his last years as he began to fail, James was often removed from the most bitter public controversies, moderating where he could and urging Synod to raise funds for the academy. He tutored divinity students in Hebrew and counselled others. But he also turned to other causes – and to great productivity. Those literary, scientific, agricultural, and charitable ventures, along with his continued commitment to the academy and the Gospel, remain to be examined.

Chapter Eighteen

The Dissenter as Moderator

MacGregor's last sixteen years were extraordinarily productive in view of his age and declining health. His long missions drew to a close, but he adapted readily to other projects. Pictou Academy survived on hotly contested annual government grants, and until Edward Mortimer's death in 1819 he and James raised £2,000 in Pictou town alone. At Synod's request, James and Duncan Ross prepared a "Memorial" asking the lieutenant governor for uninterrupted support for the academy and an endowment of a professorship of divinity "for the Presbyterian Church of Nova Scotia." It was a bold stroke, but Dalhousie, a Kirkman, was ambitious for his own college and denied both requests.[1]

James now had more time to reflect, to enjoy his children, to write, to farm, and to serve the church in new directions. During this period he wrote several addresses, three of which illustrate his persistent support of missions and education, the themes that most mark his ministry.

The tone of the first contrasts with that of McCulloch's disastrous mission to Scotland.[2] During an eighteen-month absence, McCulloch had unilaterally prepared a "Memorial" to the Scottish Kirk summing up all the best arguments for a liberal-based academy and divinity hall at Pictou, but in highly confrontational language, this address being one of what he called "my furious philipics [*sic*]."[3] With this rocket he signalled outright war, and his Scottish supporters formed an extravagantly named "Glasgow Society for Promoting the Interests of Religion and Liberal Education among the Settlers of the North American Provinces." The two societies and their central, strong personalities – Robert Burns, secretary of the Glasgow Colonial Society (GCS), and Thomas McCulloch – sharpened the struggle between the Scottish Kirk and the PCNS.

By contrast, as Moderator, James tried to reduce the conflict. In 1824 he wrote to "the United Secession Synod [of Scotland] in behalf of The Literary Institution [Academy] at Pictou."[4] Stressing the urgent need for general education and outside support, he reviewed the pattern of recent immigration with remarkable candour:

> The value of education is not understood in British America ... Even in Pictou where our chief strength lies, the effective friends of the Academy are not what you would imagine from its population. Were its whole population from the Lowlands of Scotland, ... we would carry on pretty well without foreign aid ... But ... the majority ... consists of emigrants from the counties of Inverness, Ross, and Sutherland ... Presbyterians [Kirkmen] by birth, yet there is a necessity of forming societies in the Lowlands to assist them in common school education in their native country ... [T]hey will need the same assistance here ... Something may be expected of their descendants, for they will be scholars, but of themselves little or nothing.[5]

He linked the divinity hall, however, to a larger goal: "But it is not merely a Divinity Hall ... We wish for the means of a liberal education to enable our descendants to fill every useful office in the society respectably, as well as that of the ministry."[6]

This was the spirit of Glasgow's Enlightenment, of John Millar, of Archibald Bruce, of Jacob Drummond's social harmony, and of John Witherspoon at Princeton, whose aim had been to produce "ornaments of the State as well as the Church." An earlier and more philosophic Thomas McCulloch had spoken similarly at the opening of the academy, arguing that a liberal education was not an end in itself but that it could affect the kind of society and governance a community or nation enjoyed.

MacGregor, McCulloch, Ross, Keir, Graham and the others were as one in this goal.[7] They differed in approach, but Synod did little to meet their requests.

MacGregor's second initiative was to write diplomatically a letter to Burns and the GCS to be delivered by McCulloch's hand, but he seems not to have done so. No response remains in the records. In it James adopted a conciliatory tone: "Though my sentiments may not coincide wholly with your views, still they may be of some benefit."[8] Reminding Kirkmen of their common Presbyterianism, he alerted them to Presbyterian "feebleness" in New Brunswick. He suggested five mission fields where Kirkmen and Secessionists need not conflict – indeed, where the Kirk could pursue its own goals. He had visited them all: Scoodic, St Andrew's, Nashwaak, Miramichi, and Cape Breton, which was experiencing heavy Scottish immigration. It was a territorial trade-off in areas where the sharpest needs for worship were recognized and where the Kirk could anticipate great growth.

True to his earliest principles, James cautioned that they must be ready to establish schools, for schools and churches went hand in hand on the frontier. He ended by suggesting that some might then receive theological training at Pictou. Thus, he would yield the initiative to the Kirk in New Brunswick and Cape Breton, while the PCNS would set the pace in mainland Nova Scotia and continue working closely with John Keir's Island Presbytery.[9] Counselling the Kirk and the GCS to consider the divisive effect of patronage in a new country that was so far free of it, he adverted to its unhappy effects in Scotland. A territorial division, he suggested, would allow both churches to work together towards a common Presbyterian community.[10]

But McCulloch and Burns had left no room for conciliation. It has been claimed that McCulloch had become the "undisputed leader" of the PCNS.[11] Admittedly, he served briefly as moderator between James's two terms, but had he really been "leader," why would he not have continued in the position after James's death, which was not far distant? And why would he leave Pictou and the academy for the lustre of Halifax and Dalhousie College, with its Kirk attachments?

The truth is that McCulloch had been too intemperate for Pictou's moderate presbytery and church. His bitter differences with Rev. Robert Burns of the GCS – a clash between two strongly opposed temperaments – banished the spirit of compromise and alienated many in the district. Academy and seminary were doomed, and regardless of whether MacGregor's letter reached Burns or not, his pleas and Keir's voice of reason and accommodation were lost among whirlwinds of contention.

It is difficult to credit the assertion that "Thomas McCulloch ... *almost single-handedly* built the Pictou Academical Institution and fought its long and losing battle to achieve degree-granting status."[12] Many others had striven to create it – MacGregor, Ross, Keir, Graham, the Baptist Chipman, the Anglican Speaker Robie, Mortimer, the Dicksons, Archibald, and the PCNS generally, lay and ministerial – several of whom did McCulloch's mission work for him – and in the aftermath, when the legislature began to abandon it, those many tried to save it.

Meanwhile, MacGregor proposed a church journal, modelled on *The Christian Magazine*, to which he had long been a columnist. A local journal, however, would better promote PCNS activities. He even received a printing press from his philanthropic correspondent, Mrs. Forbes of Inverness, Scotland.[13] In 1824, however, a newly arrived and bristly Kirk minister, Rev. K.J. MacKenzie, joined the fiery Kirk leader, now moderator of the new Kirk Synod, Rev. Donald Allan Fraser, and together they raised they raised the ante by aiming at a more ambitious and public journal for the Kirk.[14]

Here, however, McCulloch did MacKenzie's work for him, becoming so obdurate that he spiked MacGregor's house-organ project by becoming a hidden columnist for a new Pictou newspaper, *The Colonial Patriot*. Its volatile editor, Jotham Blanchard, McCulloch's former student, persuaded him secretly to substitute as editor during Blanchard's absences. By 1829, rumours of McCulloch's journalistic activities were so strong that he was forced into the open in the pages of the increasingly radical *Colonial Patriot*.[15] Between McCulloch, the *Patriot*, and Howe's *Novascotian*, and the new Kirk journal, the battle between the PCNS and the Kirk would become more entrenched than ever.

But by now McCulloch had moved so beyond compromise that his plans for recruiting *all* Dissenters to the academy's support became too rich for the province's conservative culture, and he was undermining much else on Synod's agenda. Although no longer holding a pulpit, in 1827 he pressured the PCNS to make the pyrrhic sacrifice of foregoing a permanent government grant for the Academy if the government trustees were not removed. It was a vain gesture from one who by his own admission was not a cheerful beggar, habitually leaving to others the arduous task of making collections.

Thus, McCulloch's intransigence scuttled a compromise that might have been built on during the Kirk's time of troubles in the so-called Disruption of the 1840s, when Rev. Thomas Chalmers reprised Ebenezer Erskine's earlier secession from the Kirk, and Pictou would witness a remarkable flight of the recent Kirk clergy to desirable posts now vacated at home. That reduction in forces should have greatly reduced the Kirk Synod's impact on Pictou's fortunes and the academy's. But it was not to be.

Instead, following the election of 1830 and James's death early in the same year, K.J. MacKenzie succeeded where James had not, launching and editing the *Pictou Observer and Eastern Advertiser*. For a decade, then, until the Disruption, the Kirk enjoyed a greatly increased presence in

Pictou while the academy's old, bold prospects slipped away, leaving only a distinguished college preparatory school. The theological college was resurrected for a time at West River under John Keir but in 1860 was transferred to Halifax, much later becoming Pine Hill Divinity Hall of the United Church of Canada – and today's Atlantic School of Theology.

Thus, McCulloch had significantly been the author of his own undoing – and of the academy as originally conceived.

While James lived, however, he remained loyal to the academy. On 28 June 1825 he preached the synod sermon to the PCNS. His text was "The Prosperity of those who Love Jerusalem," from Psalm 122:14.[16] In it he stressed the need for cooperation in domestic missions and that the academy should be located at Pictou.

In McCulloch's absence, MacGregor and Ross assisted Rev. John McKinlay, teaching Latin, Greek, and Hebrew and counselling the students. On 26 January 1826 MacGregor gave a spirited address to the students, seated as at Glasgow in their red merino gowns.[17] Tracing the academy's uniqueness and the importance of education in an ordered society, he praised McCulloch for advancing both. He then told of a current initiative already begun at Glasgow and Edinburgh and adopted that year at London, "where mechanics are turned into a sort of philosophers."[18] This was George Birkbeck's idea of "Mechanics Institutes," an experiment in adult education. MacGregor was always on the cusp of new learning, and five years later, Howe presented the first paper to a Halifax branch.

One stirring passage from MacGregor's address to the students reflected his passion for learning, although it also betrays his anti-Catholicism:

> I believe that without knowledge people cannot be good; neither good Christians nor good citizens; neither good servants to God, nor good neighbours to men; and I believe that this Institution is well calculated to maintain, to increase, and diffuse knowledge.
>
> Gentlemen, we all see this country fast increasing in population ... Without such an institution what will all these millions be? They will be ignorant, they will be poor, they will be slaves, – they will be worse, they will be vicious; for such is the end of every country destitute of learning ... They will not know their own rights, as rational human beings, nor be qualified to assert and defend them. And though we leave them the sweet inheritance of liberty, they will not be able to retain it. They will gradually degenerate into Austrians, Spaniards, and Portugese.[19]

His continuing concern lay in the ignorance of many North Highland immigrants, including Kirkmen and those who were so in name only. Arguing that they threatened the consensus that would yoke education and religion, he feared the loss of a synergy he had long encouraged:

> I can easily excuse the hostility of ... opposers. Neither they nor their fathers ever learned a letter, and many think the suppression of this institution the most effectual method to bring back the good old times when the country was not burdened with schools or learning at all. But it is cruel and unnatural for anyone who knows the benefit of learning to oppose it ... It would give [their children] ignorance, poverty, and degradation, in preference to learning, wealth and character.[20]

In February 1826 he tried to mend fences with the Baptist leader Rev, Edward Manning. For, at McCulloch's request, Manning had convened four colleagues to provide advice for McCulloch in his overseas mission.[21] But McCulloch had not waited for Manning's report, leaving MacGregor to try to soothe Manning's offended spirit. Manning felt no animus towards James, however, assuring him of his personal goodwill and readiness to cooperate "as emergencies may require." Hoping anxiously to preserve Manning's support for the academy, James replied with a wondrously mixed metaphor urging interdenominational cooperation:

> The Dissenters need to be active. You see with what colours the Bishop [John Inglis] sails ... The stone cut out of the mountain with our hands shall break in pieces the kingdom of gold, silver, brass, iron and clay, and make them into the chaff of the summer threshing floor, and itself shall fill the whole earth.[22]

He did his best, but three years later Manning laid the cornerstone of Horton Academy at Wolfville, from which would emerge Acadia University. Although Joe Howe mocked the Baptists for "nursing their sour sectarianism on a hill in Horton," the damage to Baptist support for Pictou Academy had been done.

MacGregor found great pleasure in encouraging the students of the Academy in person, and one of the brightest was William (later Sir William) Dawson, son of a local elder. In addition to becoming distinguished in the field of geology, he became the widely hailed principal of McGill, winning for it and himself an international reputation.

Further, he was widely regarded for his criticism of Darwin's "god-lessness." For explanation, his biographers observe that Dawson's "religious convictions were to be an integral part of his life, profoundly influencing his views on science and education," and they acknowledge that MacGregor had been his guide in forming those beliefs.[23]

One underachiever, John Campbell, was the son of poor, illiterate farm parents who spoke only Gaelic but had the Bible nearly by heart. Under James's guidance, young Campbell entered the ministry, but James did not live to see this chronically ill man's courageous lifetime succession to his own old ministry at St Marys – or his happy marriage to his brave wife, Annabella, who supported him through a pain-wracked mission life. Annabella was James's first child by Janet Auld Gordon.[24]

However, while James's contracts with young people gave him pleasure, these were not easy times. He was losing friends over the academy dispute, and old friends were dying. In 1823 he suffered a mild stroke, and a year later required surgery for cancer on the upper lip. Nonetheless, he missed not a Sabbath at public worship. On 26 May 1826 he lost his dearest friend, Donald MacKay, at seventy-six. He himself was now sixty-seven. They had known forty years of intimate friendship during which James had drawn continually on Donald for strength. He would have no other conduct the funeral, preaching on David's text, "Know ye not that there is a prince and a great man fallen this day in Israel" (2 Samuel 3:38).

In the same year, he suffered several other troubling losses. His long-time, intimate correspondent Sam Gilfillan of Comrie died. Then the faithful Robert Marshall took his leave. His friend John Lulan, the Boat Cove Mi'kmaq chief, departed at ninety-seven. Soon after came the turn of his farmer father-in-law, Rod MacKay, the last survivor of the *Hector*. Archibald Bruce, John Buist, the squire, the deacon, and Edward Mortimer were long gone. The ranks were thinning, he was faltering, and he could travel no more.

Instead, in his final years he turned his attention to other forms of mission with remarkable energy and success.

Chapter Nineteen

An Enduring Spirit

In his last years MacGregor was deeply engaged in founding new societies and in supporting charitable and educational ventures, many funded out of his own pocket. If his missions were now often vicarious, they still covered a surprising range. To support the divinity hall, he urged his correspondents, "Pray continually ... Solicit donations for it from all sorts of persons, especially rich bachelors, let them leave something handsome in their wills for it."[1]

Since 1808, he and Hugh Graham had together received Bibles from the British and Foreign Bible Society (BFBS),[2] and each had formed new branches in every congregation.[3] But with the American war, support waned, and at the return of peace, collections barely recovered.[4] Now it was said that James *was* the Bible Society, for the campaign for Pictou Academy eclipsed subscriptions to other causes. He apologized to the BFBS in London that the local chapter was "really dead," but while the BFBS commiserated, they commended him so warmly for his initiative that he was spurred to new effort. Soon, his colleagues dubbed him "The Prince of Beggars" because he remitted £50 sterling annually to the BFBS, the first colonial auxiliary to send money home.[5] Always the ecumenist in such matters, he gave £50 to the Baptist Bible society for use in Burma,[6] lauding the "efficacy" of such societies because "they have taught and exemplified the great lesson of harmony and unanimity."[7] Rev. John Mitchell wrote admiringly from Anderston:

> You are giving a bend and a tone to the public mind in your part of the world, which it may long retain ... You are on an equal footing with others, and your superior knowledge and education gives you, as Teacher of

religion, an ascendancy & influence in Society, which is in great measure lost in a country that has been long settled.[8]

James must have been gratified, for it was the very message that he had directed to young Scots ministers in his impassioned recruitment "Letter of 1793."

He became so widely recognized as an authority on the Gaelic that next the Scottish Bible Society asked him to edit a Gaelic Bible and other publications for use in the Highlands. (Part of his Bible manuscript can be found in Glasgow University's Special Collections.) Always thorough in editing, he corrected three hundred misuses of the apostrophe in a single work.[9] John Mitchell commended him, but lamented that "religion ... is declining in the Highlands."[10] James continued to give the BFBS advice and sent £50 sterling annually for overseas missions, with another £25 for work in the Highlands.

Once, Patterson tells us, James fell asleep at an inn where he and his colleagues had stopped for lunch. Elder John Douglass goaded McCulloch, "If you want to awaken him just begin talking about some religious society." McCulloch laughed, and spoke loudly of establishing schools for Catholic foundlings in Ireland. James sat up abruptly, saying, "Oh yes we ought to do more for that society than we are doing." Everyone burst into laughter.[11]

Forming a local branch of Scotland's Gaelic Tract Society proved less attractive, for their publications appeared largely in English! In 1815, after waiting impatiently for a reply, after six years he received an apologetic answer, the writer blithely promising to do better, for "the Gaelic Language in this Country is beginning to be more thought of." MacGregor did not bother to respond;[12] instead, he turned to the Edinburgh Tract Society, who sent him five thousand tracts in Gaelic and eleven hundred in English.[13]

James also strongly supported the Gaelic School Society in promoting Gaelic instruction and culture in the Highlands, sending £60 sterling and promising more. And he became their adviser, rendering their publications into Gaelic. So, the wheel had come full circle: he was doing what he and his father had planned to do together so many years before, advancing the church and encouraging Highland culture at home in Scotland, especially in the Highlands.[14]

Soon, in the Presbyterian way, the catechists in his own presbytery – all lay workers – undertook Sabbath schools, inviting MacGregor to deliver their first annual sermon and looking to him for continued support and advice. By 1827 there were seventy-seven schools in the county, with over two thousand pupils and two hundred teachers.[15]

Although MacGregor and Ross were always wary of "irking the priests" in trying to assist the Mi'kmaq,[16] they became so alarmed over the exploitation of the Indians and their abuse of alcohol that they founded an unfortunately named "Indian Civilization Society" as an adjunct to the settlers' Temperance Societies – "unfortunately" because the title did not reflect James's underlying respect for the dignity of Chief Lulan and his people. But they received little support, perhaps because Lulan had recently died, but probably largely because the academy issue had become the cowbird displacing all others from the nest. MacPhie remarks that while the academy was on "the brink of ruin" – attracting money and calumny – little attention was given to anything else.[17]

No Jews arrived at Pictou until much later, but in 1815 James persuaded the women in his flock to send £12 to London's Society for Promoting Christianity among the Jews.[18]

His greatest immediate concern, however, was Home Missions, urging Synod, with Duncan Ross's support, to establish a placement bureau, a "Domestic Mission Society" for divinity graduates, to help in "supporting preachers, and supplying weak, scattered, and destitute settlements."[19] His liberal approach is manifested in the second of two goals he set for the society: first, "the Diffusion of Evangelical Doctrine and Presbyterian principles in Nova Scotia, and the adjacent Provinces"; and second, "obtaining Ministers, either from the Presbyterian Church in Nova Scotia, or from *any denomination of Presbyterians in Scotland.*" It was a courageous and generous proposal, but in the current climate of recrimination the United Scottish Church balked at an ecumenism that would reach beyond Dissenter ranks even to the Kirk.[20]

Unfazed, and with the Island now a separate presbytery from Pictou, he wrote as moderator of the PCNS to John Keir, "I send you one hundred and fifty-six copies of a plan of a Domestic Missionary Society ... to dispose of to the best of your judgment ... A Missionary Society should be formed in every congregation."[21] Ever the evangelical, he believed that spreading the Gospel remained the churches' and each Christian's first duty, overriding even the academy cause. Synod expressed "cordial approbation" but effectively shelved the project, directing that he and Duncan Ross further define it. Even his own presbytery accorded him support only in principle in this instance, the dispute over the academy having consumed and embittered so many. James was disappointed, but unwaveringly he attended to other affairs of church and society as if he were preparing them all to endure his passing.

Causes and missions, however, were not the only stuff of James's final years. He was aware of changing times in the villages and farmlands upriver, and especially in the throbbing life of New Glasgow, which was arising just downriver from his home in what is now Stellarton. In 1821, presented with a gig, he often urged his horse up the East River to Angus MacGillivray's charge, where he preached under the MacGregor Elm, for the "MacGregor braes," as they were long called, would continue into the twentieth century.

Often he drove the short distance to New Glasgow, where progress was everywhere – shipbuilding, tanning, and other industries. The example may have led him again to invention, but once, it almost pushed him too far. Noticing "hydrogen gas" (methane) bubbling up in his brook, he confined it under a half-barrel, and to the delight of his children and guests, he drew out the stopper and ignited it with a burst of flame and a loud report. An idea was born, and he commissioned wooden pipes to conduct the gas to his house. To William Young – Agricola's son, an importer, and later Sir William Young, chief justice of Nova Scotia – he wrote, "I have burned small quantities of it in a room without feeling any smell … But I'd like to have two or three pieces of lead pipe [for entry through the walls] … with a cock to open and shut better than a wooden plug."[22] But in the days before duct tape, wooden conduits could not be properly sealed, and Young reported that the costs would be prohibitive. The venture was abandoned before he became the founder of Union Gas of New Glasgow – or blew himself up.[23]

In 1822, Thomas McCulloch was granted an honorary DD from Glasgow in recognition of his literary achievements and for his role in promoting the academy. He was embarrassed – as he might have been – and in a gesture that does him credit, he asked Rev. John Mitchell, who had replaced John Buist, to help obtain similar recognitions for MacGregor, S.G.W. Archibald, and Simon Bradstreet Robie, Speaker of the assembly and an Anglican, all of whom had been critically important Academy supporters. Writing to Mitchell, McCulloch cited James's qualifications:

You know already that he has founded the Presbyterian church and brought it to its present extent and prospects, and besides he is the warmest friend which our academy possesses. Few men have done so much for the best

An Enduring Spirit   187

interest of the human race ... I must not desert ... the work of his hands [the extension of the Academy], a work near his heart, and the object of his daily prayers.[24]

Shortly after, James received a DD, and McCulloch wrote again to Mitchell, "Never was honour more deservedly conferred, and I may add that honour has been rarely borne with such meekness."[25]

The honour was granted him in absentia, however, for by this time McCulloch was bound for Scotland on his fruitless diplomatic mission, and at home James could not be spared to return to Scotland to receive the honour. It was probably his only opportunity to see his old land again, but if he needed it, which is doubtful, he could find gratification at home in Nova Scotia because all but the oldest now greeted him as "Doctor," not "Father."

Further, he had time to keep up with current reading, to answer enquiries from other ministers and Gaelic scholars, to write reviews, and to compose poetry. He often set his own works and those of others to music, singing lustily in his strong tenor voice. And he still pursued the origins of language with his old passion. In 1823, he wrote to his old college friend Rev. John Jamieson, now a distinguished etymologist, philologist, and Seceder leader, who was widely recognized for having brought out the first Gaelic dictionary and for playing a central role in uniting the Scottish Secession synods.

To the widely acclaimed John Jamieson, James enclosed a sixty-page handwritten manuscript in hardboard ends, entitled "Analogy of the Gaelic and Hebrew Languages, illustrated ... To which is added, A Collection of Gaelic Words derived from the Hebrew." Their common purpose, as Jamieson had once set it out, was "not to master a dead, but to revive a dying language."[26] MacGregor inscribed the manuscript to "John Jamieson from his Friend, Dr. James MacGregor, Pictou, Nova Scotia, F.S.A. [Fellow of the Society of Antiquaries]."[27]

Jamieson received James's manuscript warmly, endorsing it:

It is, in my opinion, a Clever, ingenious performance, the production of Labour, Study & and intimate Acquaintance with the Hebrew and Gaelic languages. Were the treatise translated into Latin & French, or Latin only & transmitted to foreign Antiquarian Societies & Universities, it might Assist to Establish both the Antiquity & reputation of the Gaelic.[28]

It appears not to have been published, but it affirms that despite a busy life in the bush, James had remained the scholar – enough to have retained the respect of the most acclaimed authority on Gaelic in Enlightenment Scotland.

Jamieson also reported with pleasure having dined with "your young American plants" – three Pictou divinity graduates sent to Glasgow to be judged for their New World training. Their visit had been a triumph, and Jamieson was particularly impressed with John McLean's "solid Gospel tone."[29] He asked McLean to deliver to MacGregor his own most recent book, *Hermes Scythicus,* a controversial study of the affinity between the Gothic and classical languages. With it came the wistful note, "It will remind you of our old lucubrations about the Hebrew and Gaelic."[30]

Since his youth MacGregor had been collecting Gaelic poems, but he had also written many himself. Once, a rider came upon him on horseback at night, "humming over portions of his poems as he composed them."[31] He would recite or sing on any occasion, and although known as "The Apostle of Nova Scotia," he was more familiarly recognized as "Poet MacGregor." A Cape Bretoner reported that at weddings James enjoyed the singing and verse but disapproved of dancing, for "such were the weddings he liked best – in which he was the piper himself."[32] The Canadian Gaelic scholar J.B. MacLean observed, "It was in the language of the Gael that he wooed the Muse, and it was in this ancient and musical tongue that he gave expression to its beauty and the warmth of his kindled imagination."[33]

In 1814 James wrote to Edinburgh regarding publication of a book of his Gaelic songs, for which the publisher then went about unilaterally having translated into English and testing them out on Scottish readers. He loftily reported back: "The translation has met the unqualified approbation of the most eminent judges in this country … [and] they have experienced a favourable reception from the Public … As for your disposing of your M.S. to a printer, none of them will risk anything in Gaelic."[34]

James was discouraged. He had had no intention of publishing in English, hoping that the songs would be sung "wherever the auld tongue can be found." It was not until 1819 that the verses appeared in Gaelic as *Dain a chomhadh crab-huidh: searmonaich an t-soisgeil 'an American muthuath,* or *Poems to Promote Religion.*[35] Although he met criticism, he had set the twenty-three verses to traditional, secular Gaelic tunes in order to link "the best lessons with the sweetest melodies of his native land."[36] As an experienced communicator, he knew that a gospel message sung to a popular tune would stick more easily with the listener.

Avoiding pastoral or romantic themes like those of Robert Burns, he found inspiration in the Gospel and in the Presbyterian views of grace, good works, the resurrection, and atonement. One, on "Education," opens with these words:

> The Gael were ignorant, blind.
> Education was scant in their midst.
> Their knowledge so shallow and backward
> That their loss they could not comprehend.
> They didn't believe it gain or advantage
> To give prime education to their children,
> Though they might daily perceive
> It was this gave the Sassanach a chance.[37]

Years later Patterson sought an expert opinion of the *Dain* and was assured that the poems demonstrated "a minute and comprehensive knowledge of the whole Gaelic language … literally a 'speaking from the heart to the heart.' It is almost impossible for a Highlander to read them … unaffected or unmoved."[38]

James gave copyright to the Tract Society, and one of its agents, his nephew Rev. Sam McNab, who had recently introduced himself in a letter, assured him that "they will be very extensively circulated in the Highlands."[39] The *Dain* went through seven Tract Society editions, were reissued in Glasgow in 1825 and 1831, later in Pictou in 1861 and in Edinburgh in 1870.[40] In midcentury, when George Patterson was travelling about northern Scotland, he learned that mothers still crooned them to their children.[41]

Two generations later the *Dain* won the approval of Alexander Maclean Sinclair, grandson of John Maclean, bard of the laird of Coll and creator of Nova Scotia's best-known Gaelic poem, "*A Choille Ghrua-maic*," or "The Gloomy Forest." Maclean had arrived in Pictou in 1819, the year of the *Dain*'s first publication. In 1880 his grandson, A.M. Sinclair, published six additional poems by MacGregor in his anthology *Dain Spioradail*, or *Spiritual Songs*.[42] In 1905 in the *Oban Times*, the younger Sinclair affirmed, "As an accurate writer of Gaelic, he had no superior in his own day, either in Scotland or out of it."[43]

In 1936 it was reported that A.M. Sinclair had acquired from a "Mrs. Campbell of Sherbrooke" (who was married to a grandson of Rev. John Campbell and Annabella MacGregor) a notebook containing some of MacGregor's secular verse, including "an excellent love-song

[that to Anna Buchanan in 1785]; a song composed by Dr. MacGregor
in 1785 ...[and] a song praising the MacGregors because that in a clan
fight they had killed a lot of men."[44] Apparently, the Highland heart of
romance had beat strong in the young James. The notebook appears to
have been lost: how many other poems had he written down?

Professor Donald MacLean of Edinburgh's Free Church College
wrote, "His poetry is a reasoned, scholarly, systematic presentation of
religious truths; that of the bards is spontaneous." He further ranked
MacGregor "next to Dugald Buchanan as the poet of the sublime.
The great doctrines of grace formed his themes."[45] In 1982 Kenneth
MacDonald, executive editor of *The Historical Dictionary of Scottish
Gaelic*, ranked Dugald Buchanan as "the outstanding Gaelic poet of the
evangelical movement of the eighteenth century," and MacGregor first
among four nineteenth-century successors.[46]

Only one Canadian edition of the *Dain* has appeared, issued in Pictou
in 1861.[47] For a long time only MacGregor's inclusion in Sinclair's *Dain
Spioradail* remained to confirm his literary output. Then, for twelve
years from 1892, there appeared in Cape Breton a Gaelic periodical,
Mac-Talla (*Echo*), published by Jonathan MacKinnon of Whycogomagh,
with more of MacGregor's secular poetry.[48] In 1923, on the one hundred
and fiftieth anniversary of the coming of the *Hector*, a commemorative
volume, *Pictou Poets*, appeared, containing two of James's poems.[49]
In 2002 an American, Michael Newton, in a stimulating book entitled
*We're Indians Sure Enough: The Legacy of the Scottish Highlanders to the
United States*, cited James's importance in North American Highland
poetic output.[50]

John MacInnes, in a 1988 essay on Gaelic poetry in the nineteenth
century,[51] traces the bardic tradition that celebrated the Gael in romantic
tales of warriors, clan wars, and vainglorious imperial military victories. It was, he argued, the stuff of establishmentarian and of Moderate Kirk spokesmen. Against this, he set the voice of the Evangelical
Seceder poets who witnessed the collapse of the old social order, decrying its chauvinism and deriding its romanticized heroes. To illustrate
the Evangelical mode, MacInnes chose a Gaelic stanza written by
MacGregor, published in 1825:

> Not a tale of Ossian of the Fian,
> nor any hero in a host,
> not a tale of plundering the Lowlanders
> by the catarans of the glens and the mountains,

nor any tale of roaming the glens in the dress
that does not impede the knees,
nor a tale of brave clans
who would fight and never surrender until death:
Clan Gregor who were strong, and ignorant;
Clan Donald whose delight was the Red Hand;
Clan Cameron who were bold, without sense.
None of these, but the news of the gospel of grace
spreading in every airt all around.

James's later poetic production, then, was subsumed in his compelling Gospel purpose, as he rejected the old Highland culture of male warriors, rivalry, and widespread destruction. One wonders how much the recent North Highland and Kirk immigration to Pictou had coloured James's changing aesthetic.

Rev. Donald Sinclair singles out MacGregor's verse for another and practical significance: "Theological books especially were rare in Pictou … Dr. MacGregor proposed to remedy the defect by preparing a course of theology in verse. It is almost as comprehensive as Hodge's 'Systematic Theology.'"[52] (Thomas Hodge of Princeton University wrote the standard three-volume work on the subject in the nineteenth century.) Theology-presented-in-poetry suggests James's effective pedagogy, for at a time when the number of books was limited, learning presented in verse was more easily accessible and retained. A sample of his titles (from the Gaelic) confirms their comprehensiveness: *The Confession of Faith, The Psalms, The Ten Commandments, Praise of the Law, The Covenant of Works, The Covenant of Grace, The Gospels, Unbelief, One Heaven, On the Resurrection, Death, The Last Judgement,* and *The Work of the Holy Spirit.* Sinclair notes the unusual length of each: thirty-six stanzas each of eight lines. Yet they seem not to have attracted the interest of theology historians. Nor do we know whether the students of Pictou Academy employed them, although they would have effectively complemented McCulloch's brilliant lectures.

At home, when not on pastoral visits or missions, James read and wrote constantly. As translator and editor, he was no less prolific. In addition to work for the Bible Society, the Gaelic Society, and the Tract Society, he produced Gaelic translations of most of the *Book of Psalms,* the 1781 *Scottish Paraphrases of the Scriptures,* and the *Westminster Confession of Faith.* Many had never before been available in the Gaelic, and it is a mark of his achievement that they could now reach those who spoke only that language. Had his production appeared in English, he would be hailed as one of Canada's most prolific writers. He was a consecrated poet and translator, and a dedicated correspondent.

While MacGregor wrote poetry and song in these years, McCulloch, too, his finances having worsened and he being dispirited over the academy issue, in frustration took once more to creative writing. But the lively spirit and light satire of *The Stepsure Letters* were gone. He still addressed the immigrant's adjustment to the New World, but the focus and tone had become sombre.[53] In 1826 he published two novellas, "William" and "Melville," as *Colonial Gleanings*, in which he contrasts two Scots raised in radically different social circles and coming to different ends in the New World.[54] Seven years later, however, he could find no publisher for a third emigrant tale, "Morton," exploring the same themes but even more deeply and soberly – and with strong MacGregor associations.[55] The manuscript rests in NSA.

In it young Morton's harrowing journey to Pictou from Halifax is literally James's account of his initial trip to Truro and Pictou. Confronted with the wildness and challenge of nature, the sceptical Morton, more explicitly than the earlier Melville who also met a preacher, finds peace and strength in the words and example of "the Rev. James MacGregor" and in the acts of his faithful follower "Honest Robert Marshall." McCulloch does not disguise his models. Many incidents in "Morton" appear in the sequence and detail of James's *Memoir*, even Robert Marshall's account of his people's encounter with the Island mice.

McCulloch wrote to his Scottish agent, "I have three little tales on the stocks ... which I contrived partly ... for the purpose of commemorating ... that good man, Dr. MacGregor.[56] In them he puts aside the polemics of the day and as Gwen Davies suggests, offers three moral tales rooted in Romantic juxtaposition concerning the evils of the crowded city and of nature's "gigantic provocations," stirrings that led to yearnings for the sanctity of grace and the promises of the grave. All three stories, but especially "Morton," suggest McCulloch's reflections on Covenanter self-examination and on the intensity of a Seceder clergyman's urge to return to his primary role as shepherd. At times it appears almost self-accusatory. There is a familiar tone as "MacGregor" wins Morton back to Calvinist values, presenting himself as both Enlightenment minister and dominie, bringing reason, order, and faith out of Morton's confusion. For Morton, as Davies suggests, the bewilderingly romantic frontier and the ruggedly "picturesque" setting yield ground as "MacGregor infuses compassion, learning, an appreciation of natural history, and biblical grace."[57] "Morton" is the deeply troubled McCulloch's tribute to the wise old man he wished he could have been.

In the single-mindedness of his mission, MacGregor's correspondence with his Scottish family still suffered. In 1824 his nephew Duncan Ferguson reminded him that he had not written for two years and reported that his Aunt Elizabeth Donaldson and her husband, Donald, had left Strathearn for Upper Canada, "together with a great many more." He added news of the shaky new Scottish Seceder Union, which was barely perfected by 1847 when the United Secession Church merged with the Relief Church to form the United Presbyterian Church.

Whether James replied to Duncan is uncertain, but his name does not appear again in James's papers.[58] Yet after forty years of separation,[59] James, it appears, may not even have written to Elizabeth in Upper Canada. And perhaps, because the Donaldsons travelled in steerage, they chose or could not afford to present themselves at Pictou. Patterson reports that during their passage,

> on passing the coast of Nova Scotia, [Elizabeth] expressed a wish that she were … with her brother. One asked who was her brother there? She replied, "Doctor MacGregor, a minister in Pictou." The cook having heard this, told them that he once landed at Pictou, after being shipwrecked, that the Doctor himself had come down to the wharf and taken off his own top coat and given it to him. He had also provided him with employment during the winter. The poor fellow was so grateful for his kindness that, during the rest of the voyage, he could not do enough for them.[60]

In January 1822, MacGregor was advised by Lieutenant Governor Sir James Kempt that his right to "raise coals," dating to Governor Wentworth's day, was revoked.[61] New interests were inspecting the East River fields, and knowing that his land stood over coal and that he had never received his promised glebe lot, he applied for compensation. Early in April, he received 50 acres and was advised that if he had "a Son of age, His Excellency will take his claims … into his consideration … [for] the Board [Council] is disposed to forward your views."[62] James's foresight would soon bear handsome fruit.

Single entrepreneurs had tried to open the coalfields, but little happened until 1825, when a lease was confirmed with an English consortium, later called the General Mining Association. Underwritten by the fabulously wealthy London firm of Rundell, Bridge and Rundell, "Jewelers and Goldsmiths to the King,"[63] the company made offers to those whose lands straddled the field. For his 800 acres James received £1,150, more than enough to satisfy what Patterson called "his temporal necessities."[64] In fact, he realized a few hundred more by reducing his stock and selling off farm equipment. With the proceeds he moved across the river to a hilltop that afforded a view of his beloved river (and of the new colliery and model village). There, he built a cottage that Janet and the children would inherit. He also provided enough capital to set up young James and Rod as general merchants in New Glasgow. He ensured the other children's education, and he provided enough to maintain Janet in comfort for the rest of her days.[65]

By 1827 James and Janet were regularly entertained by the company's enterprising manager, Richard Smith, at "Mount Rundell," an imposing brick mansion newly built in a landscaped park.[66] Ironically, James's father had fled the industrial congestion and exploitation of Alloa, but his son became the industrialist, Smith's adviser and friend, an association that proved of great benefit to both.

The first workers were experienced English miners brought out to open the shafts. Like many British mining companies, Smith's firm was paternalistic. A company village was undertaken, and it and other facilities and benefits were accorded the employees, albeit they were required to share the costs by a check-off system. James was consulted by Smith as streets were laid out, rows of workers' houses raised, and medical facilities, a chapel, and on James's advice, a worker's reading room and schoolhouse built.[67]

James was ambitious for this "Albion Mine" in what would later be called Stellarton, for unlike the earlier back-to-the-land movement he had advocated with Ross and McCulloch during the timber craze, it offered the prospect of large-scale industry, prosperity, and continuity that timber had not. Here, then, was no romantic, nostalgic agrarian Highlander but a leader for new times and new opportunities, welcoming technology, applied science, training, and industry.

Richard Smith moved quickly, sinking shafts to a depth of over 61 metres (200 feet) through the "big" seam, so swiftly that the first coal was raised early in September 1827. On 7 December he introduced the first steam engine in the province. On the same day Jotham Blanchard's radical *Colonial Patriot* appeared – a second great engine, a reform engine designed, like the first, to project huge new energy into the community. Pictou was entering strenuous times.

Production quickened at the Albion Mine when several seams were found resting above each other. One of the richest, deepest (153 metres, or 500 feet), and thickest (3.8 metres, or 12 feet) lay under James's old lands. They called it the MacGregor Seam, which stirred James to new interest and curiosity. Applying his knowledge of geology more intensely than ever, he took the General Mining Association venture much further than had been anticipated.

For thirty years he had called for the opening up of the coal fields. Now, after he had carefully explored again the territory around the mine, as James M. Cameron notes,

> Dr. James MacGregor discovered iron ore near McLennan's Brook, but a short distance from the General Mining Association Colliery ... [A] favourable report having been made to the Company's chemists, a deeper interest was aroused in the latent possibilities of the country, and the General Mining Association set aside 1,000 pounds for experimenting with iron smelting.[68]

When he also discovered red hematite nearby, an essential to smelting, his friend Richard Smith began to consider unanticipated opportunities: samples were sent home, a blast furnace was set up, and a year later the first pig iron appeared. Farther up the East River, brown hematite was found at Bridgeville, and later, iron ore at Eureka and Ferrona. Accordingly, one of the company's chief mines was named "The MacGregor."

Rev. James Robertson's proverb based on Job, which he had cited at James's ordination in Glasgow in 1786, still resonated in his life: "Great events have often small beginnings." Within only months of his death, James was still combining the drive and curiosity of his youth with the spiritual resources and "useful learning" of Glasgow's Enlightenment – and of his own long life.

Although he suffered a severe stroke on 13 February 1828, he made a remarkable recovery in a matter of weeks. He was left with partial paralysis on the right side, a limp, minor impairment of his speech and right hand, and some loss of memory. Sometimes he could not remember his children's names, but he continued to preach, and if he forgot his text he improvised.[69] Like Jacob before him, he kept up his pastoral visits, catechizing for another two years. His spirit was irrepressible, his optimism persistent. He had said it years before and still acknowledged his good fortune: "I account it the happiest thing that ever befell me, that I was sent to America."

Now, sitting comfortably at home, rich in years and memories, he welcomed visitors and dozed quietly. From time to time he was awakened by the chime of the clock and exclaimed in Gaelic, still his favoured tongue, "I have been here another hour!"[70] A daughter, probably Annabella, told him she dreamed he had been crowned a king, to which he replied cheerfully, "I will soon be far better than a king, and wear a crown of glory." In Jotham Blanchard's published version of this story, James replied that he was already far better than a king, "for I am one of God's Priests."[71] But he had never flaunted the vainglorious MacGregor motto "Royal is my race."

One Sunday in 1830 he preached a sermon "with more than ordinary vigor," rested the next day until evening, and then tutored a divinity student in Hebrew. But as he prepared for bed, anticipating one of Presbytery's lively meetings next morning, he suffered a severe stroke. He died two days later, on Wednesday, 3 March, at seventy.

Kenneth Forbes, joiner, talked proudly all his life of having fashioned the coffin for Dr MacGregor. Thomas McCulloch wrote the inscription for his obelisk: "First Minister of Pictou County / Whose praise is in the Gospel / Throughout all the churches." Nearly two thousand people came to send him off, and Rev. John McKinlay recalled "a dark dense cloud of mourners" against the glistening snow.[72] It was the largest funeral in Nova Scotia to date. He was buried beside Ann, on a knoll just above the river. Only a few paces away lay his cherished companion, Donald MacKay. They built a new church nearby, and called it James Church.

His children had grown up and were scattered about the district. Robert and James had become thriving partners as general merchants in New Glasgow, although James later became a successful hardware merchant and Robert a tanner. Roderick entered provisioning and shipping as R. MacGregor & Sons, where he accumulated the second largest fortune in a very prosperous town. His son, James Drummond MacGregor, became first president of Nova Scotia Steel, which introduced the Siemens process of steel production to North America. "J.D." also succeeded in public life as mayor of New Glasgow, Nova Scotia MLA, Canadian senator, and lieutenant governor. Christy-Ann married Abram Patterson, one of New Glasgow's most successful businessmen; their son was Pictou's future historian, Rev. George Patterson, editor of the *Memoir*. Janet married "Elder Charles" Fraser, grandson of another *Hector* arrival. Sarah married Capt. George R. MacKenzie, also an

MLA, whom McPhie declares as "foremost among the shipbuilders of New Glasgow ... [He] built the largest vessels of the day, commanded several of them ... [and] probably did more than anyone else to make the town."[73]

Of James's three children with Janet Auld Gordon, Annabel married Rev. John Campbell, supporting him in gravely poor health through many brave missions from Sherbrooke for the rest of her life. Mary married Rev. John Cameron, who inherited Nine Mile River, part of Alex Dick's demanding pastoral charge.

The youngest child, Peter Gordon MacGregor, thirteen at his father's death, pursued a distinguished social gospel ministry at Halifax, and with his friend and fellow academy graduate George Grant (once Kirk minister of St Matthew's in Halifax, and later Queen's University's acclaimed principal) and their mutual friend Sandford Fleming became a driving force behind the 1875 formation of the Presbyterian Church in Canada. Peter's son, James Gordon MacGregor, became professor of physics at Dalhousie and was later named to the Chair in Natural Philosophy at Edinburgh. His children, Archibald and Janet, in turn pursued successful academic careers at Edinburgh and Manchester.

On a sweltering Thursday, 23 July 1936 – a century and a half to the day after James's first sermon in Squire Patterson's barn – a cairn was unveiled at Pictou, the speeches later appearing as the *MacGregor Celebration Addresses.*[74] A great-granddaughter, Edith Read, principal of Toronto's Branksome Hall, donated to Bloor Street United Church a stained glass window picturing James on mission.

But long before that, the new widow wrote sadly to her sister in Falkirk:

> I am now left a lonely widow with my Father's children. I have lost a Dear Partner. You need not wonder at how I am affected by the loss of a kind and affectionate husband. Nor does religion require us to repress our feelings, [but allows] us to indulge in moderate sorrow ... Hoping you will remember at a throne of grace a desolate widow with my Fatherless children.[75]

Janet Auld Gordon MacGregor lived out her life with her son-in-law James and daughter Mary Cameron in the manse at Nine Mile River in the Douglas district. She died at seventy-two in 1851 and was buried with her husband and Ann in the Pioneer Cemetery, New Glasgow.

The MacGregor Cairn. Erected at Pictou by Synod of the Maritime Provinces of the Presbyterian Church in Canada to commemorate the one hundred and fiftieth anniversary of the arrival in Nova Scotia of Rev. James Drummond MacGregor, DD, 1936. (Author's collection.)

All of MacGregor's great energy had been committed to this new country and to his flock as shepherd to individuals and congregations, as leader of a remarkable band of missionaries who brought to Pictou and beyond the spirit of their old faith and the optimism of the Glasgow Enlightenment, and as unifier in the cause of the Presbyterian Church, helping it to grow beyond a narrow sectarian spirit. He was a man of deep social conscience and a distinguished linguist, poet, tribal storyteller, amateur scientist, and musician.

Along the way, he had contributed to the wider community, encouraging social and political change; pursuing scholarship, science, technology, poetry, music, and invention; giving generous support to Scottish and overseas religious and cultural missions; and always encouraging people to pursue mind and soul at every level and in many directions.

The epitome of the Scottish Enlightenment as it flowered at Glasgow, he amply bore out the observation of a later North Shore Presbyterian minister: "Our ancestors believed that the salvation of one's soul came about through the enlightenment of one's mind!"[76] On hearing the news of MacGregor's death, Thomas McCulloch declared, "Nova Scotia has lost her best man."[77]

The Liberal lawyer-politician Hon. Duncan Cameron Fraser observed at the centenary of MacGregor's arrival, held at New Glasgow in 1886: "He was a social reformer from the first. Whatever tended to improve the congregation socially, financially, or otherwise, had his warm support, indeed, he generally initiated the social reform."[78]

The minister as public servant was his legacy – and it fell to no one more than to his son, Rev. Peter Gordon MacGregor, who would die at sixty-nine in James's centenary year, 1886.

Notes

Preface and Acknowledgements

1 Rev. J.B. MacLean, "Dr. MacGregor of Pictou," in Rev. Frank Baird, ed., *Addresses at the Celebration of the One Hundred and Fiftieth Anniversary of the Arrival in Nova Scotia of Rev. James Drummond MacGregor, D.D., by the Synod of the Maritime Provinces of the Presbyterian Church in Canada* (Toronto: Presbyterian Publications ,1937; Reprinted 2013 by Formac Press, Halifax), 42–3 (hereafter, *Celebration Addresses*).

2 Rev. George Patterson, *Memoir of the Rev. James MacGregor, D.D. ...* (Philadelphia: Joseph M. Wilson, 1859) (hereafter, *Memoir*).

3 Rev. George Patterson, ed., *A Few Remains of the Rev. James MacGregor, D.D.* (Philadelphia: Joseph M. Wilson, 1859) (hereafter, *Remains*).

4 Rev. James Robertson, *History of the Mission of the Secession Church to Nova Scotia and Prince Edward Island* (Edinburgh, 1847).

5 Thomas McCulloch, *Colonial Gleanings* (Edinburgh: Oliphant, 1826); "Morton," [untitled] [n.d.], in Nova Scotia Archives (hereafter, NSA), Thomas McCulloch Papers, MG 1, vol. 555, no. 76, [n.p.].

6 Frank Baird, *Rob MacNab: A Story of Old Pictou*, illus. C.W. Jefferys (Halifax: Royal Print & Litho Ltd., 1923; reissued by Formac Press, Halifax, 2013)

Historiographical Introduction

1 John Webster Grant, "The Presbyterian Tradition in the Maritime Provinces," unpub. paper quoted and referred to in Neil Gregor Smith, "The Presbyterian Tradition in Canada," in *The Churches and the Canadian Experience: A Faith and Order Study of the Christian Tradition*, ed. John Webster

Grant (Toronto; Ryerson Press, 1961), 38–52. See also Neil Gregor Smith, "James MacGregor and the Church in the Maritimes," in *Enkindled by the Word: Essays on Presbyterianism in Canada* [A Biographical History of the Presbyterian Church in Canada], comp. Centennial Committee of the Presbyterian Church in Canada (Toronto: Presbyterian Publications, 1966), 9. A more recent contribution to this genre is Peter Bush, "James Drummond MacGregor: The Pioneer of Pictou," in *Called to Witness: Profiles of Canadian Presbyterians, A Supplement to Enduring Witness*, vol. 3, ed. John S. Moir (Hamilton: Presbyterian Publications, 1999), 1–9.

2 Quoted in James Greenlee, *Sir Robert Falconer: A Biography* (Toronto: University of Toronto Press, 1988), 3.

3 Baird, *Celebration Addresses*.

4 D.C. Harvey, "The Intellectual Awakening of Nova Scotia, " in *Dalhousie Review* 13, no. 1 (April 1933): 13–14.

5 H.H. Walsh, *The Christian Church in Canada* (Toronto: Ryerson, 1956), 131.

6 Ann Gorman Condon, "1783–1800: Loyalist Arrival, Acadian Return, Imperial Reform," 202.

7 D. Campbell and R. MacLean, *Beyond the Atlantic Roar: A Study of the Nova Scotia Scots* (Toronto: McGill-Queen's University Press, 1974), 39.

8 Charles W. Dunn, *Highland Settler: A Portrait of the Scottish Gael in Nova Scotia* (Toronto: University of Toronto Press, 1953). .

9 Duff Crerar, "'Crackling Sounds from the Burning Bush': The Evangelical Impulse in Canadian Presbyterianism before 1875," 126.

10 See essays by Cameron and Sutherland in R.H. Campbell and Andrew S. Skinner, eds., *The Origins and Nature of the Scottish Enlightenment* (Edinburgh, Taylor & Francis, ltd., 1982). For the "Scottish legacy" in Canadian context see A.B. McKillop, *A Disciplined Intelligence: Critical Inquiry and Canadian Thought in the Victorian Era* (1979; Montreal & Kingston, 2001 [repr.]).

11 Royal Society of Canada Transactions, 1927 (Part II), 7–20. Falconer, whose ancestor arrived in Pictou before MacGregor, was himself a product of the MacGregor tradition.

12 *Concise Oxford Dictionary*.

13 Buggey, *DCB* 6, 462.

14 Buggey, *DCB* 7, 540.

15 Selected papers, edited by George Rawlyk and Charles H.H. Scobie, were published by McGill-Queen's University Press in 1997 as *The Contribution of Presbyterianism to the Maritime Provinces of Canada*.

16 William Klempa, ed., *The Burning Bush and a Few Acres of Snow* (Ottawa: McGill-Queen's Press, 1994), 6, 194–5, 197.

17 Rev. George Patterson, *More Studies in Nova Scotia History* (Halifax: Imperial Publishing, 1941), 63.
18 D.B. Mack, "George Munro Grant: Evangelical Prophet" (unpub. PhD diss., Queen's University, 1992). See also Mack's article on Grant in *Dictionary of Canadian Biography*, vol. 8, 403–9.

1. Awaiting the Verdict

1 *Memoir of the Rev. James MacGregor, D.D. ...*, ed. Rev. George Patterson (Philadelphia: Joseph M. Wilson, 1859), 47 (hereafter, *Memoir*).
2 Gordon Donaldson, *The Scots Overseas* (London: Robert Hale, 1966), 53.
3 T.M. Devine, "A Conservative People? Scottish Gaeldom in the Age of Improvement," in *Eighteenth Century Scotland: New Perspectives*, ed. T.M. Devine and J.R. Young (East Lindon, Scotland: Tuckwell, 1999), 232.
4 James Hunter, *The Making of the Crofting Community* (Edinburgh: John Donald, 1979), 12.
5 I.F. Grant, *Highland Folk Ways* (London: Routledge & Kegan Paul, 1975), 12.
6 J.M. Bumsted, "The Scottish Diaspora: Emigration to British North America, 1763–1815," in *Nation and Province in the First British Empire: Scotland and America, 1600–1800*, ed. Ned Landsman (Lewisburg, PA: Bucknell University Press, 2001); Devine, "A Conservative People?," 228–9.
7 David Daiches, *Scotland and the Union* (London: John Murray, 1977), 192.
8 See Wallace Notestein's insightful essays in *The Scot in History ...* (New Haven, CT: Yale University Press, 1946).
9 Alexander Murdoch and Richard B. Sher, "Literary and Learned Culture," in *People and Society in Scotland*, vol. 1, *1760–1830*, ed. T.M. Devine and Rosalind Mitchison (Edinburgh: John Donald, 1988), 128.

2. Honour Thy Father

1 Rosalind Mitchison, *Lordship to Patronage: Scotland, 1603–1745* (London: Edward Arnold, 1983), 165–9.
2 Ibid., 165.
3 Christopher Whatley, "The Dark Side of the Enlightenment: Sorting Out Serfdom," in *Eighteenth Century Scotland: New Perspectives*, ed. T.M. Devine and J.R. Young (East Linton, Scotland: Tuckwell, 1999), 264.
4 T.M. Devine, "Highland Migration to Lowland Scotland, 1760–1790," in *Scottish Historical Review* 63 (1983): 137–49.
5 Whatley, "Dark Side," 264–6.
6 Mitchison, *Lordship*, 172–3.

7 Donaldson, *Scots Overseas*, 132–4; N. Murray, *The Scottish Handloom Weavers, 1790–1850* (Edinburgh: Donald, 1978).
8 Whatley, "Dark Side," 263.
9 Ibid., 264–6.
10 See originals in Sackville, NB: United Church of Canada Archives, Maritime Conference, James MacGregor Papers, Family & Individual Papers, box F&I et seq. (hereafter, MCA, JMP, box F&I …). Most originals are also in NSA on microfilm.
11 An able summary of the changing Kirk and its friction with the Secessionists is T.C. Smout, *A History of the Scottish People, 1560–1830* (London: Fontana, 1998), chap. 9, sec. 3, "Change and Division in the Kirk," 213–22.
12 A useful review of the Moderates appears in Ian D.I. Clark, "From Protest to Reaction: The Moderate Regime in the Church of Scotland, 1752–1805," in *Scotland in the Age of Improvement: Essays in Scottish History in the Eighteenth Century*, ed. N.T. Phillipson and Rosalind Mitchison (Edinburgh: Edinburgh University Press, 1970), 200–24.
13 Notestein, *The Scot*, 203–4.
14 David Daiches, *The Paradox of Scottish Culture: The Eighteenth Century Experience* (London: Oxford University Press, 1964); David Daiches, Peter Jones, and Jean Jones, eds., *A Hotbed of Genius: The Scottish Enlightenment, 1730–1790* (Edinburgh: Edinburgh University Press, 1986), 13; Calum Brown, "Religion and Social Change," in *People and Society in Scotland*, vol. 1, ed. T.M. Devine and Rosalind Mitchison (Edinburgh: John Donald, 2004), 145.
15 Brown, "Religion and Social Change," 149.
16 Smout, *History*, 214.
17 Richard J. Finlay, "Keeping the Covenant: Scottish National Identity," in *New Perspectives*, 125.
18 Brown, "Religion and Social Change," 143–62. The Seceders, rooted in seventeenth-century Puritan and Covenanting ways, reaffirmed their old ways. We may associate evangelicals with exhortation and joyous conversion, but many offered little more than reproof and denunciation. In the 1690s the Kirk had urged all clergy and elders to visit regularly to ensure a godly home atmosphere. On the Sabbath, "seizers" or monitors entered homes at will. Spying was encouraged, and the congregation invited to inform on the wayward. "Loose" walking on Sunday was "vagueing." On the Sabbath, the minister publicly rebuked the accused, after which the offenders were required to sit on the "kirk stool"– a kind of ecclesiastical stocks – until they should repent. The Moderates sought to

replace what they saw as regressive practices with fines or requirements to give to the poor. See also Smout, *History*, 214.

19 Notestein, *The Scot*, 210.
20 Daiches, *Scotland and the Union*, 188.
21 Finlay, "Keeping the Covenant," 128.
22 Quoted in W. Ferguson, *Scotland, 1689 to the Present* (Edinburgh: Oliver & Boyd,1968), 123.
23 Brown, "Religion and Social Change," 149–50.

3. New Beginnings for Father and Son

1 David Alston, "The Nigg Revival," in "Social and Economic History of the Old Shire of Cromarty, 1650–1850" (unpub. PhD diss., University of Dundee, 1999); Calum Brown, *The People in the Pews: Religion and Society in Scotland since 1780* (Glasgow: Economic and Social History Society of Scotland, 1993), chap. 11.
2 A good description of the Highland border country appears in Ian Finlay, *The Highlands* (London: Batsford, 1963), 41–53.
3 For the trysts, see A.R.B. Haldane, *The Drove Roads of Scotland* (Edinburgh: Berlinn, 1997).
4 Sarah Murray, *A Companion and Useful Guide to the Beauties of Scotland* (London, 1799).
5 Jacob appears in church records as "James," and in his son's Glasgow University records as "Jacob." I have used "Jacob" to avoid confusion with his son. In the same local records, his wife is listed as Jannet "Dochartach," usually contracted to Dochart. Their first child was born on 1 October 1749 and also named Jannet. Thanks to Terris C. Howard, "A Survey of Deserted Settlements in Glen Lednock, Including Glentarken and Other Locations," (from Comrie Parish records, [USA, privately printed]).
6 *Memoir*, 16.
7 Ibid., 26.
8 MCA, JMP, box F&I-023/1/Q2.
9 *Memoir*, 36.
10 Ibid., 15–16.
11 Ibid., 16.
12 Innerpeffray Library, *Register of Borrowers*.
13 *Memoir*, 25.
14 Told me by Mrs. Janet McColl Oxley, Halifax, 1953.
15 Erskine Duncan, *Dunblane; St Blane's: A History*. Privately printed, Dunblane, 2002.

4. Glasgow and Alloa

1 A.L. Brown and Michael Moss, *The University of Glasgow, 1451–1996* (Edinburgh: Edinburgh University Press, 1996).
2 Smout, *History*, 452.
3 David Daiches, "The Scottish Enlightenment," in *A Hotbed of Genius*, ed. David Daiches, Peter Jones, and Jean Jones (Edinburgh: Edinburgh University Press, 1986), 18.
4 N.E. Phillipson, "Scottish Enlightenment," in *A Companion to Scottish Culture*, ed. David Daiches (New York: Edward Arnold, 1982), 342–3.
5 See the excellent range of essays in N.T. Phillipson and Rosalind Mitchison, eds., *Scotland in the Age of Improvement: Essays in Scottish History in the Eighteenth Century* (Edinburgh: Edinburgh University Press, 1970).
6 R.N. Smart, "Some Observation on the Provinces of the Scottish Universities," in *The Scottish Tradition: Essays in Honour of Ronald Gordon Cant*, ed. G.W.S. Barrow (Edinburgh: Scottish Academic Press, 1974), 101.
7 Roger Emerson, "The Contexts of the Scottish Enlightenment," in *The Cambridge Companion to the Scottish Enlightenment*, ed. Alexander Broadie (Cambridge: Cambridge University Press, 2003), 9–30, 20–1 (hereafter, *CCSE*).
8 Ibid., 23.
9 Phillipson, "Scottish Enlightenment," 343. Cf. Daiches, "The Scottish Enlightenment," 1.
10 The best recent account of Glasgow is Irene Maver, *Glasgow* (Edinburgh: Edinburgh University Press, 2000).
11 Ibid., 16–34.
12 Ibid., 131; Smout, *History*, 340.
13 Robert Turnbull, *The Genius of Scotland*, 4th ed. (New York, 1848), 204; the west front is pictured in Brown and Moss, *University of Glasgow*, 10–11.
14 Maver, *Glasgow*, 31.
15 Ibid.; Notestein, *The Scot*, 214–5.
16 Smout, *History*, 218.
17 Maver, *Glasgow*, 31.
18 Ibid., 34–5.
19 Roger L. Emerson, "Politics and the Glasgow Professors, 1690–1800," in *The Glasgow Enlightenment*, ed. Andrew Hook and Richard B. Sher (Phantassie, Scotland: Tuckwell, 1987), 21–39.
20 Ibid., 29.
21 John Millar, *Origin of the Distinction of Ranks; or, An Inquiry into the circumstances which give rise to Influence and Authority, in the different*

members of society, 4th ed. (1771; corrected ed., Glasgow, 1806), "Introduction."

22 Daiches, *Hotbed*, 18. Such, too, in the author's experience was the new philosopher George Grant at Dalhousie University in the 1940s.

23 Aaron Garrett, "Anthropology: The 'Original' of Human Nature," in *CCSE*, 80.

24 Richard B. Sher, "Introduction," in *Scotland and America in the Age of Enlightenment*, ed. Richard B. Sher and Jeffrey R. Smitten (Princeton, NJ: Princeton University Press, 1990), 17.

25 Smart, "Provinces," 105.

26 Donald J. Withrington, "Schooling, Literacy and Society," in *People and Society*, vol. 1, *1760–1830*, ed. T.M. Devine and Rosalind Mitchison (Edinburgh: John Donald, 1988), 166, 170.

27 Women did not play a direct part in the Scottish Enlightenment, in contrast to their prominence in France at this time. By the end of the eighteenth century, however, they were active in literary writing and criticism, chiefly novels, while some "audited" university courses. At Edinburgh the Select Society, a noted debating group, considered issues such as woman's place in marriage and society. At Glasgow, Adam Smith, Thomas Reid, and John Millar all lectured and wrote about women's role in economic, social, and cultural terms.

28 Mitchison, *Lordship*, 169–70.

29 W.C. Lehmann, *John Millar of Glasgow, 1735–1801: His Life and Thought and His Contributions to Sociological Analysis* (Cambridge, MA: Harvard University Press, 1960), 14.

30 Mitchison, *Lordship*, 169; Bruce Lennan, *Integration, Enlightenment, and Industrialization: Scotland, 1746–1832* (London: Edward Arnold, 1981), 94.

31 Thanks to Dr. Charles Scobie for this memory of his days at Glasgow.

32 *Memoir*, 25. For James MacGregor's record at Glasgow, see W. Innes Addison, comp., *A Roll of the Graduates of the University of Glasgow, 1792–1897* (Glasgow, 1898), Glasgow University Library, Special Collections.

33 Thomas Miller, "Francis Hutcheson and the Civic Humanist Tradition," in *The Glasgow Enlightenment*, ed. Hook and Sher, 42–9.

34 Alexander Broadie, "The Human Mind and Its Powers," *CCSE*, 73–4.

35 Samuel Fleischaker, "The Impact on America: Scottish Philosophy and the American Founding," *CCSE*, 329.

36 Daiches, *Hotbed*, 31.

37 Garrett, "Anthropology," *CCSE*, 81.

38 Quoted in Broadie, "The Human Mind," *CCSE*, 71.

39 See, for example, his mss "The numbers, order, & names of the Irish letters, according to Forcharn's Uraiceuct" and "The number, order & names of the Letters according to O'Flaherty," Glasgow University Library, Special Collections, MS Gen 526/32, J.D. MacGregor.

40 Withrington, "Schooling," 164.

41 Lehmann, *Millar*, 31; L.B., "John Millar, 1759–1838," *DNB* 13, 402–3.

42 John Rae, *Life of Adam Smith* (London: Macmillan, 1895), 14.

43 Lehmann, *Millar*, 31.

44 John W. Cairns, "Legal Education in Glasgow, 1761–1801," in *The Glasgow Enlightenment*, ed. Hook and Sher, 151.

45 Anand C. Chitnis, *The Scottish Enlightenment & Early Victorian English Society* (London: Croom Helm, 1986), 15.

46 Murray H.G. Pittock, "Historiography," *CCSE*, 258–79, 264.

47 Lehmann, *Millar*, Foreword by R.M. McIver, viii; Lehmann, *Millar*, 50–1.

48 Ibid., 3.

49 Quoted in ibid., 373–4.

50 David Allan, *Virtue, Learning and the Scottish Enlightenment* (Edinburgh: Edinburgh University Press, 1993), 194. Allan also explores this idea in its Calvinist roots.

51 Ibid.; Richard B. Sher, *Church and University in the Scottish Enlightenment: The Moderate Literati of Edinburgh* (Edinburgh: Edinburgh University Press, 1985), 191.

52 Lehmann, *Millar*, 81.

53 Chitnis, *Scottish Enlightenment*, 14.

54 Ibid., 6.

55 Emerson, "Politics and Professors," *CCSE*, 34.

56 *Memoir*, 26–7.

57 Grant, *Folk Ways*, 131–2.

58 W.J. Watson, *Scottish Verse from the Book of the Dean of Lismore* (1937), xvii, quoted in Grant, *Folk Ways*, 132.

59 *Memoir*, 37. Patterson misspells "Morison" here.

60 Addison, *Roll of the Graduates*, [n.p.].

5. In Passage

1 *Memoir*, 47.

2 NSA, MacGregor Papers, MFM 10876, folder X, no. 2, "Petition from Pictou"; *Memoir*, appendix A, "Petition from Pictou," 512.

3 Ibid.; *Memoir*, 511–12.

4 Ibid.; *Memoir*, 511.

5 NSA, MacGregor Papers, MFM 10876, folder X, no. 2, "Petition to the Presbytery of Perth"; *Memoir*, 512–13.

6 *Memoir*, 44.

7 MCA, JMP, "Excerpts from Correspondence, Diaries, Sermon Notes, 1786–1811," box F&I-023/4; *Memoir*, 43–5.

8 Ibid., box F&I-023/4/4; *Memoir*, 47.

9 NSA, MFM 10875, "Diary of Rev. James MacGregor," [n.p.] (hereafter, NSA, MFM 10875, Diary); *Memoir*, 47–8.

10 *Memoir*, 50.

11 Ibid., 49; Rev. James Robertson, *History of the Mission of the Secession Church to Nova Scotia and Prince Edward Island, From its Commencement in 1765* (Edinburgh, 1847), 76.

12 NSA, MFM 10876, folder S, 1–19, "Correspondence with John Buist."

13 NSA, MFM 10876, folder X, no. 2, "Rev. John Buist Notes," 30 May 1786; *Memoir*, "Extract of Ordination … ," 514–16.

14 *Memoir*, 53.

15 Ibid., 52.

16 NSA, MFM 10875, Diary; *Memoir*, 59–60.

17 NSA, MFM 10875, Diary.

18 Ibid.

19 NSA, MFM 10876, folder L, no. 22, "MacGregor, Halifax, to Robert Patterson, Pictou, 13 July 1786."

20 NSA, MFM, 10875, Diary.

21 Ibid.

22 Ibid.

23 Ibid.

24 Ibid.

25 Ibid.

26 *Memoir*, 117–18. See also Rev. John MacKerrow, History of the Secession Church, 2 vols., Edinburgh: Wm. Oliphant, 1839. 1, 434.

27 NSA MFM 10876, folder S, no. 6, "Buist to MacGregor, 2 March 1790."

28 NSA, MFM 10875, Diary.

29 Ibid.

30 Arthur E. Betts, *Our Fathers in the Faith: Maritime Presbyterian Ministers* (Halifax: Maritime Conference Archives, 1983), 28; Robertson, *Mission*, 19–24.

31 Robertson, *Mission*, 34.

32 Ibid., 32.

33 NSA, MFM 10875, Diary.

34 Ibid.

35 Ibid.
36 Ibid.
37 Ibid.
38 Ibid.
39 NSA, MFM 10876, folder X, no. 2. He brought with him a letter of
    introduction from Pagan and Buchanan addressed to the two Pattersons:
    "Pagan and Buchanan to Messrs Robert and John Patterson, 2 June 1786,"
    MCA, JMP, box F&I-023/4/23.

6. Orienting

 1 Rev. George Patterson, *A History of the County of Pictou* (Belleville, ON:
    Mika, 1972 [repr.]). 22 (hereafter, PH). "Pictou" is pronounced "Pick-toh."
 2 See D. Campbell & R.A. MacLean, *Beyond the Atlantic Roar: A Study of
    the Nova Scotia Scots* (Toronto: McClelland & Stewart, 1974). This is still
    the best condensed source for a discussion of Scottish development in
    northeastern Nova Scotia and Cape Breton Island (hereafter, *Beyond*).
 3 *Memoir*, 74–80; PH, 56.
 4 The Archibald party named two of Pictou's landmarks, Mount Thom
    and Mount Ephraim, after members of this party. Samuel Archibald
    was the author's four-times great-uncle, and his wife's four-times great-
    grandfather.
 5 W. Frank Craven, "John Witherspoon," in Alexander Leitch, *A Princeton
    Companion* (Princeton, NJ: Princeton University Press, 1978).
 6 Frank Patterson, *John Patterson: The Founder of Pictou Town* (Truro: Truro
    Publishing, 1955), 5.
 7 Ibid., 9.
 8 Ibid., 2.
 9 *Memoir*, 78–80; J.P. MacPhie, *Pictonians at the Home and Abroad* (Boston:
    Pinkham, 1914), 14–22.
10 *Memoir*, 79.
11 PH, appendix D., 457.
12 PH, 80–1.
13 PH, 14–19; *Memoir*, 78–80; James M. Cameron, *Pictou County's History*
    (Pictou: Pictou County Historical Society, 1972), 10–12.
14 Bernard Bailyn, *The Peopling of British North America: An Introduction* (New
    York: Knopf, 1986), 12–14.
15 *Memoir*, 511.
16 Ibid.
17 Frank Patterson, *Patterson*, 14.

18 *Memoir*, 96.

19 Ibid., 107.

20 NSA, MFM 10875, Diary.

21 While teaching at Johns Hopkins, Newcomb designed and operated the largest telescope in the United States, at the Naval Observatory. He became the dean of American mathematical astronomers, gaining world recognition.

22 NSA, MFM 10875, Diary; *Memoir*, 131–2, 220.

23 *Memoir*, 101.

24 Strict Anti-Burghers objected to anything but the human voice, and to Watts's New Testament "hymns." Like the Catholics, they clung to familiar, metrical forms and the awesome justice of the old psalms. Later, James mounted a long, turgid defence of the original psalms, reprinted by Patterson as "A Defence of the Religious Imprecations and Denunciations of God's Wrath, Contained in the Book of Psalms, against the Enemies of the Gospel," in *A Few Remains of the Rev. James MacGregor, D.D.*, comp. rev. George Patterson (Philadelphia: Joseph M. Wilson, 1859), 1–97 (hereafter, *Remains*).

25 NSA, MFM 10875, Diary.

26 John Witherspoon, also a Dissenter, strove for simplicity in his sermons. He gave his opinion of the typical Kirk sermon of the day as "an ostentatious shell of words, or a painted ornamental foppery of style, so ill suited to the gravity of the pulpit; an abstracted, refined or philosophical disquisition, which, if it has any meaning at all, perhaps not three in the audience can understand." Quoted by Sher, *Church and University*, 169.

27 NSA, MFM 10875, Diary.

28 *Memoir*, 101.

29 Ibid., 200.

30 For example, the case of Kenneth Fraser. See *Memoir*, 106.

31 Robertson, *Mission*. See also Donald MacLean Sinclair, "Dr. MacGregor as Gaelic Poet," in *Celebration Addresses*, 20.

7. Settling In and Broadening Out

1 NSA, MFM 10875, Diary.

2 MacPhie, *Pictonians*, 10.

3 It was not until late in life that James found time to revise the paper. It appeared in print posthumously, revised and published by Patterson as "A Guide to Baptism, Being An Attempt to Guide the Plain Christian Unto the Scripture Doctrine and Practice of Baptism, Written about the Year

1826," in *Remains*, 135–65. See draft in NSA, MacGregor Papers, MFM 10876, folder X, no. 7.

4 *Memoir*, 34–5.

5 MacPhie, *Pictonians*, 149; NSA, MFM 10875, Diary; PH, 146. According to *The Fifth Head of the First Book of Disciplines* (1560), "A certain time must be appointed to reading and to learning the catechism, a certain time to the grammar, and to the Latin tongue; a certain time to the arts, philosophy, and to the tongues; and a certain [time] to that study in which they intend chiefly to travail for the profit of the commonwealth."

6 B.F. MacDonald, "Intellectual Forces in Pictou, 1803–1843" (MA thesis, University of New Brunswick, 1977), 11, 20. Compare, too, the able account of Rev. Samuel Elder, who later added to the "genteel Baptist tradition" in New Brunswick. See "Samuel Elder: A Formal and Genteel Evangelical Ministry," chap. 8 in Daniel C. Goodwin, *Into Deep Waters: Evangelical Spirituality and Maritime Calvinistic Baptist Ministers, 1790–1855,* (Montreal: McGill-Queen's University Press, 2010), 207–33.

7 NSA, MFM 10875, Diary.

8 Ibid.

9 Ibid.

10 MacLaren, *Pictou Book*, 168–73.

11 NSA, MFM 10875, Diary.

12 Gordon Robertson, "History of Churchville … 1784–1934," *New Glasgow Evening News*, 21 October 1957, in Gray Box Collection, NG-Ref, New Glasgow Public Library, New Glasgow, NS; *Memoir*, 121.

13 The elm was felled for safety's sake. A historic plaque was removed to a nearby church.

14 *Memoir*, 198.

15 Ibid., 140.

16 NSA, MFM 10875, Diary.

17 Rev. Samuel Gilfillan to MacGregor, 13 August 1808, NSA MFM 10876, folder U.

18 Susan Buggey, Barry Cahill, and Jenni Calder are recent exceptions to the judgment that MacGregor was inflexible. Calder calls him "open-minded": Jenni Calder, *Scots in Canada* (Edinburgh: Luath Press, 2003), 42–3.

19 NSA, MFM 10875, Diary. Italics mine.

20 Ibid.

21 Ibid.

22 Ibid.

23 Ibid., *Memoir*, 27; Michael F. Hennessey, ed., *The Catholic Church in Prince Edward Island, 1720–1979* (Summerside, PE: Roman Catholic Episcopal

Corporation, 1979), 287–8; NSA, MFM 10875, Diary; PH, 163; Duncan Campbell, *History of Prince Edward Island* (Charlottetown, 1875), 188–90; John M. MacLeod, *History of Presbyterianism on Prince Edward Island* (Chicago: Winona, 1904), 257.

24 Norman D. Kennedy, "Dr. James MacGregor: An Apostle," in *Celebration Addresses*, 106.

25 NSA, MFM 10875, Diary.

26 David Alston, "Social and Economic History of the Old Shire of Cromarty, 1650–1850." Unpublished PhD dissertation, University of Dundee, Scotland, 1999, "The Nigg Revival."

27 NSA, MFM 10875, Diary; MCA, JMP, "Dr. MacGregor's First Session Book, 17 September 1786–3 June 1804," 6 May 1787, box F&I.

28 NSA, MFM 10875, Diary; James Drummond to James McGregor, 7 April 1788, MCA, JMP, box F&I-023/12/7.

29 NSA, MFM 10875, Diary.

30 Ibid.

31 Frank Patterson, *Patterson*, 56; *Memoir*, 146.

32 NSA, MFM 10876, folders Q & R; "The Rev. James MacGregor, Personal Accounts & Receipts, 1792–1803, 'Edward Mortimer, Merchant.'"

33 NSA, MFM 10875, Diary.

34 Ibid.

35 Ibid.

36 Ibid., an early Canadian challenge to bilingualism.

37 Ibid.

38 Roland H. Sherwood, *The Log Church at Loch Broom* (Hantsport, NS: Lancelot, 1986). A replica of the church stands at the site today.

39 NSA, MFM 10895, Diary.

40 Ibid.

41 Kennedy, "MacGregor: An Apostle," in *Celebration Addresses*, 119.

42 Ibid.

43 Ibid.

44 Ibid.; *Memoir*, 182–3, 184–5.

45 [Hon.] D.C. Fraser, Address, *Proceedings at the Centennial Celebration of James Church Congregation, New Glasgow, September 17th, 1886* (New Glasgow: S.M. Mackenzie, 1886), 41 (hereafter, *Proceedings*, 1886).

46 D.C. Harvey, "The Intellectual Awakening of Nova Scotia," *Dalhousie Review* 13 (1933): 1–22.

47 *Memoir*, 123–4.

48 Ibid., 129.

49 At an outdoor meeting, when a rain-filled cloud advanced on them, James called for calm and prayer, beseeching divine intervention. Whereupon "the cloud which appeared coming right upon them was diverted from its course, but passed so near them, that they could see the heavy drops falling." *Memoir*, 201–2.

50 NSA, MFM 10875, Diary.

51 Ibid.

52 MCA, JMP, "Dr. MacGregor's First Session Book, 17 September 1786–3 June 1804," box F&I.

8. Letter to a Minister

1 See, too, the case of "Mungo" and Dr. Harris, *Memoir*, appendix D, 516.

2 Rev. J. Barlas to MacGregor, 30 March 1792, NSA, MFM 10876, folder U, no. 5.

3 *Memoir*, 150–8. The full text of MacGregor's attack appears as "A Letter to a Clergyman, Urging Him to Set Free a Black Girl he held in Slavery," reprinted in *Remains*, 167–88; see also Barry Cahill, "The Antislavery Polemic of the Reverend James MacGregor: Canada's Proto-Abolitionist as 'Radical Evangelical,'" in *The Contribution of Presbyterianism to the Maritime Provinces of Canada*, ed. Charles H.H. Scobie & G.A. Rawlyk (Montreal: McGill-Queen's University Press, 1997), 132–43; Barry Cahill, "Mediating a Scottish Enlightenment Ideal: The Presbyterian Dissenter Attack on Slavery in Late Eighteenth-Century Nova Scotia," in *Myth, Migration and the Making of Memory: Scotia and Nova Scotia c. 1700–1990*, ed. Marjory Harper and Michael E. Vance (Halifax: Gorsebrook Research Institute & Fernwood Books; Edinburgh: John Donald, 1999), 189–201; and Harper and Vance, "Myth, Migration and Memory," in ibid., "Introduction," 14–48.

  Note: Richard Kidston, Halifax, acknowledged receipt of MacGregor's manuscript, assuring him that it would be published as a "Small Pamphlet by itself, which will be done this week." Kidston to MacGregor, 14 July 1788, NSA, MFM 10876, folder N, no. 1.

4 *Memoir*, 151.

5 Cameron, *Pictou County's History*, 211.

6 NSA, MFM 10876, folder S, No.7, Buist to MacGregor, 20.8.98.

7 J. Watt, "Ramsay, James (1733–1789)," in *New Oxford Dictionary of National Biography*, online ed. (Oxford: Oxford University Press, 2006).

8 NSA, MFM 10876, folder 9, No. 2, Smith to MacGregor, 14 July 1788 & 28 February 1789; reprinted in *Remains*, 167–8.

9 Ibid., "Letter," 170.
10 Ibid., 170–1.
11 Ibid., 171–7.
12 Ibid., 172–5.
13 Ibid., 174–5.
14 Ibid., 177.
15 Ibid., 178.
16 Ibid., 179–80.
17 Ibid., 180.
18 Ibid., 181.
19 Ibid., 181–2. Emphasis mine.
20 Ibid., 183.
21 Ibid.
22 Ibid.
23 Ibid., 183–4.
24 Cahill, "Polemic," 139.
25 *Remains*, "Letter," 188.
26 Robin Winks, "Negroes in the Maritimes: An Introductory Survey," *Dalhousie Review* 48 (1968): 461.
27 Robin Winks, *The Blacks in Canada: A History*, 2nd ed. (Montreal: McGill-Queen's University Press, 1997), 103; see Smith's ripostes, NSA, MFM 10876, folder S, no. 2. Smith to MacGregor, 14 July 1788 & 25 February 1789.
28 *Memoir*, 152–3.

9. On the Road

1 MCA, JMP, "Dr. MacGregor's First Session Book, 17 September 1786–3 June 1804," various entries, box F&I.
2 *Memoir*, 137.
3 Sher, "Introduction," *Scotland and America*, 15.
4 Leith Eric Schmidt, "The Scottish Context of Presbyterian Revivalism in America," in ibid., 65–80; see also Laurie Stanley-Blackwell, *"Tokens of Grace": Cape Breton's Open Air Communion Tradition* (Sydney: Cape Breton University Press, 2006).
5 Schmidt, "Context," 71.
6 Ibid., 72.
7 Stanley-Blackwell, *Tokens of Grace*, 193–202.
8 Ibid., 195; See also Laurie Stanley-Blackwell, "Tabernacles in the Wilderness": The Open-Air Communion Tradition in Nineteenth

and Twentieth Century Cape Breton," in *Contribution*, ed. Scobie and Rawlyk, 96.

9 Interview with Mrs. Janet McColl Oxley, Halifax, 1953.

10 Quoted in George Shepperson, "Andrew Brown, 1763–1834," *DCB* 6, 87–8.

11 Ibid., 87.

12 Andrew Brown to MacGregor, 31 January 1793, MCA, JMP, box F&I-023/3/5–6.

13 Donald A. Fergusson, ed., *Beyond the Hebrides, Including the Cape Breton Collection* (Halifax: Lawson Graphics, 1977), 292–5.

14 *Memoir*, 298–9; Rev. J. Barlas to MacGregor, 26 April 1789, NSA, MFM 10876, folder U. no. 4.

15 *Memoir*, 202–3.

16 Ibid., 255–6.

17 Ibid., 179–80.

18 Ibid., 181.

19 Quoted in *One Hundred and Fifty Years in the Life of the First Presbyterian Church, New Glasgow* (Toronto: Presbyterian Publications, 1939), 63.

20 *Memoir*, 275.

21 Ibid., 234–5.

22 Ibid., 165.

23 Ibid., 193.

24 Ibid.; cf. Peter Burroughs, "Ramsay, George, 9th Earl of Dalhousie, 1770–1838," *DCB* 7, 722.

25 *Memoir*, 167.

26 Ibid., 187.

27 Ibid., 231.

28 See, for example, ibid., 108.

29 William McCulloch, Address, *Proceedings*, 1886, 22.

30 Ibid., 227–8.

31 Ibid., 178. The best short account of Henry Alline and the Nova Scotia New Lights remains J.M. Bumsted, *Henry Alline, 1748–1784*, Canadian Biographical Series, ed., Alan Wilson (Toronto: University of Toronto Press, 1971).

32 Ibid.

33 Ibid., 190–1.

34 Robert Archibald to MacGregor, MCA, JMP, "Correspondence 1791–1816," box F&I-023/5/MI-3 & in typescript, 023/5/MI-4; ibid., M2/1–2; ibid., M3/1–2. I have omitted the many [sics] that the letter warrants.

35 Ibid., M3 [n.d.]; *Memoir*, 178; Thomas Millar, *Historical and Genealogical Record of … Colchester County* (Halifax, 1873), 76 (hereafter, Millar, *Record*);

Cameron, *Pictou County's History*. Millar is now often questioned in its details, but it remains a remarkable pioneering narrative and genetic jigsaw.

36 Susan Buggey in her fine article on MacGregor in the *DCB* lists only four visits to the Island, but there were at least ten: 1791, 1794, 1800, 1806, 1808, 1815, 1816, 1817, 1819, and 1821. Susan Buggey, "James Drummond (MacGregor) MacGregor, 1759–1830," in *DCB* 6, 458; J.L. MacDougall, *History of Inverness County, Nova Scotia*. Belleville, ON, Mika Facsimile Edition, 1972).

10. Years of Trial

1 For his extended problems over stipends, see *Memoir*, 139–50.
2 Quoted by William McCulloch, "Address," in *Proceedings*, 1886, 25. James was meticulous in keeping an account of every parishioner's assets in land, house, buildings, and animals – those elements on which an estimate of their assessment for his stipend would be based. See, for example, "Personal Accounts, 1787–1794," MCA, JMP, box F&I-023/9/Q5-30.
3 A.H. Clark, *Three Centuries and the Island: A Historical Geography of Settlement and Agriculture in Prince Edward Island, Canada* (Toronto: University of Toronto Press, 1959); Campbell, *History of Prince Edward Island*; F.W.P. Bolger, ed., *Canada's Smallest Province: A History of Prince Edward Island* (Halifax: Nimbus, 1991); G.N.D. Evans, *Uncommon Obdurate: The Several Public Careers of J.F.W. DesBarres* (Toronto: University of Toronto Press, 1969), 44–58.
4 Robert Critchlow Tuck, "Theophilus DesBrisay, 1754–1823," *DCB* 6, 197–8.
5 *Memoir*, 219; William Gregg, *History of the Presbyterian Church in the Dominion of Canada* (Toronto: Presbyterian Print and Publishing, 1885), 100.
6 *Memoir*, 212.
7 Ibid., 213.
8 Ibid., 213–14.
9 Ibid., italics his, 214–18.
10 Ibid., 219, fn.
11 Ibid., 220.
12 Ibid., 245–50.
13 Ibid., 246–9.
14 Ibid., 252; "Letter to the General Associate Synod. Originally Published by the Order of Synod in the Year 1793, with Explanatory notes by a Committee of Synod," in *Remains*, 189–203.
15 *Remains*, 193.

16 Ibid., 194.
17 Ibid., 197–201.
18 Ibid., 201–2.
19 *Memoir*, 262–4.
20 Winthrop Bell, *The "Foreign Protestants" and the Settlement of Nova Scotia* (Toronto: University of Toronto Press, 1961), 99–101, 550–2.
21 Evans, *Uncommon Obdurate*, 51.
22 *Memoir*, 189.
23 MacDonald, "Intellectual Forces," 20.
24 *Memoir*, 189.
25 Ibid., 274.
26 Gilfillan to MacGregor, 22 April 1795, MCA, JMP, box F&I-023/31/7/8.
27 *Memoir*, 273.
28 Ibid., 276.

11. A Threefold Cord and a Wedding

1 *Memoir*, 276.
2 MCA, JMP, "Dr. MacGregor's First Session Book, 17 September 1786–3 June 1804," entry for 3 July 1793.
3 *Memoir*, 276.
4 Ibid., 287.
5 Cited in David Brown, *Life of the Late John Duncan, LL.D. …*, 2nd ed., rev. (Edinburgh: Edmonston & Douglas, 1872), 25. If Bruce was quick in his stride, he was not so in the pulpit. David Brown repeats the elder M'Crie, saying that "in the pulpit his measured slowness would in our day be scarcely endured even by the most patient."
6 *Memoir*, 289. Italics his.
7 Consult Robert Gaston Hall, "Archibald Bruce of Whitburn (1746–1816) With Special Reference To His View Of Church and State"(unpub. PhD diss., University of Edinburgh, November 1954), 292 pp. Although Hall does not treat Bruce's interest in overseas missions or his contacts with MacGregor, which this biography seeks to do, Hall's thesis is invaluable in understanding the eccentric Bruce. For a treatment of Bruce more relevant to this study, see Jack C. Whytock, *"An Educated Clergy": Scottish Theological Education and Training in the Kirk Secession, 1560–1850* (Milton Keynes, UK: Paternoster, 2007), 272–85.
8 Rev. Thomas M'Crie, *Life of Thomas M'Crie, D.D. … By His son* (Edinburgh, 1840), 56; Rev. Graham Mitchell, "Parish of Whitburn," in A.M. Bisset *History of Bathgate and District* (Bathgate: District Council, 1906), 154–7;

Rev. Dr. Sherman Isbell, "Bruce, Archibald," in *Dictionary of Scottish Church History & Theology* (Edinburgh: T&T Clark,1993), 103; Derek B. Murray, "Bruce, Archibald," *Dictionary of National Biography* (Oxford: Oxford University Press, 2004).

9 *Memoir*, 363.

10 Rev. W.B. McMartin, *A History of the Congregation of Brucefield Church, Whitburn, 1857–1957*, ms, Whitburn Public Library, West Lothian, Local History Collection; M'Crie Jr, *M'Crie*, 55, fn.

11 MacGregor to William Young, Philadelphia, 11 August 1803, in *Memoir*, 336.

12 Quoted in Brown, *Duncan*, 24.

13 Ibid., 24–5.

14 M'Crie Jr., *M'Crie*, 55.

15 Cahill, "Mediating," 189–201.

16 McCrie Jr, *McCrie*, 57.

17 Alexander MacKenzie, "The Editor in Canada," *The Celtic Magazine* (Inverness, Scotland) 5 (1879–80): 69.

18 *Memoir*, 289–90.

19 MCA, "Presbytery of Truro Minutes, 1786-1875," vol. 1, 1786–1826, [n.p.]; *Memoir*, 407.

20 *Memoir*, 294.

21 Ibid., 295–6.

22 Ibid., 295.

23 Ibid., 290–2.

24 Ibid.

25 Ibid., 296–7.

26 Rev. Robert Grant, "East River Worthies," originally in Eastern Chronicle Series, now in Pictou County GenWeb, 24 August 2005. Thanks to Web Editor Richard MacNeill: http://www.rootsweb.com/~nspictou.

27 Chain Rock is still a popular swimming and picnicking site on the Northwest Arm, Halifax.

28 Robertson, *Mission*, 181.

29 Rev. Robert Grant, "East River Worthies"; Barry Cahill, "The Reverend James MacGregor Marriage Scandal," *Nova Scotia Genealogist* 13, no. 3 (1995): 134–6.

30 *Memoir*, 303.

31 Terence M. Punch, comp., *Religious Marriages in Halifax, 1766–1841, From Original Sources*, GANS Publication no. 16 (Halifax: Formac, 1996), cited in Cahill, "MacGregor Marriage Scandal," 134.

32 Judith Fingard, "Robert Stanser, 1760–1828," *DCB* 6, 731.

33 *Memoir*, 304.

34 Ibid., 305. Italics his.

35 MacGregor to Mrs. Forbes, Inverness, Scotland, [1805] MCA, JMP, "Correspondence, 1786–1811," box F&I-023/4/13.

12. East Side, West Side

1 J. Murray, *History of the Presbyterian Church in Cape Breton* (Truro: News Publishing Company, 1921), 236; Evans, *Uncommon Obdurate*, chap. 17; Laurie Stanley-Blackwell, *The Well-Watered Garden: The Presbyterian Church in Cape Breton, 1798–1860* (Sydney: University College of Cape Breton Press, 1983), 37–8; Robert J. Morgan, *Early Cape Breton: From Founding to Famine* (Sydney: Breton Books, 2000), chaps. 1 & 2.

2 Grant, *Folk Ways*, 137–8.

3 Quoted in *The Presbyterian Witness*, 5 May 1850.

4 McIllwharnell to MacGregor, 24 March 1801, MCA, JMP, box F&I-023/12/T17.

5 Donaldson to MacGregor, 24 March 1801, MCA, JMP, box F&I-023/12/1.

6 *Memoir*, 326.

7 Ibid., 333.

8 Reprinted as "Essay on the Duration and Character of the Millennial Age of the Church," in *Remains*, 99–134; original in *The Christian Magazine*, vol. 4.

9 J. Roger, *Buffon: A Life of Natural History*, ed. L.P. Williams, trans. S. Lucille (Ithaca, NY: Cornell University Press, 1997). Its several volumes first appeared in an English translation between 1790 and 1799, by William Smellie.

10 Paul Wood, "Who Was John Anderson?" in *Glasgow Enlightenment*, ed. Hook & Sher, 111–32.

11 "Essay on Millennial," in *Remains*, 111–12. Italics his.

12 "View of Nature," in "Essay on Millennial," in *Remains*, 116.

13 Ibid., 116.

14 Ibid., 134.

15 *Memoir*, chap. 14.

16 Rev. T. Chalmers Jack, "Days of the Fathers in East Hants," in *Centennial Celebration of the Ordination and Induction of the Late Rev. Alexander Dick, Presbyterian Minister, Maitland, Hants County, Nova Scotia, June 21st and 23rd* " (Halifax: Maitland Centennial Celebration Committee, 1903), 55; Betts, *Our Fathers*, 33; Rev. E.V. Forbes, *Address Given by the Rev. E.V. Forbes in St. David's Church, [Maitland, NS], June 19, 1953; Marking the 150th Anniversary of the Church*, [1953], [pp. 2–5].

17 The point is made in Susan Buggey and Gwendolyn Davies, "Thomas McCulloch, 1776–1843," *DCB* 7, 529–41; see also Leslie Armour and Elizabeth Trott, *The Faces of Reason: An Essay on Philosophy and Culture in English Canada, 1850–1950* (Waterloo, ON: Wilfrid Laurier Press, 1981), 64.

18 "Thomas Dick, 1774–1857," in *DNB* 15, 17–18; *Concise Dictionary of National Biography*, 789–90.

19 Jack, "Fathers," 56.

20 Rev. John Currie, "A Stone of Memorial," in *Centennial Celebration of the Ordination and Induction of the Late Rev. Alexander Dick, Presbyterian Minister, Maitland, Hants County, Nova Scotia, June 21st and 23rd "* (Halifax: Maitland Centennial Celebration Committee, 1903), 7–18.

21 McCulloch to Rev. Dr. John Mitchell, 17 February 1831, in NSA, vol. 553; Michael Gauvreau, however, subscribes unreservedly to the heroic McCulloch model, not even mentioning MacGregor in his account of Pictou's and the Pictou Academy's roots in the Scottish Enlightenment and advancing that McCulloch both "founded" and "powerfully reinforced" them. See Gauvreau, "Between Awakening and Enlightenment: The Evangelical Colleges, 1820–1860," in *The Evangelical Century*, ed. G.A. Rawlyk, chap. 1 (Montreal: McGill-Queen's University Press, 1991), 13 et seq.

22 *Memoir*, 377; "One Hundred and Fifty Years," 63.

23 Thomas McCulloch, "Morton" [unpub. ms], NSA, Thomas McCulloch Papers, MG1, vol. 555, no. 76, [n.p.].

24 On Pictou's economy and social growth, see R.M. Guy, "Industrial Development and Urbanization of Pictou County to 1900" (unpub. MA thesis, Acadia University, Wolfville, NS, 1962); Campbell and Maclean, *Beyond*, 76–78; Cameron, *Pictou County's History*, chaps. 7–9.

25 George MacLaren, *The Pictou Book: Stories of Our Past* (New Glasgow: Hector, 1954), 265.

26 *Memoir*, 106–7, emphasis mine. Current Scottish historians question the assumption that the Highlands were wastelands of ignorance and indifference to education. See the work of Donald Withrington and others.

27 3 August 1790, Robertson to MacGregor, MCA, JMP, 023/12/T19.

28 *Memoir*, 267.

29 The benefactor was a "Mr. Alice/Ellis" of Paisley. James Alice to MacGregor, 27 February 1795 & 1796, MCA, JMP, box F&I-A0173A/14/1&2; Rev. James Watt to MacGregor, 18 March 1796, ibid., box F&I-A0173A/16/V6. 30.

30 John MacKay, "Reminiscences of a Long Life," Grey Box Collection, New Glasgow Public Library, New Glasgow, NS.

31 PH, 157.

32 D.C. Harvey, "Early Public Libraries in Nova Scotia," *Dalhousie Review* 15 (January 1935): 429–43.

33 *Memoir*, 143.

34 Ibid., 144.

35 Ibid., 322. One of the tools he invented was on view at the province's Ross Farm Museum.

36 Dunlop, "Duncan Ross, 1770–1834," *DCB* 6, 659; G. M. Grant, "James MacGregor," in *Celebration Addresses*, 32.

37 Guy, "Industrial Development," 28; Michael. "Coal in the History of Nova Scotia," in *Industry and Society in Nova Scotia: An Illustrated History*, ed. James E. Candow (Halifax: Fernwood, 2001), 57–79.

38 *Memoir*, 321. J.S. Martell dates this fireside chat to the 1793 election, but that was before James built his house and began experimenting with coal: Martel, "Early Coal-Mining in Nova Scotia," *Dalhousie Review* 5, no. 25 (April, 1945) 156–72.

39 Isabella McCulloch, "Dr. Thomas McCulloch," in *Celebration Addresses*, 185.

40 Susan Buggey, "John Keir, 1780–1858," *DCB* 8, 451–3; *Memoir*, 359; George Patterson, *A Brief Sketch of the life and labours of the late Rev. John Keir, D.D.* (New Glasgow: S.M. MacKenzie, 1859).

41 MacLaren, *Pictou Book*, 168–73.

42 Douglas C., "The Story of Pictou Presbytery from Its Beginning to the Union of 1875" (unpub. M.Div diss, Atlantic School of Theology, Halifax, NS, May 1973), 90.

43 *Memoir*, 399.

44 Ibid., 391. One recent young scholar misses MacGregor's wry wit here, his unfailing generosity, and his thin purse consequent on his extensive charities and large family and accuses him of meanness in this instance. McCulloch acknowledged James as the largest fundraiser and one of the most generous in support of the Pictou Academy. A frontier minister seldom received the cash owing him and often got only indifferent produce unfit for resale. In cash terms, it was not meanness but poverty.

45 *Memoir*, 391.

46 Ibid.

13. New Places, New Faces

1 Duncan Ferguson to MacGregor, 29 July 1806 & 4 June 1824, MCA, JMP, boxes F&I-023/4/18, 023/3/11 & A0173A/16/10.

2 MCA, JMP, diary entries, box F&I-023/4/18; *Memoir*, 338–49. Susan Buggey lists only his first visit to Miramichi in 1797, but he went again in 1807 and 1816: Buggey, "MacGregor," *DCB* 6, 458; *Memoir*, 358.

3 Ibid., 340; interview with Mrs. Janet McColl Oxley, Halifax, 1953.

4 Ibid., 342.

5 Ibid., 344–5.

6 Ibid., 347.

7 Ibid.

8 *The Christian Magazine*, x; *Memoir*, 351.

9 *Memoir*, 234.

10 Ibid., 353–6.

11 John M. MacLeod, *History of Presbyterianism on Prince Edward Island* (Chicago: Winona, 1904), 57–60.

12 Ibid., 59; *Memoir*, 356.

13 Rev. S. Gilfillan to MacGregor, 24 July 1806, MCA, JMP, box F&I-A0173A/14/8; Patterson, "Pioneers," NSA, MG 1, vols. 741–3, [unpub. ms].

14 *Memoir*, 357.

15 Patterson, "Pioneers," NSA, MG 1, vol. 743.

16 "Minutes of Presbytery of Truro, 1786–1875," 14 October 1808, MCA, MF-51.

17 Gordon at "John Thomsons, P.E.I.," to Janet Gordon, 22 October 1808, MCA, JMP, box F&I-A0173A/16/8; also in NSA, MFM 10876, folder Z [pt. 2], Gordon Letters, z. 23; P. Gordon to Janet Gordon, 22 October 1808; Gordon at Malpeque to Janet Gordon, 28 March 1809, ibid., folder Z. 25; Hugh Graham to Peter Graham, 7 July 1809, NSA, Rev. Hugh Graham Fonds, MG 1, B 1, 332B; NSA, Patterson, "Pioneers," MG 1, vol. 742.

18 Rev. S. Gilfillan to MacGregor, 13 August 1808, MCA, JMP, box F&I-A1073A/14/9.

19 Buggey, "John Keir," *DCB* 8, 451–3; *Memoir*, 359; George Patterson, *Brief Sketch*.

20 Bruce to MacGregor, 27 March 1815, MCA, JMP, box F&I-A1073A/17/3.

21 *Memoir*, 364.

22 Betts, *Our Fathers*, 95–6.

23 G. Lawson Gordon, *River John: Its Pastors and People* (New Glasgow: G. Lawson Gordon, 1911).

24 Glenelg (Forks of St. Marys) "Pre-1900 Houses," [unpub., "Introduction"], Sherbrooke Branch Library, Sherbrooke, NS, Local History Collection, 1975. ("St Marys" was then spelled so.)

25 *Memoir*, 365.

26 Inscription on MacGregor tombstone in Pioneer Cemetery, New Glasgow, NS.
27 *Memoir*, 365.
28 Ibid., 367; see also MacGregor to Keir, 20 December 1811, MCA, JMP, box F&I-023/1/5.
29 Patterson, "Pioneers," NSRM, MG 1, vol. 743.
30 Thanks to Edith Patterson, Truro, for a copy of this letter.
31 Bruce to MacGregor, 27 March 1815, MCA, JMP, box F&I-A0173/17/3. Bruce also comments on Napoleon's escape from Elba three weeks earlier.

14. Pictou and Progress

1 See James J. Cameron's several books on the district; on lumbering, consult Alton A. Lomas, "The Industrial Development of Nova Scotia, 1830–1854" (unpub. MA thesis, Dalhousie University, 1950), 4, 13, 31, 87. See Pictou County map.
2 MacLaren, *Pictou Book*, 236.
3 James M. Cameron, *Industrial History of the New Glasgow District* (New Glasgow: Hector, [1961]), chap. 2.
4 Campbell and MacLean, *Beyond*, 53–5.
5 Cameron, *Industrial History*, chap. 8; Campbell & MacLean, *Beyond*, 44; Lomas, "Industrial Development," 36.
6 Susan Buggey, "Edward Mortimer, 1768–1819," *DCB* 5, 611–12.
7 PH, 251.
8 Mortimer is an enigmatic figure. His portrait shows him to be tall and commanding and suggests a soft, fleshy face, prominent forehead crowned by curly light hair, penetratingly clear eyes, a strong nose, a small, girlish mouth, a double chin, and the corpulence that betrayed his love of good wine and fine food. See the Field portrait in the Art Gallery of Nova Scotia; a photograph of the painting is available at NSA.
9 Judith Fingard, "Sir John Wentworth, 1737–1820," *DCB* 5, 850; Brian Cuthbertson, *The Loyalist Governor* (Halifax: Petheric Press, 1980).
10 Mortimer to MacGregor, 11 & 15 December 1799, MCA, JMP, box F&I-023/3/9 & 10; ibid., 023/7/06. Although Mortimer asked MacGregor to arrange for "cheese, meat & bread" to be available at an East River meeting, he first apologized ["I am making too free with you but I beg your excuse"] and then asked him to alert several men to arrange for additional "refreshment" on their coming out of the woods. There is no record of James's reply or subsequent action, but these were Highlanders and it was long before James's temperance days.

11 Judith Tulloch, "William Cottnam Tonge, 1764–1832," *DCB* 6, 780; Fingard, "Wentworth," *DCB* 5, 850.

12 Tonge to MacGregor, "November," 1799, MCA, JMP, box F&I-023/7/05.

13 David Sutherland, "Michael Wallace, 1744–1831," *DCB* 6, 327–9.

14 Two decades later, with its usual resilience, Pictou County had diversified and was prospering again in textiles, hardwood, furniture-making, milling, coalmining, leather works, foundries, and an industrial railway. MacLaren, *Pictou Book*, 232; Lomas, "Industrial Development," chap. 6. James's son Robert was apprenticed to Lippincott's tannery, later entering the trade himself.

15 *Memoir*, 317–18, 369–71.

16 Cf. Armour and Trott, *The Faces of Reason*, 63–5; Thomas McCulloch, *The Stepsure Letters*, ed. John A. Irving and Douglas Lochhead, New Canadian Library Series (Toronto: McClelland & Stewart, 1960). McCulloch initiated the tradition of Canadian satirical humour. Perhaps he had learned from his old teacher, Archibald Bruce, a master of satire: see his first question in "The Catechism Modernized" (1791): "What is the chief end of a Moderate Probationer? The chief end of a Moderate Probationer is to secure the Favour of a patron and procure a Kirk."

17 Bernard Pothier, "Jean-Mante, 1763–1844," *DCB* 7, 800–6.

18 *Memoir*, 369; emphasis mine.

19 Dunlop, "Ross," *DCB* 6, 659. Gordon Donaldson, *Scots Overseas*, 149, refers only to Ross and John Young in tracing Scottish contributions to agricultural reform in Nova Scotia, but MacGregor had begun experimenting with seeds, fertilizers, and implements well before Ross and Young's arrival; he was more inventive, and his provincial connections were wider than Ross's. Graeme Wynn cites MacGregor extensively: Graeme Wynn, "Exciting a Spirit of Emulation among the 'Podholes': Agricultural Reform in Pre-Confederation Nova Scotia," *Acadiensis* 20 (Autumn 1990), 5-51.

20 MacGregor to John Young, 19 April 1822, Report of East River Agricultural Society, NSA, RG 8, vol. 6, no. 144; Wynn, "Exciting," 15.

21 MacGregor to Young, 6 January 1820, NSA, MG 8, vol. 67, no. 129. See, for example, MacGregor to Young, 6 April 1820, NSA, MG 1, vol. 6, no. 116.

22 Wynn, "Exciting," 37.

23 Ibid., 21.

24 MacGregor to Young, RG 8, vol. 8, no. 5 & 6, January 1820; RG 8, vol. 6, no. 129; and, 31 January 1826, NSA, RG 6, vol. 5, no. 65.

25 Ross to Young, 28 November 1818, cited by MacLaren, *The Pictou Book*, 214–15.

26 MacGregor to Young, NSA, RG 8, vol. 6, nos. 131, 144, 143, 130, 131, 140, respectively; MacLaren, "John Young," *DCB* 7, 930–5.
27 Wynn, "Exciting," 16.
28 Ibid., 20–1. Julian Gwynn questions the early movement's long-term effects, but in selected regions continued benefits were felt, and it had also encouraged coalitions of leaders from scattered communities to turn to joint purposes. See Julian Gwynn, *Excessive Expectations, Maritime Commerce and the Economic Development of Nova Scotia, 1740–1870* (Montreal & Kingston: McGill-Queen's University Press, 1998), 67–73. Cf. Wynn's critique of Gwynn, "Exciting," 15, fn 31.
29 MacPhie, *Pictonians*, 222.
30 Frank Patterson, *Patterson*, 84.
31 Ibid., 27–8.
32 *Memoir*, 372.
33 Ibid., 372, 374.
34 Ibid., 374; William McCulloch, Address," *Proceedings*, 1886, 26.

15. Onward Christian Soldiers

1 Duncan Campbell, *Nova Scotia in Its Historical Mercantile and Industrial Relations* (Montreal, 1873), 279–81.
2 See NSA, Hugh Graham Fonds, MG 1, B 1, 332B. Graham's personal letters, addressed to various members of his family, contain only a few early and critical references to MacGregor, dating from 1793 to 1795. Further correspondence was probably burned in an early fire he suffered. See also James E. Candow, "Hugh Graham, 1758–1829," *DCB* 6, 293–4; Robertson, *Mission*, 34–46. See Maria A. Darragh, "Roots in Nova Scotia: The Story of a Canadian Family: Rev. Hugh Graham (1758–1829)," vol. 3 (2006). Thanks to Maria A. Darragh for making available this extraordinary collection, along with an edited version of Graham's letters. See, too, John M. Gammell, "Graham and MacGregor: What Formed These Heralds of the Early Church?" (paper presented to the Canadian Society of Presbyterian History, Toronto, 29 September 2007). Thanks to John Gammell for providing a copy and for his encouragement.
3 See "Presbytery of Truro Minutes, 1786–1875," vol. 1, various entries, MCA, MF-51.
4 Hugh Graham to John Young, 12 January 1826, Report of Stewiacke Agriculture Society, NSA, RG 8, vol. 5, no. 57; Gammell, "Graham and MacGregor," 27–8.

5 Rev. John Brown, Whitburn, to MacGregor, 2 September 1820, MCA, JMP, box F&I-A0173/W6.
6 Hugh Graham to William Hamilton, Whitburn, 26 February 1820, NSA, MG 1, B 1, 332B; Hugh Graham to Peter Graham, 29 September 179[5], NSA, Hugh Graham Fonds, MG 1, B1, 332B.
7 *Memoir*, 409.
8 Ibid., 296.
9 Ibid., 409; MacGregor to John Keir, 6 October 1814, MCA, JMP, box F&I-023/4/3; for Kent, see Thomas Miller, *Historical and Genealogical Record of … Colchester County* (Halifax, 1873), 349.
10 Patterson gives the text of the sermon in full, *Memoir*, 425–32; see the congregation's letter of apology to Presbytery, "Petition from Upper Settlement, East River," [n.d.], MCA, JMP, box F&I-023/4/6.
11 George More, Edinburgh, to MacGregor, 23 March 1814, MCA, JMP, box F&I-A0173/14/4.
12 *Memoir*, 413–14. See one clergyman's enthusiastic response, in ibid.
13 MacGregor to Keir, 6 October 1814, MCA/FIP, JMP, box F&I-023/14/3.
14 Graham to "My Worthy Dear Friend," 26 February 1820, NSA, MG 1, B 1, 332B; Minutes of Joint Synod, 29 June 1819, in "Patterson Scrapbook, 1824–1897," NSA, MG 9, vol. 31, MFM 170.
15 *Memoir*, 466.
16 Hugh Graham to Peter Graham, 30 May 1818; Hugh Graham to William Hamilton, Whitburn, 26 February 1820, NSA, MG 1, B 1, 332B. Robert Marshall appears in McCulloch's unpublished novella "Morton" under his own name and just as he was, a humble, caring man.
17 See chaps. 18 and 19, this volume. MacGregor was still very active in church, academy, missions, and related affairs – which must have figured in his re-election as moderator and leader. McCulloch had served the second term as moderator, but then MacGregor was returned. McCulloch then became absorbed single-mindedly in his fierce and tireless lobbying for the academy and in advancing a commendably broad provincial approach to education. Leadership, however, is not a one-issue responsibility: Synod may have passed him over for a second term for that reason. Cf. Buggey and Davies, "McCulloch," *DCB* 7, 529–41; Armour and Trott, *The Faces of Reason*, 63–5; B. Anne Wood, "Schooling for Presbyterian Leaders: The College Years of Pictou Academy, 1816–1832," in *The Burning Bush and a Few Acres of Snow: The Presbyterian Contributions to Canadian Life and Culture*, ed. William Klempa,19–37, Carleton Library Series no. 180 (Ottawa: Carleton University Press, 1994), 20.

18 16 July 1817, MacGregor to Keir, MCA, JMP, box F&I-023/1/16; Gregg, *History Presbyterian Dominion*, 231.

19 MCA, MF-51, "Presbytery of Truro Minutes, 1786–1875," vol. 1, 1 October 1816.

20 Ibid., 117; *Memoir*, 408.

21 Glasgow Colonial Society, *Selected Correspondence of the Glasgow Colonial Society, 1825–1840*, ed. E.A.K. McDougall and John S. Moir, Champlain Society Publication no. 58 (Toronto: Champlain Society, 1994). Yet, in 1843, at the time of the Chalmers-led Disruption of Scotland, of the eight Kirk ministers sent so hurriedly to Pictou in the 1820s, one went over to the Wee Frees and six returned to Scotland to take up livings left empty by Chalmers's Seceders.

22 Glasgow Colonial Society, *Correspondence*, ed. McDougall and Moir, "Introduction," xiiii; John S. Moir, *The Church in the British Era: From the British Conquest to Confederation* (Toronto: McGraw Hill Ryerson, 1972), 26; W.B. Hamilton, "Thomas McCulloch: Advocate of Non-Sectarian Education," in *Profiles of Canadian Educators*, ed. Robert S. Patterson et al., 21–37 (Toronto: 1994), 26.

23 Glasgow Colonial Society, *Correspondence*, ed. McDougall and Moir; Wood, "Schooling for Presbyterian Leaders," 19–37.

24 Murray Beck, "S.G.W. Archibald, 1777–1846," *DCB* 8, 21–5.

25 Wood, "Schooling for Presbyterian Leaders," 36, n18.

26 R.A. MacLean, "Norman (MacLeod) McLeod, 1780–1866," *DCB* 9, 517.

27 "MacGregor to the United Secessionist Church, and others, in behalf of the Literary Institution in Pictou, NS, East River, Pictou, 22 August 1825," Reverend George Patterson's Scrapbook, NSA, MG 9, vol. 31, MFM 170; MacLean, "MacLeod," *DCB* 9, 517.

28 MacLean, "MacLeod," *DCB* 9, 517.

29 "Letter to the Friends of the Glasgow Society (In Connection with the Established Church of Scotland) For Promoting the Religious Interests of the Scottish Settlers in British North America," [n.d.], in *Remains*, 258.

30 MacLeod's saga continued when six shiploads of people followed him, at seventy-one, from St Ann's to New Zealand in 1851.

16. Last Calls

1 Betts, *Our Fathers*, 107–8. His grandson Dr. George C. Pidgeon was first moderator of the United Church of Canada in 1925.

2 Ibid., 106.

3 MacGregor to Bruce, [n.d.]. MCA, JMP, box F&I-023/4/15.

4 *Memoir*, 402–6.

5 Ibid., 443–7; see Stephen Hornsby, "Scottish Emigration and Settlement in the Early Nineteenth Century," in *The Island: New Perspectives on Cape Breton History, 1713–1990*, ed. Kenneth Donovan (Fredericton, NB: Acadiensis Press, 1990), 49–70.

6 Rev. Murdoch Maxwell MacOdrum, "The Presbyterian Pioneers of Cape Breton," in *Celebration Addresses*, 244.

7 I first heard this story when, aged seven, I was staying at Mariner Smith's Inn at Margaree.

8 MacOdrum, "Presbyterian Pioneers," in *Celebration Addresses*, 244.

9 *Memoir*, 442–4; Phyllis Blakeley, "The History and Development of Sherbrooke in Guysborough County, Nova Scotia," Halifax: Nova Scotia Museum, [n.d.].

10 *Memoir*, 453.

11 Sherbrooke Branch Library, Local History Collection, "Registration of Marriages for Saint Marys River Settlement," entry, 10 May 1809, 1.

12 Miller, *Record*, 50–1.

13 Ibid., 76.

14 Joseph Howe, *Western and Eastern Rambles: Travel Sketches of Nova Scotia*, ed. M.G. Parks (Toronto: University of Toronto Press, 1973), 194.

15 *Memoir*, 443.

16 The story did not end happily for the calf. It was presented to the governor, who shipped it off to the Tower of London Zoo, where it languished among other colonial exotica. Rev. Robert Grant, "East River Worthies," originally in Eastern Chronicle Series, now in Pictou County GenWeb, 24 August 2005.

17 Ibid.

18 Note by late Rod McColl in possession of the writer.

19 William Simpson, Manchester, to MacGregor, 3 April 1819, MCA, JMP, box F&I-023/6/N7

20 A.C. Jost, *Guysborough Sketches and Essays* (Guysborough, NS: [Privately printed], 1950), 192.

21 Allan C. Dunlop, "Thomas Dickson, 1791–1855," *DCB* 8, 222; cf. Gwynn, *Excessive Expectations*, 175–6.

22 Jost, *Guysborough*, 107.

23 Gregg, *History Presbyterian Dominion*, 236–7.

24 Campbell, *History of Prince Edward Island*, 193.

25 MacLeod, *History of Presbyterianism*, 60.

17. Erring Shepherds

1 Campbell and MacLean, *Beyond*, 197.
2 Howe, *Rambles*, 145–7.
3 Address to Synod, Glasgow, [n.d.], "Patterson's Scrapbook, 1824–1897," NSA, MG 9, vol. 31.
4 Thomas McCulloch to Rev. Dr. John Mitchell, 29 May 1819, NSA, MG 1, vol. 553, McCulloch Papers, 7.
5 Anne Wood gives a good account of the reckless accusations and encroachments of the Glasgow Colonial Society and its agents in Nova Scotia in these years. Wood, "Schooling," 24–7.
6 *Memoir*, 485.
7 MacGregor to Rev. John MacLennan, [1824–5], MCA, JMP, box F&I-023/4/16.
8 *Memoir*, 475–6.
9 Gene Morrison, "The Brandy Election of 1830," in Nova Scotia Historical Society *Collections*, 30, 1954, 151–83; Hector Centre Archives, Pictou, MG 19, 345d, 29–31, John Oliver, "Sketches and Recollections of the Past," [unpub.], 1880; interview with Mrs. Janet McColl Oxley, Halifax, 1953.
10 James Fraser, "Autobiography" (London, Ontario: [Unpub.], 1867), NGPL, R-NG.
11 Ibid.
12 Ibid.
13 Ibid.
14 William Scarfe Moorsom, *Letters from Nova Scotia: Comprising Sketches of a Young Country* (London, 1830), 352–3.
15 Susan Buggey, "Churchmen and Dissenters: Religious Toleration in Nova Scotia" (unpub. MA thesis, Dalhousie University, Halifax, NS, 1981), 230.
16 Anne Wood, "Schooling," 24–7.

18. The Dissenter as Moderator

1 Gregg, *History Presbyterian Dominion*, 244.
2 Rev. E. Ross, Address, *Proceedings*, 1886, 33.
3 *A memorial from the committee of missions of the Presbyterian Church of Nova Scotia, to the Glasgow Society for Promoting the Religious Interests of the Scottish Settlers in British North America* (Edinburgh, 1826); McCulloch to Rev. Dr. John Mitchell, 10 November 1822, NSA, MG 1, vol. 553, McCulloch Papers.

4 Repr. in *Remains*, 205–14.
5 Ibid., 211.
6 Ibid., 213.
7 Thomas McCulloch, *The Nature and Uses of a Liberal Education Illustrated* (Halifax: A.B. Holland, 1819).
8 "Letter to the Friends of the Glasgow Society (In Connection with the Established Church of Scotland) For Promoting the Religious Interests of the Scottish Settlers in British North America," [1825], *Remains*, 247–62.
9 Because no one was keeping Pictou Presbytery's minutes at the time, it is impossible to determine how far MacGregor was acting on his own.
10 Ibid.
11 Buggey and Davies, "McCulloch," *DCB* 7, 531.
12 Armour and Trott, *The Faces of Reason*, 64.
13 *Memoir*, 474 fn; MacLaren, *Pictou Book*, 178; Gammell, "Graham and MacGregor," 8. The press was later moved to the New Hebrides with the great Pictou County missionary John Geddie.
14 Buggey and Davies, "McCulloch," *DCB* 7, 532; Pamela Bruce, "Donald Allan Fraser," in *DCB* 7.
15 Murray Beck, "Jotham Blanchard, 1800–1839," *DCB* 7, 81–5; Buggey and Davies, "McCulloch," *DCB* 7, 534.
16 "'The Prosperity of Those who love Jerusalem,' A Sermon. Preached at the opening of the Synod of the Presbyterian Church of Nova Scotia, 16th June 1825," in *Remains*, 215–35.
17 "Address to the Students of The Pictou Academy, January 2nd, 1826," in *Remains*, 237–46. MacGregor looked to a progressive future, not the re-creation of a static ancien régime rural world as the Abbe Sigogne was calling for at Pointe d'Eglise.
18 Ibid., 245.
19 Ibid., 239–40.
20 Ibid., 242.
21 McCulloch to Manning, 12 May 1825, NSA, MG 9, vol. 31, MFM 170, "Patterson Scrapbook, 1824–1897," no. 48.
22 MacGregor to Manning, 18 August 1826, NSA, MG 9, vol. 31, MFM 170, "Patterson Scrapbook, 1824–1897," no. 47.
23 Peter R. Eakins and Jean Sinnamon Eakins, "Sir John William Dawson," in *DCB* 10.
24 George Patterson, *Sketch of the Life and Labours of Rev. John Campbell of St. Marys, N.S.* (New Glasgow: S.M. McKenzie, 1889).

19. An Enduring Spirit

1 *Memoir*, 460.
2 Ibid., 380.
3 Ibid., 381–2; Gammell, "Graham and MacGregor," 26–7.
4 Robertson, *Mission*, 188.
5 PH, 271; *Memoir*, 382–90.
6 *Memoir*, 399–400.
7 "Observations on the efficacy of the British and Foreign Bible Society," [n.d.], MCA, JMP, box F&I-023/4/19; *Memoir*, 464–6; PH, 271, 312.
8 Mitchell to MacGregor, 23 May 1813, MCA, JMP, box F&I-A0173A/16/11; emphases his.
9 *Memoir*, 382.
10 Rev. John Mitchell, Anderston, to MacGregor, 23 May 1813, MCA, JMP, box F& I-A0173A/16/7.
11 *Memoir*, 399–400.
12 G. MacDonald, Edinburgh, to MacGregor, 27 March 1815, MCA, JMP, box F&I-A0173A/17/12.
13 *Memoir*, 395–7.
14 Ibid., 397–8.
15 Ibid., 468–70; PH, 311–12.
16 Ibid., 193; PH, 193.
17 MacPhie, *Pictonians*, 139.
18 *Memoir*, 398.
19 MacGregor to Secretary, BFBS, 6 July 1823, in *Memoir*, 464–5.
20 Ibid.
21 Ibid., 466–67; MacGregor to John Keir, 17 May 1824, MCA, JMP, box F&I-023/4/10.
22 MacGregor to John Young, enclosure to William Young, May 1821 & 19 April 1822, NSA, RG 6, nos. 136 & 144.
23 *Memoir*, 488.
24 McCulloch to Dr. John Mitchell, 24 November 1821, NSA, MG 1, vol. 553, McCulloch Papers.
25 McCulloch to Mitchell, 10 May 1822, ibid. See also Glasgow University Archives, "James Drummond MacGregor," in "Records of education and awarding of honourary D.D., 1822." The vellum scroll and the university's great seal are in Sackville, New Brunswick, in MCA, JMP, box F&I-A01373A. This episode again illustrates the dual nature of Thomas McCulloch, who could be driven by his passions into a fruitless war with

his Scottish GCS counterpart Rev. Robert Burns, which ultimately undid the academy, or he could be as straightforward and self-effacing as this episode suggests. By contrast, a late registrar of Dalhousie University, H.L. Scammell, in a paper entitled "Why Did McCulloch Come to Dalhousie?," published in Nova Scotia Historical Society's *Collections* 36 (1957): 68, wrote that McCulloch was a "short, frustrated, waspish little man in whom an enlarged ego was continually assailed by a strong interest in self preservation."

26 Thomas Bayne, "Jamieson, John," *DNB* 29 (1892): 237–8; 24 August 2005, online, "Significant Scots," and online, "John Jamieson," 1–3.

27 Glasgow University Library, Special Collections, MS Gen. 895.

28 Ibid.

29 24 February 1825, John Jamieson, Edinburgh, to MacGregor, MCA, JMP, box F&I-A0173/17/W11; MacPhie, *Pictonians*, 43.

30 Ibid.; *Memoir*, 38–9.

31 *Memoir*, 448–55.

32 Ibid., 333.

33 J.B. Maclean, "MacGregor of Pictou," in *Celebration Addresses*, 54.

34 MacFarlane to MacGregor, 4 October 1814, MCA, JMP, box F&I-A0173A/14/19.

35 *Seumas Macgrhiogair, Dain a chomhadh crabhuidh: searmonaich an t-soisgeil' an America mu thuath, Clo-Bhuailte Le Og & Gelie* (Glascho, 1819).

36 *Memoir*, 448.

37 J.D. Logan, comp., *Pictou Poets: A Treasury of Verse Selected from the Poems of James MacGregor, D.D., George Frederick Cameron, et al, Selected and Prefaced with Biographical Selections and Appreciations*, illustrated (Pictou: Press of the Pictou Advocate, 1923), 17.

38 *Memoir*, 450–2.

39 Rev. Sam McNab, Saltcoats, to MacGregor, 17 April 1820, MCA, JMP, box F&I-023/3/15–16.

40 Sinclair, "MacGregor as Gaelic Poet," in *Celebration Addresses*, 68.

41 *Memoir*, 452.

42 A. MacLean Sinclair, comp., *Dain Spioradail* ("Spiritual Songs") Edinburgh: 1880); Kenneth E. Nilsen, "Alexander MacLean Sinclair, 1840–1924," *DCB*, online ed., 23 August 2005,

43 Quoted in J. Ralph Watson, *MacGregor of Pictou* (Pictou, [n.d.]), 16.

44 A.M. Sinclair, quoted by J.B. MacLean, "MacGregor of Pictou," in *Celebration Addresses*, 55–7.

45 Quoted in J.B. MacLean, "MacGregor of Pictou," in *Celebration Addresses*, 57.

46 K.D. MacDonald, "Dugald Buchanan," in *A Companion to Scottish Culture*, ed. David Daiches (New York: 1982), 45.

47 "The Gaelic Poems of the late Rev. James MacGregor, D.D., just published and for sale by J.D. McDonald, Pictou," in *Eastern Chronicle*, 3 April 1862.

48 "Lament for Thomas Fraser," *MacTalla*, vol. 3, 5, and vol. 9, 35, second verse omitted; "Advice to Tolmie," vol. 3, 27; and "Song to MacGregor," vol. 9, 30. Thanks to Effie Rankin, Mabou.

49 J.D. Logan, comp., *Pictou Poets*.

50 Michael Newton, *We're Indians Sure Enough: The Legacy of the Scottish Highlanders to the United States* (Alexandria, VA: Thistle and Shamrock Books, 2002).

51 John MacInness, "Foreword" in Michael Newton, *From the Clyde to the Callender: Gaelic Songs, Poetry, Tales and Traditions* (Stornoway, Scotland: Acair, 1999); see also MacInness, *The Evangelical Movement in the Highlands of Scotland, 1688 to 1800* (Scotland: Aberdeen University Press, 1951).

52 Donald M. Sinclair, "MacGregor as Gaelic Poet," in *Celebration Addresses*, 64.

53 Cf. the emigrant novels of John Galt, commissioner of the Canada Land Company from his headquarters in Guelph, Upper Canada.

54 Thomas McCulloch, *Colonial Gleanings*. See Isabella McCulloch's personal copy in Dalhousie University, Killam Library, Special Collections; Buggey and Davies, "McCulloch," *DCB* 7, 538–9.

55 "Morton," [untitled ms., n.p., n.d.], in NSA, Thomas McCulloch Papers, MG 1, vol. 555, no. 76.

56 Thomas McCulloch to James Mitchell, 9 November & 29 December 1833, NSA, vol. 553, McCulloch Papers, nos. 56 & 58.

57 Gwendolyn Davies, "Thomas McCulloch's Fictional Celebration of the Reverend James MacGregor," in *Contribution*, ed. Scobie & Rawlyk, 24.

58 Duncan Ferguson to MacGregor, 4 June 1824, MCA, JMP, box F&I-A0173A/16/10.

59 John McIllwharnell to MacGregor, 13 April 1789, MCA, JMP, box F&I-023/2/17.

60 *Memoir*, 378.

61 Office of the Lieutenant Governor to MacGregor, 14 January 1822, MCA, JMP, box F&I-023/7/14 & 023/3/19–20.

62 Ibid.

63 PH, chap. 18; Michael Earle, "Coal in the History of Nova Scotia," in *Industry and Society in Nova Scotia: An Illustrated History*, ed. James E. Candow, 57–59 (Halifax: Fernwood, 2001).

64 *Memoir*, 489.

65 His estate was probated at £1,150, of which £400 were to be shared by the six children of his first marriage, the rest entrusted to Janet and her three children. The executors were James MacGregor Jr. and Thomas McCulloch. NSA, MFM no. 19959, estate file no. 158.

66 David Frank, "Richard Smith, 1783–1868," *DCB* 9, 730–2; interview with Mrs. Janet McColl Oxley, Halifax, 1953.

67 Interview with Mrs. Janet McColl Oxley, Halifax, 1953; Marilyn Gerriets, "The Rise and Fall of a Free-Standing Company in Nova Scotia: The General Mining Association," *Business History* 34 (July 1992): 16–48.

68 Cameron, *Industrial History*, vol. 3, 1–2.

69 *Memoir*, 491.

70 Ibid., 492.

71 Ibid.; editorial, *Colonial Patriot*, 27 March 1830.

72 *Memoir*, 496.

73 J.P. MacPhie, *Pictonians*, 224; Guy, "Industrial Development," 32–4.

74 *Celebration Addresses*, ed. Rev. Frank Baird.

75 Janet MacGregor to Mrs. Peter McIndoe, enclosed in Hugh Ross to Mrs. Peter McIndoe, 17 June, MCA, JMP, "Correspondence, 1793–1830," box F&I-023/8/11.

76 Quoted by Rev. D.I. MacEachern, in "Introduction" to R. Sheldon Mackenzie, *Gathered by the River: The Story of the West River Seminary and Theological Hall, 1848–1858* (New Glasgow: Hignell, 1999).

77 Isabella McCulloch, "Dr. Thomas McCulloch," in *Celebration Addresses*, 180.

78 Hon. D.C. Fraser, Address, in *Proceedings*, 1886, 39.

Bibliography

Archival Sources

British and Foreign Bible Society. London "Foreign Correspondents," BSA/
 X/M, 1794–1897, 15 letters from Pictou, Nova Scotia (Canada), 1807–27.
Glasgow University Archives. *James Drummond MacGregor*. "Records of
 education and awarding of honourary D.D., 1822."
Glasgow University Library. Special Collections. Addison, W. Innes, comp.
 Roll of the Graduates of the University of Glasgow, 1727–1897. Glasgow: 1898.
Glasgow University Library. Special Collections. MS Gen. 526/32, MacGregor,
 James D. Fonds, J.D. MacGregor, "The numbers, order, & names of the
 Irish letters, according to Forcharn's Uraiceuct" and "The number, order &
 names of the Letters according to O'Flaherty," mss.
Glasgow University Library. Special Collection. MS Gen. 526/33, MacGregor,
 James D. Fonds, Rev. James MacGregor, "Analogy of the Gaelic and Hebrew
 Languages, illustrated ... To which is added, A Collection of Gaelic Words
 derived from the Hebrew." Unpublished manuscript, boards.
Glasgow University Library, Special Collections, MS Gen. 895.
Hector Centre Archives, Pictou, NS. MG 19, 345d, 29–31. John Oliver.
 "Sketches and Recollections of the Past." Unpublished manuscript, 1880.

United Church of Canada Archives, Maritime Conference Archives,
Sackville, NB

MCA. JMP. James MacGregor Papers. Family & Individual Papers. Box F&I
 et seq.
MCA. JMP. "Dr. MacGregor's First Session Book, 17 September 1786–3 June
 1804," 6 May 1787.

MCA. JMP. "Excerpts from Correspondence, Diaries, Sermon Notes, 1786–
    1811." Box F&I-023/4.
MCA. JMP. "Correspondence, 1786–1811." Box F&I-023/4/13.
MCA. JMP. "Correspondence, 1791–1816." Box F&I-023/5/M1–3 and in
    typescript, 023/5/M1–4.
MCA. JMP. "Correspondence Received, 1788–1825." Box F&I-023/6/Na.
MCA. MF-51. "Presbytery of Truro Minutes, 1786–1875." Vol. 1, 1786–1826.

Nova Scotia Archives, Halifax

NSA, MacGregor Papers, MFM 10876, folder X, no. 2, "Petition from Pictou";
    Memoir, appendix A, "Petition from Pictou," 512.
NSA. MFM 10875. "Diary of Rev. James MacGregor." [N.p.].
NSA. MFM 10876. Folder S, 1–19, "Correspondence with John Buist."
NSA. MFM 10876. Folders Q & R, "The Rev. James MacGregor, Personal
    Accounts & Receipts, 1792–1803, 'Edward Mortimer, Merchant.'"
NSA. MFM 10876. Folder X, no. 2, "Rev. John Buist Notes."
NSA. MFM 10876. Folder z [pt. 2], "Rev. Peter Gordon Letters."
NSA. MG 1, B 1, 332B. Rev. Hugh Graham Fonds.
NSA. MG 1, vol. 553. McCulloch Papers.
NSA. MG 1, vols. 741–3. Patterson, Rev. George, "Pioneers." Unpublished
    manuscript.
NSA. MG 9, vol. 31, MFM 170. "Patterson Scrapbook, 1824–1897."
NSA. MG 9, vol. 31, MFM 170. No. 44, "Joint Synod Meeting Minutes, 1817."
    [PCNS].
NSA. RG 8, vol. 5. No. 57, Report of Stewiacke Agriculture Society.
NSA. RG 8, vol. 6. No. 144, Report of East River Agricultural Society.

Private and Public Libraries, Museums

Carmichael Stewart House Museum, New Glasgow, NS.
Hector Exhibit Centre, Pictou, NS.
Innerpeffray Library, nr. Creiff, Scotland. *Register of Borrowers.*
Leighton Library, Dunblane, Scotland. Local History Collection.
New Glasgow Public Library, New Glasgow, NS. Grey Box Collection. John
    MacKay. "Reminiscences of a Long Life." Unpublished manuscript.
New Glasgow Public Library, New Glasgow, NS. NGPL, R-NG. James Fraser.
    "Autobiography." Unpublished manuscript, London, ON, 1867.
Old Courthouse Museum, Guysborough, NS.
Sherbrooke Branch Public Library, Sherbrooke, NS. Local History Collection.

Whitburn Public Library, Whitburn, West Lothian. Local History Collection.
Whitburn Public Library, Whitburn, West Lothian. W2.929.5 "Register
  of South Parish Church Inscriptions on Headstones in the Kirkyard."
  Unpublished manuscript.

Miscellaneous

Howard, Terris C. "A Survey of Deserted Settlements in Glen Lednock,
  Including Glentarken and Other Locations." From Comrie Parish records.
  USA, privately printed.
Oxley, Mrs. Janet McColl. Interview, Halifax, NS, 1953.
Punch, Terence M. *Religious Marriages in Halifax, 1768–1841*, from original
  sources.
GANS Publication no.16. Halifax: Formac, 1991.
Pictou County GenWeb: www.rootsweb.ancestry.com/~nspictou/..

MacGregor's Published Materials

"Address to the Students of The Pictou Academy, January 2nd, 1826."
  Remains, 237–46.
"Address to the United Secession Synod in behalf of The Literary Institution
  at Pictou. Written in the year 1824." *Remains*, 205–14.
Dain a Chomhadh Crabhuidh: Searmonaich an T-Soisgeil 'an America Mu. Thuath
  Le Seumas Macgrhiogair Clo-Bhuailte Le Og & Galie. Glascho: 1819. [23
  religious songs].
"A Defence of the Religious Imprecations and Denunciations of God's Wrath,
  Contained in the Book of Psalms, against The Enemies of the Gospel. ..."
  Remains, 1–97.
"Essay on the Duration and Character of the Millennial Age of the Church."
  Remains, 99–134; *Christian Magazine* 4.
A Few Remains of the Rev. James MacGregor, D.D. Comp. Rev. George
  Patterson. Philadelphia: Joseph M. Wilson, 1859. [Essays, addresses, and
  letters].
The Gaelic Poems of the late Rev. James MacGregor, D.D. Pictou: J.D. McDonald,
  1862.
"A Guide to Baptism Being An Attempt to Guide the Plain Christian Unto the
  Scripture Doctrine and Practice of Baptism, Written about the Year 1826."
  Remains, 135–65.
"Lament for Thomas Fraser." *MacTalla*, vol. 3, p. 5, and in vol. 9, p. 35, second
  verse omitted [In Gaelic.]

"Advice to Tolmie." *MacTalla*, vol. 3, p. 27. [In Gaelic.]

"Song to MacGregor." *MacTalla*, vol. 9, p. 30. [In Gaelic.]

"A Letter to a Clergyman, Urging him to Set Free a Black Girl he Held in Slavery." *Remains*, 167–88; Halifax: John Howe, 1788.

"Letter to the General Associate Synod. Originally Published by the Order of Synod in the Year 1793, with Explanatory notes by a Committee of Synod." *Remains*, 189–203.

"Letter to The Friends of the Glasgow Society (In Connection with the Established Church of Scotland) For Promoting the Religious Interests of the Scottish Settlers in British North America." [1825]. *Remains*, 247–62.

Memoir of the Rev. James MacGregor, D.D., Missionary of the General Associate Synod of Scotland to Pictou, With Notices of the Colonization of British America, and of the Social and Religious Condition of the Early Settlers. Ed. Rev. George Patterson. Philadelphia: Joseph M. Wilson, 1859.

"Private Letters." *Remains*, 263–8.

"'The Prosperity of Those Who Love Jerusalem,' A Sermon. Preached at the Opening of the Synod of the Presbyterian Church of Nova Scotia, 26th June, 1825." *Remains*, 215–35.

"Translation of a Portion of One of His Gaelic Poems" ["The Gospel"]. Ed. Rev. John McKennon. *Remains*, 269–74.

Original Sources

"The Fifth Head." In *The First Book of Disciplines*. 1560.

Bruce, Rev. Archibald. *The Catechism Modernized: And Adapted to the Meridian of Patronage and Late Improvements in the Church of Scotland: With Suitable Creeds and Prayers*. Whitburn, Scotland: 1791, self-published; available Online at *Eighteenth Century Collections Online (ECCO)*, 2010.

Fraser, James. "Autobiography." London, ON: [Unpublished], 1867. New Glasgow Public Library, Grey Box Collection, R-NG.

Glasgow Colonial Society. *Selected Correspondence of the Glasgow Colonial Society, 1825–1840*. Edited by E.A.K. McDougall and John S. Moir. Champlain Society Publication no. 58. Toronto: Champlain Society, 1994.

Howe, Joseph. *Western and Eastern Rambles: Travel Sketches of Nova Scotia*. Edited by M.G. Parks. Toronto: University of Toronto Press, 1973.

Logan, J.D., comp. *Pictou Poets: A Treasury of Verse Selected from the poems of James MacGregor, D.D., George Frederick Cameron, et al, Selected and Prefaced with Biographical Selections and Appreciations*. Illustrated. Pictou: Press of the Pictou Advocate, 1923.

McCulloch, Thomas. *Colonial Gleanings*. Edinburgh: Oliphant, 1826. [Combines two novellas, "William" and "Melville."]

– *A memorial from the committee of missions of the Presbyterian Church of Nova Scotia, to the Glasgow Society for Promoting the Religious Interests of the Scottish Settlers in British North America*. Edinburgh, 1826.

– "Morton." [Unpublished manuscript]. In NSA, Thomas McCulloch Papers, MG 1, vol. 555, no. 76, [n.p.].

– The Nature and Uses of a Liberal Education Illustrated. Halifax, NS: A.B. Holland, 1819.

– *The Stepsure Letters*. Edited by John A. Irving and Douglas Lochhead. New Canadian Library Series. Toronto: McClelland & Stewart, 1960.

Millar, John. *The Origin of the Distinction of Ranks*. Reprinted in *John Millar of Glasgow*. Edited by William C. Lehmann, 173–332. Cambridge: Cambridge University Press, 1960. [See also,

John Millar, *Origin of the Distinction of Ranks; or, An Inquiry into the Circumstances Which Give Rise to Influence and Authority, in the Different Members of Society*, 4th ed. (1771; corrected ed., Glasgow, 1806)].

Moorsom, William Scarfe. *Letters from Nova Scotia: Comprising Sketches of a Young Country*. London, 1830.

Oliver, John. "Sketches and Recollections of the Past. ..." [Unpublished], 1880. Hector Centre Archives, Pictou, MG 19, 345d, 29–31.

Reid, Thomas. *An Inquiry into the Human Mind on the Principles of Common Sense*. Edited by D.R. Brookes. Edinburgh: Edinburgh University Press, 1997.

Roger, J. *Buffon: A Life in Natural History*. Edited by L.P. Williams. Translated by S. Lucille. Ithaca, NY: Cornell University Press, 1997.

Sinclair, A. MacLean, comp. *Dain Spioradail [Spiritual Songs]*. Edinburgh, 1880. [Contains several of MacGregor's poems.]

Smith, Adam. *The Theory of Moral Sentiments*. Edited by Knud Haakonssen. Cambridge: Cambridge University Press, 2002.

Newspapers

The Acadian Recorder (Halifax).
The Christian Magazine (Glasgow).
The Colonial Patriot (Pictou).
The Eastern Chronicle (New Glasgow).
The Enterprise (New Glasgow).
Evening News (New Glasgow).
The Presbyterian Witness (Halifax).

Secondary Works

A.G. "Thomas McCrie." *Dictionary of National Biography* 35 (1886): 12–14.

Aitchison, Peter, and Andrew Cassell. *The Lowland Clearances: Scotland's Silent Revolution, 1700–1830*. East Linton, Scotland: Tuckwell, 2003.

Allan, David. *Virtue, Learning and the Scottish Enlightenment*. Edinburgh: Edinburgh University Press, 1993.

Alston, David. "Social and Economic History of the Old Shire of Cromarty, 1650–1850." PhD diss., University of Dundee, Scotland, 1999.

Archibald, Donald Eldon. "The History of Education in the Municipality of Sherbrooke, Guysborough County, N.S." EdM thesis, Acadia University, Wolfville, NS, 1970.

Archibald, Frank. "Contribution of the Scottish Church to New Brunswick Presbyterianism from Its Earliest Beginnings until the Time of the Disruption and Afterwards, 1784–1852." PhD diss., University of Edinburgh, 1933.

Armour, Leslie, and Elizabeth Trott. *The Faces of Reason: An Essay on Philosophy and Culture in English Canada, 1850–1950*. Waterloo, ON: Wilfrid Laurier Press, 1981.

Bailyn, Bernard. *The Peopling of British North America: An Introduction*. New York: Knopf, 1986.

Baird, Frank, ed. "Addresses at the Celebration of the One Hundred and Fiftieth Anniversary of the Arrival in Nova Scotia of Rev. James Drummond MacGregor, D.D., by the Synod of the Maritime Provinces of the Presbyterian Church of Canada." Toronto: Synod of the Maritime Provinces of the Presbyterian Church of Canada, 1937. Reprinted 2013 by Formac Press, Halifax.

– ed. "The MacGregor Family." *Celebration Addresses*, 301–10.

– *Rob: A Story of Old Pictou*. Illustrated by C.W. Jefferys. Halifax: [Privately printed], 1923. [Novel in which Jefferys portrays a preacher, based on MacGregor, driving the half-pays from the squire's barn; another illustration shows MacGregor presiding over a prayer meeting, but MacGregor wore no beard.]

Bayne, Thomas Wilson. "Jamieson, John." *Dictionary of National Biography*. London, England: Smith, Elder & Co., 1885–1900.

Beck, Murray. "Jotham Blanchard, 1800–1839." *DCB* 7, 81–5.

– *The Politics of Nova Scotia*. Toronto: University of Toronto Press, 1957.

– "S.W.G. Archibald, 1777–1846." *DCB* 8, 21–5.

Bell, Winthrop. *The "Foreign Protestants" and the Settlement of Nova Scotia*. Toronto: University of Toronto Press, 1961.

Betts, Arthur E. *Our Fathers in the Faith: Maritime Presbyterian Ministers.*
 Halifax: Maritime Conference Archives, 1983.
Bisset, A.M. *History of Bathgate and District.* Bathgate, Scotland: District
 Council, 1906.
Blakeley, Phyllis "The History and Development of Sherbrooke in
 Guysborough County, Nova Scotia," Halifax: Nova Scotia Museum, [n.d.].
Bolger, F.W.P., ed. *Canada's Smallest Province: A History of Prince Edward Island.*
 Halifax: Nimbus, 1991.
Broadie, Alexander, ed. *The Cambridge Companion to the Scottish Enlightenment.*
 Cambridge: Cambridge University Press, 2003.
– "The Human Mind and Its Powers." In Broadie, *The Cambridge Companion to
 the Scottish Enlightenment.*
– *The Scottish Enlightenment: The Historical Age of the Historical Nation.*
 Edinburgh: Birlinn, 2001.
Brown, A.L., and Michael Moss. *The University of Glasgow, 1451–1966.*
 Edinburgh: Edinburgh University Press, 1996.
Brown, Calum. *The People in the Pews: Religion and Society in Scotland since 1780.*
 Glasgow: Economic and Social History Society of Scotland, 1993.
– "Protest in the Pews: Interpreting Presbyterianism and Society Fracture
 during the Scottish Economic Revolution." In *Conflict and Stability in Scottish
 Society, 1700–1850.* Edited by T.M. Devine. Edinburgh: John Donald, 1990.
– "Religion and Social Change." In *People and Society in Scotland.* Vol. 1, *1760–
 1830.* Edited by T.M. Devine and Rosalind Mitchison, 143–62. Edinburgh:
 John Donald, 2004.
Brown, David. *Life of the Late John Duncan, LL.D ...*, 2nd rev. ed. Edinburgh:
 Edmonston & Douglas, 1872.
Bruce, Pamela. "Donald Allan Fraser." *DCB* 7.
Bryson, Gladys. *Men and Society: The Scottish Inquiry of the Eighteenth Century.*
 New York: Kelly, 1968.
Buggey, Susan. "Churchmen and Dissenters: Religious Toleration in Nova
 Scotia, 1758–1835." MA thesis, Dalhousie University, Halifax, NS, 1981.
– "Edward Mortimer, 1768–1819." *DCB* 5, 611–12.
– "James Drummond (McGregor) MacGregor, 1759–1830." *DCB* 6, 457–62.
– "John Keir, 1780–1858." *DCB* 8, 451–3.
Buggey, Susan, and Gwendolyn Davies. "Thomas McCulloch, 1776–1843."
 DCB 7, 529–41.
Bumsted, J.M. *Henry Alline, 1748-1784.* Canadian Biographical Series, edited
 by Alan Wilson. Toronto: University of Toronto Press/DCB, 1971.
– "The Scottish Diaspora: Emigration to British North America, 1763–1815."
 In *Nation and Province in the First British Empire: Scotland and America,*

1600–1800. Edited by Ned Landsman. Lewisburg, PA: Bucknell University Press, 2001.

Burroughs, Peter. "Ramsay, George, 9th Earl of Dalhousie, 1770–1838." *DCB* 7, 722–33.

Bush, Peter. "James Drummond MacGregor: The Pioneer of Pictou." In *Called to Witness: Profiles of Canadian Presbyterians: A Supplement to Enduring Witness*. Vol. 3. Edited by John S. Moir. Toronto: Committee on History, Presbyterian Church in Canada, 1991.

Cahill, Barry. "The Antislavery Polemic of the Reverend James MacGregor: Canada's Proto-Abolitionist as 'Radical Evangelical.'" In Scobie and Rawlyk, *The Contribution of Presbyterianism to the Maritime Provinces of Canada*.

– "Colchester Men: The Proslavery Presbyterian Witness of the Reverends Daniel Cock of Truro and David Smith of Londonderry." In *Planter Links: Community and Culture in Colonial Nova Scotia*. Edited by Margaret Conrad and Barry Moody. Fredericton, NB: Acadiensis Press, 2001.

– "Mediating a Scottish Enlightenment Ideal: The Presbyterian Dissenter Attack on Slavery in Late Eighteenth-Century Nova Scotia." In *Myth, Migration and the Making of Memory: Scotia and Nova Scotia c.1700–1990*. Edited by Marjory Harper and Michael E. Vance, 189–201. Halifax: Gorsebrook Research Institute & Fernwood Books; Edinburgh: John Donald, 1999.

– "'Nowhere to Be Seen': Blacks as an Invisible Minority at the James MacGregor Sesquicentenary Celebration of 1936." *Journal of the Canadian Church Historical Society* 40, no. 1 (Spring 1998): 5–30.

– "The Reverend James MacGregor Marriage Scandal." *Nova Scotia Genealogist* 13, no. 3 (1995): 134–6.

Cairns, John W. "Legal Education in Glasgow, 1761–1801." In Hook and Sher, *The Glasgow Enlightenment*, 133–59.

Calder, Jenni. *Scots in Canada*. Edinburgh: Luath Press, 2003.

Cameron, James K., and S.R. Sutherland. In *The Origins and Nature of the Scottish Enlightenment*. Edited by R.H. Campbell and Andrew S. Skinner. Edinburgh: Taylor & Francis, ltd., 1982.

Cameron, James M. *Industrial History of the New Glasgow District*. Vol. 3. Pictou, NS: Hector Publishing Company, 1960.

– *Pictou County's History*. Pictou, NS: Pictou County Historical Society, 1972.

Cameron, James M., and George D. Macdougall, eds. *One Hundred and Fifty Years in the Life of the First Presbyterian Church (1786–1936), New Glasgow*. Toronto: Presbyterian Publications, 1939.

Campbell, D., and R.A. MacLean. *Beyond the Atlantic Roar: A Study of the Nova Scotia Scots*. The Carleton Library, No. 78. Toronto: McClelland & Stewart, 1974.

Campbell, Duncan. *History of Prince Edward Island*. Charlottetown, 1875.

– *Nova Scotia in its Historical, Mercantile and Industrial Relations*. Montreal, 1873.

Campbell, R.H. *Scotland since 1707: The Rise of an Industrial Society*. Oxford: Oxford University Press: 1965.

Candow, James E. "Hugh Graham, 1758–1829." *DCB* 6, 293–4.

Chitnis, Anand C. *The Scottish Enlightenment & Early Victorian English Society*. London: Croom Helm, 1986.

Clark, A.H. *Three Centuries and the Island: A Historical Geography of Settlement and Agriculture in Prince Edward Island, Canada*. Toronto: University of Toronto Press, 1959.

Clark, Ian D.L. "From Protest to Reaction: The Moderates Regime in the Church of Scotland, 1752–1805." In *Scotland in the Age of Improvement: Essays in Scottish History in the Eighteenth Century*. Edited by N.T. Phillipson and Rosalind Mitchison, 200–24. Edinburgh: Edinburgh University Press, 1970.

Condon, Ann Gorman. "1783–1800: Loyalist Arrival, Acadian Return, Imperial Reform." In *The Atlantic Region to Confederation: A History*. Edited by Phillip A. Buckner and John G. Reid. Toronto; Fredericton: University of Toronto Press; Acadiensis Press, 1994.

Craven, Frank W. "John Witherspoon." In *A Princeton Companion*. Edited by Alexander Leitch. Princeton, NJ: Princeton University Press, 1978.

Crawford, Robert. *On Glasgow and Edinburgh*. Cambridge, Mass.: Belknap, 2013.

Crerar, Duff. "'Crackling Sounds from the Burning Bush': The Evangelical Impulse in Canadian Presbyterianism before 1875." In *Aspects of the Canadian Evangelical Experience*. Edited by G.A. Rawlyk. Montreal: McGill-Queen's University Press, 1997.

Currie, Rev. John . "A Stone of Memorial." In Centennial Celebration of the Ordination and Induction of the Late Rev. Alexander Dick, Presbyterian Minister, Maitland, Hants County, Nova Scotia, June 21st and 23rd, 7–18. Halifax: Maitland Centennial Celebration Committee, 1903.

Cuthbertson, Brian. *The Loyalist Governor: Biography of Sir John Wentworth*. Halifax: Petheric Press, 1980.

Daiches, David, ed. *A Companion to Scottish Culture*. New York: Edward Arnold, 1982.

– *The Paradox of Scottish Culture: The Eighteenth Century Experience*. London: Oxford University Press, 1964.

– *Scotland and the Union*. London: John Murray, 1977.

Daiches, David, Peter Jones, and Jean Jones. *A Hotbed of Genius: The Scottish Enlightenment, 1730–1790*. Edinburgh: Edinburgh University Press, 1986.

Davies, Gwendolyn. "Thomas McCulloch's Fictional Celebration of the Reverend James MacGregor." In Scobie and Rawlyk, *The Contribution of Presbyterianism to the Maritime Provinces of Canada*.

Davies, Gwendolyn, and Susan Buggey. "Thomas McCulloch, 1776–1843."
    DCB 7, 529–41.
Devine, T.M. "A Conservative People? Scottish Gaeldom in the Age of
    Improvement." In Devine and Young, *Eighteenth Century Scotland*, 225–36.
– "Highland Migration to Lowland Scotland, 1760–1790." *Scottish Historical
    Review* 63 (1983): 137–49.
– *The Transformation of Rural Scotland*. Edinburgh: John Donald, 1999.
– *To the Ends of the Earth. Scotland's Global Diaspora, 1750–2010*. Washington,
    D.C.: Smithsonian Books, 2011.
Devine, T.M., and Rosalind Mitchison, eds. *People and Society in Scotland*. Vol.
    1, *1760–1830*. 3rd ed. reprint. Edinburgh: John Donald, 2004.
Devine, T.M., and J.R. Young, eds. *Eighteenth Century Scotland: New
    Perspectives*. East Linton, Scotland: Tuckwell, 1999.
Donaldson, Gordon. *The Scots Overseas*. London: Robert Hale, 1966.
Douglas C. "The Story of Pictou Presbytery from Its Beginning to the
    Union of 1875." MDiv diss., Atlantic School of Theology, Halifax, NS,
    May 1973.
Drummond, A., and A. Bullock. *The Scottish Church, 1688–1843: The Age of the
    Moderates*. Edinburgh: 1973.
Drummond, Andrew L. "Witherspoon of Gifford and American
    Presbyterianism." *Royal Scottish Church Historical Society* 12 (1958).
Duncan, Erskine. *Dunblane; St. Blane's: A History*. Privately printed, Dunblane:
    2002.
Dunlop, Allan C. "Duncan Ross, 1770–1834." *DCB* 6, 659–60.
– "Thomas Dickson, 1791–1855." *DCB* 8, 222.
Dunn, Charles W. *Highland Settler: A Portrait of the Scottish Gael in Nova Scotia*.
    Toronto: University of Toronto Press, 1953.
Eakins, Peter R., and Jean Sinnamon Eakins. "Sir John William Dawson," in
    DCB 10.
Earle, Michael. "Coal in the History of Nova Scotia." In *Industry and Society
    in Nova Scotia: An Illustrated History*. Edited by James E. Candow, 57–59.
    Halifax: Fernwood, 2001.
Emerson, Roger. "The Contexts of the Scottish Enlightenment." In Broadie,
    The Cambridge Companion to the Scottish Enlightenment.
Evans, G.N.D. *Uncommon Obdurate: The Several Public Careers of J.F.W.
    DesBarres*. Toronto: University of Toronto Press, 1969.
Fenton, Alexander. "Lexicography and Historical Interpretation." *The Scottish
    Tradition: Essays in Honour of Ronald Gordon Cant*. Edited by G.W.S. Barrow,
    243–58. Edinburgh: Scottish Academic Press, 1974.
Ferguson, W. *Scotland 1689 to the Present*. Edinburgh: Oliver & Boyd, 1968.

Fergusson, Donald A., ed. *Beyond the Hebrides: Including the Cape Breton Collection.* Halifax: Lawson Graphics, 1977.

Fingard, Judith. "Robert Stanser, 1760–1828." *DCB* 6, 731–2.

– "Sir John Wentworth, 1737–1820." *DCB* 5, 848–52.

Finlay, Ian. *The Highlands.* London: Batsford, 1963.

Finlay, Richard J. "Keeping the Covenant: Scottish National Identity." In Devine and Young, *Eighteenth Century Scotland,* 122–3.

Forbes, Rev. E.V. "Address Given by the Rev. E.V.Forbes in St. David's Church, [Maitland, NS], June 19, 1953 Marking the 150th Anniversary of The Church." 1953.

Frank, David. "Richard Smith, 1783–1868." *DCB* 9, 730–2.

Gammell, John M. "Graham and MacGregor: What Formed These Heralds of the Early Church?" Paper presented to the Canadian Society of Presbyterian History, Toronto, 29 September 2007.

Garrett. Aaron. "Anthropology: The 'Original' of Human Nature." In Broadie, *The Cambridge Companion to the Scottish Enlightenment,* 78–93.

Gauvreau, Michael. "Between Awakening and Enlightenment: The Evangelical Colleges, 1820–1860." In *The Evangelical Century.* Edited by G.A. Rawlyk, Montreal: McGill-Queen's University Press, 1991.

Gerriets, Marilyn. "The Rise and Fall of a Free-Standing Company in Nova Scotia: The General Mining Association." *Business History* 34 (July 1992): 16–48.

Goodwin, Daniel C. Into Deep Waters: Evangelical Spirituality and Maritime Calvinistic Baptist Ministers 1790–1855. Montreal: McGill-Queen's University Press, 2010.

Gordon, G. Lawson. *River John: Its Pastors and People.* New Glasgow: G. Lawson Gordon, 1911.

Grant, Rev. G.M. "Dr. MacGregor." *Celebration Addresses,* 27–39.

Grant, I.F. *Highland Folk Ways.* London: Routledge & Kegan Paul, 1975.

Greenlee, James. *Sir Robert Falconer: A Biography.* Toronto: University of Toronto Press, 1988.

Gregg, William. *History of the Presbyterian Church in the Dominion of Canada.* Toronto: Presbyterian Print and Publishing, 1885.

Guy, Ralph Murray. "Industrial Development and Urbanization of Pictou County to 1900." MA thesis, Acadia University, Wolfville, NS, 1962.

Gwynn, Julian. *Excessive Expectations, Maritime Commerce and the Economic Development of Nova Scotia, 1740–1870.* Montreal: McGill-Queen's University Press, 1998.

Haakonssen, Knud. *Natural Law and Moral Philosophy: From Grotius to the Scottish Enlightenment.* Cambridge: Cambridge University Press, 1996.

Haldane, A.R.B. *The Drove Roads of Scotland.* Edinburgh: Birlinn, 1997.

Hall, Robert Gaston. "Archibald Bruce of Whitburn (1746–1816) with Special
    Reference to His View of Church and State." PhD diss., University of
    Edinburgh, November 1954.

Hamilton, W.B. "Educational Politics and Reform in Nova Scotia, 1800–1848."
    PhD thesis, University of Western Ontario, 1970.

– "Thomas McCulloch: Advocate of Non-Sectarian Education." In *Profiles of
    Canadian Educators*. Edited by R.S. Patterson et al., 21–37. Toronto: The Nova
    Scotia Teacher, 1974.

Harper, Marjory. *Adventurers and Exiles: The Great Scottish Exodus*. London:
    Profile, 2003.

Hart, Harriet Cunningham. *History of the County of Guysborough*. Reprint.
    Belleville, ON: 1975.

Harvey, D.C. "Early Public Libraries in Nova Scotia." *Dalhousie Review* 15
    (January 1935): 429–43.

– "The Intellectual Awakening of Nova Scotia." *Dalhousie Review* 13, no.1
    (April 1933).

Hay, Eldon. *The Chignecto Covenanters: A Regional History of Reformed
    Presbyterianism in New Brunswick and Nova Scotia, 1827–1905*. Montreal:
    McGill-Queen's University Press, 1996.

Hazlett, W. Ian P. "Ebbs and Flows of Theology in Glasgow, 1451–1843." In
    Traditions of Theology in Glasgow, 1450–1980. Edited by W.I.P. Hazlett, 1–26.
    Edinburgh: 1993.

Hennessey, Michael F., ed. *The Catholic Church in Prince Edward Island, 1720–1979*.
    Summerside, PE: Roman Catholic Episcopal Corporation, 1979.

Hook, Andrew, and Richard B. Sher, eds. *The Glasgow Enlightenment*. East
    Linton, Scotland: Tuckwell, 1997.

Hornsby, Stephen. "Scottish Emigration and Settlement in the Early
    Nineteenth Century." In *The Island: New Perspectives on Cape Breton
    History, 1713–1990*. Edited by Kenneth Donovan. Fredericton, NB:
    Acadiensis Press, 1990.

Hunter, James. *The Making of the Crofting Community*. Edinburgh: John Donald,
    1979.

Isbel, Rev. Dr. Sherman. "Bruce, Archibald." *Dictionary of Scottish Church
    History & Theology*, 103. Edinburgh: T & T Clark, 1993.

Jack, Rev. T. Chalmers. "Days of the Fathers in East Hants." In *Centennial
    Celebration of the Ordination and Induction of the Late Rev. Alexander Dick,
    Presbyterian Minister, Maitland, Hants County, Nova Scotia, June 21st and 23rd,
    1903*. Halifax: Maitland Centennial Celebration Committee, 1903.

Johnstone, Walter. *Travels in Prince Edward Island in the Years 1820–21*.
    Edinburgh: David Brown, 1823.

Jost, A.C. *Guysborough Sketches and Essays*. Guysborough, NS: [Privately printed], 1950.

Kennedy, Norman D. "Dr. James MacGregor: An Apostle." *Celebration Addresses*, 72–141.

Klempa, William. "Scottish Presbyterianism Transplanted to the Canadian Wilderness." In Scobie and Rawlyk, *The Contribution of Presbyterianism to the Maritime Provinces of Canada*.

– ed. *The Burning Bush and a Few Acres of Snow: The Presbyterian Contributions to Canadian Life and Culture*. Ottawa: Carleton University Press, 1994.

Lehmann, W.C. *John Millar of Glasgow, 1735–1801: His Life and Thought and His Contributions to Sociological Analysis*. Cambridge, MA: Harvard University Press, 1960.

Lennan, Bruce. *Integration, Enlightenment, and Industrialization: Scotland, 1746–1832*. London: Edward Arnold, 1981.

Linkletter, Michael. "*Bu Dual Dha Sin* (That Was His Birthright): Gaelic Scholar Alexander Maclean Sinclair." PhD diss., Harvard University, 2006.

Lomas, Alton A. "The Industrial Development of Nova Scotia, 1830–1854." MA thesis, Dalhousie University, Halifax, NS, 1950.

Longworth, Israel. *Life of S.G.W. Archibald*. Halifax, 1881.

MacDonald, B.F. "Intellectual Forces in Pictou, 1803–1843." MA thesis, University of New Brunswick, Fredericton, 1977. NSA, Micro. M135. I61.

MacDonald, K.D. "Dugald Buchanan." In Daiches, *A Companion to Scottish Culture*, 45.

MacDougall, J.L. *History of Inverness County, Nova Scotia*. Truro: 1922.

Mackenzie, John M. and T.M. Devine, eds., Scotland and the British Empire. Oxford, New York: Oxford, 2011.

MacKenzie, R. Sheldon. *Gathered by the River: The Story of the West River Seminary and Theological Hall, 1848–1858*. New Glasgow: Hignell, 1999.

MacKerrow, John. *History of the Secession Church*, 2 vols. Edinburgh: Wm. Oliphant, 1839.

MacInnes, Rev. John. *The Evangelical Movement in the Highlands of Scotland, 1688 to 1800*. Scotland: Aberdeen University Press, 1951.

Mack, D.B. "George Munro Grant: Evangelical Prophet." PhD diss., Queen's University, 1992.

– "George Munro Grant." In *Dictionary of Canadian Biography*, vol. 8. Toronto: University of Toronto/Université Laval, 2003.

MacLaren, George. *The Pictou Book: Stories of Our Past*. New Glasgow: Hector, 1954.

MacLaren, R.A. "John Young, 1773–1837." *DCB* 7, 930–35.

– "Norman (MacLeod) McLeod, 1780–1866." *DCB* 9, 516–17.

MacLean, Alexander. *The Story of the Kirk in Nova Scotia*. Pictou: Pictou Advocate, 1911.

MacLean, J.B. "Dr. MacGregor of Pictou." *Celebration Addresses*, 39–61.

MacLennan, Jean M. *From Shore to Shore*. Edinburgh: Knox Press, 1977.

MacLeod, John M. *History of Presbyterianism on Prince Edward Island*. Chicago: Winona, 1904.

MacLeod, Rev. John. *History of Presbyterianism on Prince Edward Island*. Chicago: The Winona Publishing Company, 1904.

MacOdrum, M.M. "The Presbyterian Pioneers of Cape Breton." *Celebration Addresses*, 242–9.

MacPhie, J.P. *Pictonians at Home and Abroad*. Boston: Pinkham, 1914.

Martell, J.S. "Early Coal-Mining in Nova Scotia." *Dalhousie Review* 5, no. 25 (April, 1945): 156–72.

Mavor, Irene. *Glasgow*. Edinburgh: Edinburgh University Press, 2000.

Mayall, Colin. *The Story of Strathearn: An Anthology of People and Place*. Crieff, Scotland: Jamieson & Munro, 2001.

McCulloch, Isabella. "Dr. Thomas McCulloch." *Celebration Addresses*, 159–86.

McCulloch, William. *Life and Times of Thomas McCulloch, D.D.* Truro, NS: Truro Publishing, 1920.

McGregor, John. *British America*. 2 vols. Edinburgh: Blackwoods, 1832.

McIntosh, John R. *Church and Theology in Enlightenment Scotland: The Popular Party, 1740–1880*. Scottish Historical Review Monograph Series, 1998.

McKerracher, Archie. *Perthshire in History and Legend*. Rev. ed. Edinburgh: John Donald, 2000.

McKillop, A.B. *A Disciplined Intelligence: Critical Inquiry and Canadian Thought in the Victorian Era*. Montreal: McGill-Queen's University Press, 2001.

McMullin, S.G. "Thomas McCulloch: The Evolution of a Liberal Mind." PhD diss., Dalhousie University, Halifax, NS, 1975.

McMurtin, Rev. W.B. *A History of the Congregation of Brucefield Church, Whitburn, 1857–1957*. Whitburn (Scotland) Public Library, Local History Collection.

M'Crie, Thomas, Rev. *Life of Thomas M'Crie, D.D. ... By His son*. Edinburgh, 1840.

Miller, Thomas. *Historical and Genealogical Record of ... Colchester County*. Halifax: 1873.

Mitchell, Rev. Graham. "Parish of Whitburn." In Bisset, *History of Bathgate and District*.

Mitchison, Rosalind. *History of Scotland*. London: Routledge, 1970.

– *Lordship to Patronage: Scotland, 1603–1745*. London: Edward Arnold, 1983.

Mitchison, Rosalind, and T.M. Devine, eds. *People and Society in Scotland, 1760–1830*. Edinburgh: John Donald, 1988/2006.

Moir, John S. *The Church in the British Era: From the British Conquest to Confederation*. Toronto: McGraw-Hill Ryerson, 1972.

Morgan, Robert J. *Early Cape Breton: From Founding to Famine*. Sydney: Breton Books, 2000.

Morison, Gene. "The Brandy Election of 1830." *Collections of the Nova Scotia Historical Society*. Vol. 30. Halifax: Nova Scotia Historical Society, 1954.

Murdoch, Alexander, and Richard B. Sher. "Literary and Learned Culture." In *People and Society in Scotland*. Vol. 1, *1760–1830*. Edited by T.M. Devine and Rosalind Mitchison, 127–42. Edinburgh: John Donald, 1988.

Murray, Derek B. "Bruce, Archibald." *Dictionary of National Biography*. Oxford: Oxford University Press, 2004.

Murray, J. *The History of the Presbyterian Church in Cape Breton*. Truro, NS: News Publishing Company, 1921.

Murray, N. *The Scottish Handloom Weavers, 1790–1850*. Edinburgh: Donald, 1978.

Murray, Sarah. *A Companion and Useful Guide to the Beauties of Scotland*. London: 1799.

Newton, Michael. *From the Clyde to the Callander: Gaelic Songs, Poetry, Tales and Traditions*. Stornoway, Scotland: Acair, 1999.

– *We're Indians Sure Enough: The Legacy of the Scottish Highlanders to the United States*. Alexandria, VA: Thistle and Shamrock Books, 2002.

Nilson, Kenneth E. "Alexander Maclean Sinclair, 1840–1924." *DCB*, online ed. 23 August 2005.

Notestein, Wallace. Th*e Scot in History* … New Haven, CT: Yale University Press, 1946.

Patterson, Frank H. *John Patterson: The Founder of Pictou Town*. Truro: Truro Publishing, 1955.

Patterson, Rev. George. *A Brief Sketch of the life and labours of the late Rev. John Keir, D.D.* New Glasgow: S.M. MacKenzie, 1859.

– comp. *A Few Remains of the Rev. James MacGregor, D.D., Missionary of the General Associated Synod of Scotland to Pictou, Nova Scotia; With Notices of the Colonization of the Lower Provinces of British America, and of the Social and Religious Condition of the Early Settlers*. Philadelphia: Joseph M. Wilson, 1859. [Essays, addresses & letters.]

– *A History of the County of Pictou*. Reprint. Belleville, ON: Mika, 1972.

– ed. *Memoir of the Rev. James MacGregor, D.D.* Philadelphia: Joseph M. Wilson, 1859.

– *More Studies in Nova Scotia History*. Halifax, NS: Imperial Publishing Company, 1941.

- "Pioneers of Presbyterianism in the Maritime Provinces of Canada (a biographical sketch of Presbyterian ministers)." Unpublished. NSA. MG 1, vols. 741–743.
- "The Rev. James MacGregor ..." In his *More Studies in Nova Scotian History*, 54–70.
- *Sketch of the Life and Labours of the Rev. John Campbell of St. Marys, N.S.* New Glasgow: S.M. McKenzie, 1889.

Phillipson, N.E. "Scottish Enlightenment." In Daiches, *A Companion to Scottish Culture*, 340–4.

Phillipson, N.E., and Rosalind Mitchison, eds. *Scotland in the Age of Improvement: Essays in Scottish History in the Eighteenth Century*. New ed. Edinburgh: Edinburgh University Press, 1997.

Pothier, Bernard. "Jean-Mante, 1763–1844." *DCB* 7, 800–6.

Proceedings at the Centennial Celebration of James Church Congregation, New Glasgow, September 17th, 1886. New Glasgow: S.M. MacKenzie, 1886.

Rae, John. *Life of Adam Smith*. London: Macmillan, 1895.

Rawlyk, G.A. "New Lights, Presbyterians, James MacGregor and Nova Scotia's First Long Communion, July 1788." In *The Canada Fire: Radical Evangelicalism in British North America, 1775–1812*, 185–206. Kingston, ON: McGill-Queen's Press, 1994.

Robertson, Gordon. "History of Churchville ... 1784–1934." *New Glasgow Evening News*, 21 October 1957. Gray Box Collection, NG-Ref. New Glasgow Public Library.

Robertson, Rev. James. *History of the Mission of the Secession Church to Nova Scotia and Prince Edward Island, From Its Commencement in 1765*. Edinburgh: 1847.

Scammell H.L. "Why Did McCulloch Come to Dalhousie?" Nova Scotia Historical Society's *Collections* 36 (1957): 68.

Schmidt, Leith Eric. "The Scottish Context of Presbyterian Revivalism in America." In Sher and Smitten, *Scotland and America in the Age of the Enlightenment*.

Scobie, Charles H.H., and George Rawlyk. *The Contribution of Presbyterianism to the Maritime Provinces of Canada*. Montreal: McGill-Queen's University Press, 1997.

Shepperson, George. "Andrew Brown, 1763–1834." *DCB* 6, 87–9.

Sher, Richard B. *Church and University in the Scottish Enlightenment: The Moderate Literati of Edinburgh*. Edinburgh: Edinburgh University Press, 1985.
- *The Enlightenment and the Book: Scottish Authors and Their Publishers in Eighteenth-Century Britain, Ireland and America*. Chicago: University of Chicago Press, 2007.

Sher, Richard B., and Jeffrey R. Smitten, eds. *Scotland and America in the Age of the Enlightenment*. Princeton, NJ: Princeton University Press, 1990.

Sherwood, Roland H. *The Log Church at Loch Broom*. Hantsport, NS: Lancelot, 1986.

Sinclair, Donald Maclean. "Dr. MacGregor as Gaelic Poet." *Celebration Addresses*, 62–71.

Smart, R.N. "Some Observations on the Provinces of the Scottish Universities." In *The Scottish Tradition: Essays in Honour of Ronald Gordon Cant*. Edited by G.W.S. Barrow, 91–106. Edinburgh: Scottish Academic Press, 1974.

Smith, Neil Gregor. "James MacGregor and the Church in the Maritimes." In *Enkindled by the Word: Essays on Presbyterianism in Canada*. Compiled by the Centennial Committee of the Presbyterian Church in Canada, 9–18. Toronto: Centennial Committee of the Presbyterian Church in Canada, 1966.

Smout, T.C. *A History of the Scottish People, 1560–1830*. London: Fontana, 1998.

Stanley-Blackwell, Laurie. *Tokens of Grace: Cape Breton's Open-Air Communion Tradition*. Sydney: Cape Breton University Press, 2006.

– *The Well-Watered Garden: The Presbyterian Church in Cape Breton, 1798–1860*. Sydney: University College of Cape Breton Press, 1983.

Sutherland, D.A. "Michael Wallace, 1744–1831." *DCB* 6, 327–9.

Thomson, William McCulloch. "Dr. Thomas McCulloch." *Celebration Addresses*, 142–58.

Tomlinson, Grace. "A Scottish Dominie in Nova Scotia." *Dalhousie Review* 46, no. 3 (Autumn 1966): 338–47.

Tuck, Robert Critchlow. "Theophilus Desbrisay, 1754–1823." *DCB* 6, 197–8.

Tulloch, Judith. "Thomas Cutler, 1752–1837." *DCB* 7, 223–4.

– "William Cottnam Tonge, 1764–1832." *DCB* 6, 778–83.

Turnbull, Robert. *The Genius of Scotland*. 4th ed. New York, 1848.

W.G.B. "Archibald Bruce." *Dictionary of National Biography* 7 (1886): 89.

Waite, P.B. *Lives of Dalhousie University*. Vol. 1, *1818–1925*. Montreal: McGill-Queen's University Press, 1994.

Watson, W.J. *Scottish Verse from the Book of the Dean of Lismore*. Edinburgh: Oliver & Boyd, 1937.

– *MacGregor of Pictou*. Montreal: Church Centre, 1986.

Watt, J. "James Ramsay (1733–1789)." *New Oxford Dictionary of National Biography*. Online ed. Oxford: Oxford University Press, 2006.

Whatley, Christopher. "The Dark Side of the Enlightenment: Sorting Out Serfdom." In Devine and Young, *Eighteenth Century Scotland*, 259–74.

– *Scottish Society, 1707–1830: Beyond Jacobitism,Toward Industrialisation*. Manchester, UK: Manchester University Press, 2000.

Whitelaw, Marjory, ed. *Dalhousie Journals*. Toronto: Oberon Press, 1978.

– *Thomas McCulloch: His Life and Times*. Halifax: Nova Scotia Museum, 1985.

Whytock, Jack C. "An Educated Clergy." *Scottish Theological Education and Training in the Kirk and Secession, 1560–1850*. Milton Keynes, UK: Paternoster, 2007.

Winks, Robin. *The Blacks in Canada: A History*, 2nd ed. Montreal: McGill-Queen's University Press, 1997.

– "Negroes in the Maritimes: An Introductory Survey." *Dalhousie Review* 48, 1968.

Withrington, Donald J. "Schooling, Literacy and Society." In *People and Society in Scotland*. Vol. 1, *1760–1830*. Edited by T.M. Devine and Rosalind Mitchison, 163–87. Edinburgh: John Donald, 1988.

Wood, B. Anne. "Schooling for Presbyterian Leaders: The College Years of Pictou Academy, 1816–1832." In Klempa, *The Burning Bush and a Few Acres of Snow*, 19–37.

– "The Significance of Calvinism in the Educational Vision of Thomas McCulloch." *Vitae Scholasticae* (Ames, IA), no. 1–2 (1985): 15–30.

– "The Significance of Evangelical Presbyterian Politics in the Construction of State Schooling: A Case Study of the Pictou District, 1817–1866." *Acadiensis* 2, no. 2 (1991): 62–85.

Wood, Paul, ed. *The Scottish Enlightenment: Essays in Reinterpretation*. Rochester, N.Y.: University of Rochester Press, 2000.

– "Who Was John Anderson?" In Hook and Sher, *The Glasgow Enlightenment*, 111–32.

Wynn, Graeme. "Exciting a Spirit of Emulation among the 'Podholes': Agricultural Reform in Pre-Confederation Nova Scotia." *Acadiensis* 20 (Autumn 1990): 5–51.

Index